C.D Cunningham

The Pioneers of the Alps

C.D Cunningham

The Pioneers of the Alps

ISBN/EAN: 9783743414808

Manufactured in Europe, USA, Canada, Australia, Japa

Cover: Foto ©ninafisch / pixelio.de

Manufactured and distributed by brebook publishing software (www.brebook.com)

C.D Cunningham

The Pioneers of the Alps

THE
PIONEERS OF THE ALPS

BY

C. D. CUNNINGHAM

AND

CAPTAIN W. DE W. ABNEY, C.B., R.E., F.R.S.

SECOND EDITION

BOSTON
ESTES AND LAURIAT.
1888

LONDON:
PRINTED BY GILBERT AND RIVINGTON, LIMITED,
ST. JOHN'S HOUSE, CLERKENWELL ROAD.

To

Sir FRANCIS OTTIWELL ADAMS, K.C.M.G., C.B.

Her Britannic Majesty's Envoy Extraordinary
and Minister Plenipotentiary to the Swiss Confederation,

&c., &c., &c.

Honorary Member of the Alpine Club

THIS VOLUME IS DEDICATED.

PREFACE.

IN the pages now presented to the reader will be found a collection of sketches of the lives and of portraits of those who first conquered the great peaks, opened out the mountain highways, and who may fairly be said to have made possible that sport which so many of us enjoy every year in the Alps —men who are, or have been in their day, undoubtedly great guides. The present is a singularly favourable time for forming such a collection, as in addition to the portraits of those guides who have perfected the Art of Climbing, and who are still among us, we are able to obtain the likenesses of many of those who took the largest share in the work of exploring the Alps after the commencement of systematic mountaineering.

The first point on which a decision was required was as to the mountain centres to which the selection of guides should be limited. For several reasons we resolved to confine ourselves to Grindelwald, Zermatt, Chamonix, and their surroundings. Had we gone further afield, there are three names at least which, as a matter of course, must have had a place in this work—Hans Grass, Gaspard *père*, and Santo Siorpaes.

The next matter was an extremely difficult one to decide, viz. the selection from among the living guides of those who should rank amongst the pioneers. Most amateurs spend the majority of their seasons in the Alps with the same leading guide, and although they may have been together on the rope with other guides, or seen them at work on the same mountain, there are but a limited number, even among the oldest and most experienced climbers, who have had opportunities of really observing and making a fair comparison between *all* the guides who may be considered to hold a foremost place in the craft. As an instance of this we may mention that the present editor of the *Alpine Journal* laughingly told one of us, that he had only once seen Melchior Anderegg, and that from a window!

It appeared to us that the most impartial course to pursue was to take the opinion of a selected number of working members of the Alpine Club, whose knowledge of the qualifications of the guides was more than ordinarily extended, and who must be considered as representative men. We accordingly requested ten members to give us their advice, and out of them the eight following responded to our invitation. Their names are a sufficient guarantee for the value and impartiality of their opinions, representing as they do the various epochs of climbing from the formation of the Alpine Club to the present time :—

        Mr. G. S. Barnes.   Mr. C. E. Mathews.
        Mr. W. E. Davidson.   Mr. A. W. Moore.
        Mr. J. Walker Hartley.   Mr. H. Pasteur.
        Mr. H. Seymour Hoare.   Mr. Horace Walker.

A skeleton list of guides was sent to each (none knew the names of the others who were giving their opinion), with the request that they would mark with a "D," as "doubtful," those guides of whom they had the slightest doubt as to their being on the list, to strike out those names which they considered should not appear, and also to add any names which our scroll-list had failed to give, but which, in their opinion, should have been inserted. The result of the balloting lists was as follows, giving a ½ mark for those names followed by a D. :—

Fifteen guides had eight votes (maximum), five guides seven and a half, two guides seven, and one guide, Josef Mooser, six and a half votes.

It would be invidious to other guides to state further the results of the ballot; we can only say that it left no possible doubt in our minds as to our having obtained a consensus of opinion strongly in favour of the twenty-two we have given, and to which number we had resolved and felt bound to limit ourselves. It will thus be seen that we ourselves have taken no part in the selection of the guides; we pledged ourselves to be bound by the opinion of our referees.

Our endeavour has been that the biographical notices of the living guides should be written either by the amateurs with whom their names will always be associated, or by those who have had ample opportunities of forming an estimate of their character and capacities. We have always asked our contributors to keep one object prominently before them—to draw the same accurate and faithful description of the guide's life and character as it has been our aim to give in the illustrations of their outward appearance. With the exception of the sketch of Emile Rey, all the biographical notices of those guides which one of us has written were submitted to those who had spent many seasons in the Alps with them, and who, although themselves indisposed to provide us with the notices, were yet kind enough to give us the benefit of their criticism upon them.

To these and to all those who have contributed biographical sketches we here formally express our thanks and sense of obligation. If there be any merit in this work, we feel that it is mainly due to their labours, which have been so freely given and largely used. The Editorial work and the revision of the proof has certainly been no light task to one of us. We feel that we must offer our most sincere and cordial thanks to Mr. W. E. Davidson, who amid a constant press of official duties has nevertheless always been ready to give us his most welcome counsel and advice as regards the scope of the work, as well as his unwearying help and assistance in the preparation of these pages for the press.

The photographic illustrations which have hitherto accompanied publications have, as a rule, been silver-prints, which are more or less fugitive, or by some permanent process in which the artistic qualities are spoiled by a vulgar gloss. It has been our object to avoid both these defects, and the portraits have been printed from plates produced by photogravure, a process almost as old as photography itself, but which has only been rendered possible for a work of this kind by recent improvements. The illustrations, being in printers' ink, will last as long as the paper on which they are printed.

PREFACE TO THE SECOND EDITION.

In issuing a Second Edition of this volume, the Authors desire to convey their sincere thanks to Mr. G. E. Foster, Mr. J. Walker Hartley, Mr. C. E. Mathows, Mr. F. F. Tuckett, and the Rev. F. T. Wethered, for the valuable criticisms they have been so good as to make regarding the First Edition. The greater part of the corrigenda we have made has been at the suggestion of these gentlemen.

The name of Mr. Thomas Middlemore was inadvertently omitted from the list of contributors in the First Edition, an error which we very much regret.

CONTRIBUTORS.

CLIFFORD ALLBUTT, M.D.
GEORGE S. BARNES.
HENRY COCKBURN.
W. M. CONWAY.
REV. W. A. B. COOLIDGE.
C. T. DENT.
W. B. DUFFIELD.
JAMES ECCLES.
G. E. FOSTER.
DOUGLAS W. FRESHFIELD.

FREDERICK GARDINER.
REV. W. S. GREEN.
J. WALKER HARTLEY.
H. SEYMOUR HOARE.
T. S. KENNEDY.
J. OAKLEY MAUND.
C. E. MATHEWS.
WILLIAM MATHEWS.
THOMAS MIDDLEMORE.
REV. F. T. WETHERED.

CONTENTS.

GROWTH AND DEVELOPMENT OF MOUNTAINEERING—

	PAGE
I. Period, 1387—1787	1
II. Period, 1788—1854	7
III. Period, 1855—1865	14
IV. Period, 1866 - 1885	26
V. Alpine Accidents	30
VI. Mountaineering without Guides	37
VII. Mountaineering in Winter	39
VIII. Ice-axe and Rope	42
IX. Guidecraft	48

THE TRAINING OF MOUNTAINEERS — 52

THE PORTRAITS — 61

GUIDES OF THE PRESENT DAY—

Melchior Anderegg	64
Johann von Bergen	68
Johann Jaun	71
Ulrich Lauener	79
Christian Lauener	81
Christian Almer	83
Johann Baumann	87
Peter Baumann	90

	PAGE
Ulrich Almer.	92
Ulrich Kaufmann.	96
Josef Imboden	97
Aloys Pollinger	100
Peter Knubel.	101
Alexander Burgener	103
François Dévouassoud	105
François Couttet.	112
Michel Payot.	115
Alphonse Payot	118
Edouard Cupelin.	120
Jean Joseph Maquignaz.	123
Jean-Antoine Carrel.	126
Emile Rey	132

"IN MEMORIAM"—

Auguste Balmat	136
Auguste Simond	140
Christian Michel	141
Peter Bohren.	143
Franz Andermatten	145
J. J. Bennen.	148
Jakob Anderegg	153
Michel Croz.	154
Peter Rubi.	157
Johann Fischer	159
Laurent Lanier	161
Andreas Maurer	163
Ferdinand Imseng	166

APPENDIX . 169

INDEX . 171

THE
PIONEERS OF THE ALPS.

The Growth and Development of Mountaineering.

I. PERIOD 1387—1787.

THE 17th of September, 1854, the date of the first ascent of the Wetterhorn from Grindelwald, is a red-letter day in the history of modern mountaineering,—of mountaineering properly so called which is undertaken for its own sake, and entirely apart from the performing of some particular feat, or from some special scientific object. If we look at the table of first ascents in Studer's 'Über Eis und Schnee,' we shall see how few of the great peaks had been conquered previous to 1854, the most important among them being the Titlis in 1737, the Buet in 1770, Mont Vélan in 1779, the Dent du Midi in 1784, Mont Blanc in 1786, the Jungfrau in 1811, the Finsteraarhorn in 1812, the Tödi in 1824, the Gross Lauteraarhorn in 1842, and at various times several of the minor peaks of the Monte Rosa *massif*. These, however, had been climbed at long and irregular intervals, while Mr. Justice Wills's ascent of the Wetterhorn was the first of a series of expeditions destined to become continuous, and distinctly marked the commencement of systematic mountaineering. Hence it is, that the anniversary of this ascent may well be termed the Founder's Day of our craft in its modern guise.

Probably the first authentic record of a mountain ascent in the Swiss Alps was in 1387, when Pilatus, or Mons Fractus as it was then called, was climbed by six *Geistliche* in defiance of the Catholic Government of Lucerne. I say the 'first authentic record,' for every district has its traditions as to its own great glacier highways having been crossed at some remote period; and these traditions, too, are rendered all the more hazy from the alternate increase and decrease in the size of the glaciers, and the consequent perplexity and confusion which were doubtless caused, when each successive generation repeated the accounts which their fathers had handed down to them. On descending from Pilatus, the unfortunate *Geistliche* were immediately seized and imprisoned, as it had been forbidden to go near the mountain owing to the legend that Pontius Pilate was wandering about on the summit, and that if any one ventured on the sides of the mountain, or threw stones into the lake, Pontius himself would appear in the neighbourhood on Good Friday. More than a century later, in 1518, at the commencement of the Reformation, Pilatus was again ascended, by Joachim von Watt, of St. Gallen, the well-known Reformer who Latinized his name as Vadianus, and three friends. They threw stones into the lake, but with no results, so far at least as inducing the much-dreaded spectre to reappear. Both these ascents were made, not only as a protest against the superstition and religious intolerance of the period, but with the object of investigating certain questions of natural science. And it is interesting to note that the two earliest recorded climbs in the Alps, were incidents in that great struggle to reach the Light from that Darkness which preceded the Reformation. The next ascent was undertaken solely for scientific purposes, probably in order to collect botanical specimens, and was made in 1555 by Gesner, then Professor of Medicine at the Carolinum of Zurich, which became in 1832 its University. Thus "Science and Religion took it in turns to deal blows at the mediæval horror of the High Alps." Gesner was at heart a mountaineer in the true sense of the word, who has recorded that he would "climb a mountain every year as long as God gave him life." Nearly two centuries now passed without a fresh ascent of any importance being made in the Alps. It was not till 1737 that the Titlis, the first snow mountain conquered in Switzerland, was climbed by a monk from the monastery at Engelberg. The second snow mountain ascended was the Buet, by the brothers De Luc in 1770. In connection with the history of the Buet, it is an interesting fact that it was the mountain on which, in 1800, the first Alpine accident occurred; it was also, as we shall afterwards see, the first mountain on which a new route was made. It had been intended to place the names of the De Lucs along with those of Bourrit and De Saussure on the sides of the little monument 'à la Nature,' at the Montanvert. This building is now used as the washhouse of the Hôtel, but was originally erected as a monument to the founders of the love of mountaineering. These were all men who undoubtedly held a foremost place among the early pioneers of the Alps. De Saussure may be taken as the man of science; Bourrit as an artist, who enjoyed far more to make sketches of the mountains, than to take scientific observations. The De Lucs were mountaineers, rather than artists or men of science. They all lived at Geneva, and were contemporaries of J. J. Rousseau, whose writings and opinions must doubtless have been the means of directing their attention to the mountains within sight of their native town; although we must recollect that any interest which Jean Jacques himself took in the peaks, was from a purely social standpoint. "He admired the mountains," Mr. Leslie Stephen tells us, "as the barriers which kept luxury from corrupting the simplicity of the native, and in some passages he expresses what may be taken for substantially the modern sympathy with savage scenery; but one still feels an uncomfortable suspicion that his love of rocks may be a particular case of his love of paradox. He admires them, we may fancy, because they are hideous; the mountains, like the noble savage, are a standing protest against the sophisticated modern taste; they are bare and wild and repulsive, but at any rate they have not taken to wearing wigs and stays, and submitted to the conventional taste of the century."

JEAN ANDRÉ DE LUC (1727—1817) and his less known brother, GUILLAUME ANTOINE DE LUC (1729—1812), the sons of a watchmaker in Geneva, made their first attempt on the Buet in 1765. A most interesting account of the early history of this mountain is given in the ninth volume of the *Alpine Journal*, and to the researches of its author I am indebted for the following details. The De Lucs failed in their first attempt, but five years afterwards (1770) they again tried to gain the summit. On this occasion they were accompanied by an 'apprentice to a hunter,' who when the party were in difficulties owing to one of the De Lucs having sprained his foot, insisted on leaving his *voyageurs* on the pretext that he was obliged to return home and milk his master's cows. The unfortunate brothers spent the night on the mountain, returning the following morning to Sixt. A month later they made another attempt, and reached Les Fonds, where in recent years the 'Eagle's Nest' has been built. They were again driven back to Sixt by bad weather, but the following day they once more started, and succeeded in reaching the summit.

MARC THEODORE BOURRIT (1739—1819), Precentor of the Cathedral of Geneva, commenced life as a miniature painter. When quite a young man he visited Les Voirons, and was so much struck with the beauty of mountain scenery, that he gave up miniature painting and took to landscape. He may be considered the first artist who succeeded in portraying with accuracy the forms of mountains. He was a friend of De Saussure, and assisted him in illustrating some of his works; the intimacy which existed between them, has been characterized, however, as being somewhat on the Johnson-Boswell lines. Bourrit's attainments in science being by no means so great as his passion for the mountains, his real delight consisted in exploring them, and recording with his brush the many beautiful forms of nature he so thoroughly appreciated. His name will always be remembered from his having been one of the first travellers who reopened the passage of the Col du Géant in 1787, the year previous to De Saussure's encampment for seventeen days on the 'Grand Col.' He is the "first inventor of that lately somewhat hardly pressed resource of climbers, 'the new route,'" and many a tourist hears Bourrit's name for the first time when in going up the Buet from Val Orsine he passes that great boulder still called 'La Table au Chantre,' where the Precentor and his party rested during the first ascent of the Buet from that side. Bourrit was the first traveller who attempted to make an ascent of Mont Blanc. Between 1784 and 1788 he made no less than four attempts, but failed on each occasion. One cannot help experiencing a certain feeling of sympathy for Bourrit's want of success in attaining what must doubtless have been the great object of his ambition.

HORACE BENEDICT DE SAUSSURE was born in Geneva, February 17th, 1740. "He may be considered as the father of experimental science," Captain Abney writes, "as studied at high altitudes. His career is most noteworthy. At the age of twenty-two he was elected Professor of Philosophy at Geneva; but his heart lay in the study of nature, as found in the grand surrounding scenery in which he lived, rather than in the drier study of logic, and his chief amusement seems to have been in travelling and making mountain ascents with a view of enlarging the conception of what we should now not inaptly call physiography. De Saussure's dream from the age of twenty was to ascend Mont Blanc, a most natural desire considering the temperament of the man, and the stimulation which the constant view of the mountain monarch from Geneva, must have afforded to it. The realization of his dream he effected, accompanied by seventeen guides, in the year following its first ascent by Balmat in 1786, having the previous year resigned his professorship to Pictet. De Saussure's first introduction of science was as a botanist, but as he made his Alpine ascents he became a geologist, mineralogist, and meteorologist. Solar radiation at high altitudes was one of his studies to which he paid the closest attention, and he carried barometers and boiling-point thermometers to the summits of such mountains as were then accessible, and when possible passed days at high elevations to continue his researches. On the Théodule, for instance, in 1792, he passed three days with his son Nicholas taking observations at an elevation of nearly 11,000 feet. As an enterprising mountaineer we have only to glance at his work which is reported in 'Voyages dans les Alpes,' to see the spirit in which he worked. We should give him the title of Prince of Scientific Mountaineers, as his mind grasped theories, which though in his day men considered as not proven, yet subsequently have been accepted as the only explanation of his experimental data. Not only did De Saussure make experiments, but he invented many of the instruments with which he undertook them, and thus shone not only as an experimenter but as an inventor."

"He played no mean part in the politico-economics of his native town. He was a staunch educationalist, and performed with the same vigour, as that with which he carried out his scientific work, his duties in the National Assembly of Two Hundred, to which he was elected. His health began to fail in 1794, and he died on January 17th, 1799, having been practically imbecile for the last three years of his life."

It is interesting to notice what a large share the Church took in the early conquest of the Alps. Mont Vélan and Monte Leone were first climbed by Austin Canons, the Titlis by a Benedictine monk, and the Dent du Midi by the Curé of Champéry. Undoubtedly the most distinguished of the monastic pioneers was PLACIDUS À SPESCHA of Disentis (1752—1835), a man of great scientific attainments and vastly in advance of the age in which he lived. In his mountain excursions Placidus was in the habit of using an ice-axe and a rope. When over seventy he made his sixth assault on the Tödi, and although he did not succeed in reaching the summit, it is pleasant to notice what genuine satisfaction the good old monk expresses at the success of his more fortunate companions. Writing of his own *tentative* he says, "Yet again my sixth attempt remained fruitless, my goal however was reached, and I thank God for it. I sent two chamois hunters from the upper huts of the Russein Alp, and by eleven o'clock they had climbed the peak. With my servant I climbed up a considerable height on the right hand, in order to witness the ascent and return of the hunters. At 4 p.m. we came together to the above-mentioned huts, where we refreshed ourselves and recounted the events of the day."

The last of the early pioneers whose name we shall mention is JACQUES BALMAT (1762—1834), who was born in the village of Los Pélerins, near Chamonix. Throughout the whole history of the conquest and exploration of the Alps, there is no pluckier or more remarkable incident than Balmat's unaided effort to reach the summit of Mont Blanc. Both Bourrit and De Saussure had already made unsuccessful attempts on the mountain, and the latter after his failure sent a party of guides to see if they could discover the route. They attained a point somewhat beyond the Dôme du Goûter, but considered it impracticable to proceed further. One of their number was Jacques Balmat, who, whether by accident or design, remained behind, while the others returned to Chamonix. Mr. William Longman, in 'Modern Mountaineering,' thus describes the difficulties Balmat had to contend with before his ultimate triumph. "He was not on good terms with his companions, and fancying he saw his way to reaching the summit of the mountain, may have wished to keep to himself the honour of discovering it. He soon lost sight of his companions; a snowstorm came on, and he was forced to bury himself in a hole in the snow and wait till morning. When daylight came, he began his explorations and discovered the route, which for a long time was the only one by which ascents were made. He ascertained that if the crevasses which border the Grand Plateau were once crossed, the way to the top of Mont Blanc was clear and unbroken. To quote his own words, "In descending (the previous day) to the

Grand Plateau, I thought that halfway down there was a steep but possible slope, which would lead to the Rocher Rouge. I determined to try it, but when I reached it I found it was so steep and the snow so hard that I could not stand on it. However, by cutting steps with my bâton I managed to climb it, but my fatigue was extreme. It was neither easy nor pleasant to hang, so to speak, on one leg with an abyss below me, and obliged to cut steps like a staircase. At length I reached the Rocher Rouge. 'Oh!' I said, 'we are nearly there. From here to the top of Mont Blanc there is nothing to stop me.' But I was half dead with fatigue, cold, and hunger. It was getting late and I was obliged to descend, but with the determination of returning the first opportunity, and I felt sure of success." He then returned to Chamonix, but was so utterly exhausted by fatigue and exposure that he at once took to his bed, and did not leave it for weeks. No one knew of his hopes of success. Out of gratitude to Dr. Paccard, who attended him during his illness, he confided the details of his attempt to him. On the 7th August the two started without other companions, and succeeded in reaching the summit. Balmat had a passion for gold-seeking which kept him a poor man all his life. In 1834, when no less than seventy-two years of age, he started on one of these expeditions, from which he was destined never to return. It is supposed that he slipped and fell, while climbing one of the precipices of Mont Ruan. A monument has, by the irony of fate, been erected to Balmat at Chamonix, within sight of the Bureau des Guides, that very institution, which, since its foundation has been the means of repressing among the younger guides of each succeeding generation, those qualities which enabled Balmat to perform that great feat, by which his name will always be remembered by mountaineers. 'Balmat' is a household word at Chamonix. It is quoted as frequently and as glibly by the mule-drivers of that village, as the name of Raphael is dinned into the ears of hesitating customers by the copyists in the Borgognissanti. Both these ornaments to their respective callings, fondly imagine that there is some link which connects them in a mysterious way with these great men.

The following year (1787), exactly four hundred years since Pilatus was climbed by the *Geistliche*, De Saussure made his memorable ascent of Mont Blanc.

Towards the end of the eighteenth century the halo of unknown terrors by which the mountains were surrounded in men's minds, that superstitious dread shared alike by the peasants who lived under the shadow of the great peaks, and the professors at the University of Bâle, was fast upon the wane. One can well imagine the feelings of the good, steady-going folk of Geneva, as they walked by the lake on a summer's evening; and saw Mont Maudit, the 'mountain of ill-omen,' as Mont Blanc was then considered, lit up by the rich warm after-glow of sunset. They doubtless conjured up in their imagination some such weird scene as Mr. Irving created on the boards of the Lyceum when he represented the summit of the Brocken in 'Faust;' and even the moral support which one would suppose the presence of men of such orthodox, well-balanced minds as Calvin and John Knox to give, did not succeed in dispelling these illusions. As a good Presbyterian, I feel bound to suppose that had John Knox been approached on the subject, he would have expressed the greatest possible contempt for all the bogies and warlocks, said to be lurking in Mont Maudit. What he said may possibly have rather lost weight, from his making unfavourable comparisons between the scene before him, and his own beloved Firth of Forth and North Berwick Law. It is strange for us in the nineteenth century to think that at so recent a date as 1723, a book was published describing the monsters of the then unexplored recesses of the Alps. In that year George I. was on the throne, England had just recovered from the scare of the South Sea Bubble, and Sir Robert Walpole had commenced his twenty-one years' ministry. The work was dedicated to The Royal Society. The illustrations, two of which were printed at the expense of Sir Isaac Newton, represented the dragons and other uncanny beasts which the author solemnly affirmed were to be met with among the Alps. Scheuchzer, one of the early Swiss travellers, and a man of considerable scientific attainments, who invented a theory of glacier motion, was the author of this book. He divides his dragons into distinct scientific classes—slimy dragons, dragons with wings, two and four-legged dragons. "He is puzzled by the question whether the crest is to be taken as a specific distinction or is merely characteristic of the male or (should we say?) the cock dragon." There is a strange fascination about these eerie creatures in Scheuchzer's illustrations, but his volume should by no means be put into the hands of nervous people near bed-time. One of the plates, 'Monster and Man,' has been reproduced in the third volume of the *Alpine Journal*, which is, perhaps fortunately, out of print. Had Milton seen the book, I fear that we must have held Scheuchzer responsible for certain passages in 'Paradise Lost.' Nor can I help suspecting that the illustrators of children's picture-books must have been greatly indebted to Scheuchzer for the anatomical proportions of the serpents who figure in their different renderings of the 'Temptation of Eve.' Scheuchzer's descriptions of the glaciers are not more accurate than what he says of the strange beings which were supposed to haunt them. In 1744 one of Dr. Pococke's and Mr. Windham's party wrote a letter which was "laid before The Royal Society," giving an account of their visit to Chamonix. He says, "Though Scheuchzer in his *Iter Alpinum* describes the Glacières that are in the Canton of Berne, yet they seem by his description to be very different from those of Savoy." Mr. Windham's expedition to Chamonix has considerable interest from its being the first occasion on which an English traveller visited the valley. Curiously enough, in their narrative written at the time, no mention is made of Mont Blanc. Mr. Windham was the leader of the party; he is said to have been a man of most powerful build, a great athlete, and was known in London as 'boxing Windham.' He met Dr. Pococke at Geneva, who had then just returned from his travels in the East, and allowed him to join his expedition.

It is interesting to follow step by step the gradual process which has taken place during the last two centuries, by which not only the mountains themselves, but mountain scenery, have lost all those weird terrors with which they were at one time associated in men's minds. The first step was the eviction of the whole tribe of dragons, by which they were supposed to be tenanted, to a permanent shelf in the property-room of Drury Lane. It is true their places were immediately filled by elves, gnomes, and dwarfs; such a crowd as we have seen on canvas in the 'Fairy Raid' or 'Oberon and Titania.' But these were infinitely more harmless beings to see disporting themselves round a boulder on a moonlight night, than "slimy" or even "cock dragons." In 1741 Mr. Windham's party were told by the people of Chamonix, "many strange Stories of Witches, &c., who came to play pranks upon the *Glacière*, and dance to the sound of Instruments." They do not seem to have paid much attention to these tales, and observe that, "As in all Countries of Ignorance, People are extremely superstitious." We might almost say that the mountain myths had kept pace with the times. Those of them that are left, are now of a very practical, matter of fact sort, quite in keeping with an age of invention and progress like the nineteenth century; as any one will probably admit who has been (for instance) in Edinburgh on May-day morning. There they may have seen troops of red-headed cooks and housemaids, shop-girls, and even elderly spinsters with some pretension to 'genteelity,' hieing off to Arthur's Seat, to wash their faces with dew, with the object not only of improving, but preserving their good looks for the next twelve months. This is a function which may perhaps be described as a sort of carnival for the straight-laced, and (I am told) is winked at, even by the sternest and most exemplary of the New Town.

One characteristic which has always been more or less associated with the mountains, has been graphically described by Mr. Ruskin in his chapter in Modern Painters on 'The Mountain Gloom.' He speaks of the feelings with which the peasants in the sunny fertile Swiss valleys looked upon the bleak barren cliffs, and weather-beaten pines under whose shadow they lived, as forming a sort of Debateable Land between them and the unknown terrors of the unexplored mountain fastnesses beyond. In a frequently quoted passage from the 'Journey to the Western Islands,' Dr. Johnson expresses this conventional eighteenth century view of mountain scenery. Boswell and he were then in the neighbourhood of Fort Augustus. "I sat down on a bank, such as a writer of romance might have delighted to feign. The day was calm, the air soft, and all was rudeness, silence, and solitude. Before me, and on either side, were high hills which by hindering the eye from ranging, forced the mind to find entertainment for itself." The following trite remarks seem to have been suggested by these surroundings. "It will readily occur that this uniformity of barrenness can afford very little amusement to the traveller, that it is easy to sit at home and conceive rocks, heath, and waterfalls, and that these journeys are useless labours, which neither impregnate the imagination nor inform the understanding." Such was the popular estimate of mountain scenery at the beginning of the century, lasting till the revival of the taste for Gothic architecture, and the founding of the romantic school of poetry by Wordsworth and by Scott. The beautiful pastorales of Wordsworth seem at once to dispel the 'Mountain Gloom,' and the hills and glens became untenanted, save by the chieftains and heroines of Sir Walter Scott's creation. As in the old days all classes shared alike the same dread of the mountains; so now does their wonderful beauty and grandeur appeal, though in widely different ways, to all sorts and conditions of men. Whether it be the recollection of long days on the moors, of scrambles with our guides on the great snow peaks, or of long hours spent in the valleys, lazily watching the ever-changing effects of light and colour on the cliffs beyond,—there are but few who will not own, how many of the best pleasures in life are to be found among the mountains.

* * * * * * * * * * * * * *

II. PERIOD 1788—1854.

DURING these sixty odd years, the science of mountaineering made little or no progress. With very few exceptions no new expeditions were made outside the Chamonix district, and more than fifty years passed from the time when the first ascent of Mont Blanc was made, before any other peak in the chain was conquered. At this time, Mont Blanc acted the part of a huge magnet, attracting to its base all the travelling public who were ambitious of boasting on their return home, that they had seen the highest mountain in

Europe. In making the Grand Tour it had become the fashion in the early part of the nineteenth century to visit some of the strongholds of the Alps, to cross the Grimsel, the Great St. Bernard, or to make an excursion from Geneva to Chamonix. This was the period at which horn-blowing became a recognized profession in the Oberland, and cannon-firing one of the regular institutions at Chamonix. Now too, appeared on the scene, that keen observer of human nature, who first started the custom of branding the names of peaks, waterfalls, or villages on bâtons; nor am I at all sure that the ill-drawn, exaggerated lithographs then published of the views from Brévent or Flégère, owed their inaccuracies to any lack of artistic power on the part of the Geneva draughtsmen; they were probably rather the results of very careful deliberation as to what the people who purchased such *souvenirs* would most like to induce their friends at home to believe they had actually seen. There is an old Cumberland Squire in whose front parlour hangs a couple of coloured Swiss views, purchased during his tour in 1821. These, together with the old gentleman's description, have annually for the last fifty years, taken away the breath (so to speak) of all the Members of the Hunt when they came to breakfast. And I should not like to say how much the good old Squire's life-long reputation for truthfulness and integrity has suffered through the superior accuracy of the same views depicted in a pair of Mr. Donkin's photographs, which have found their way to Busselthwaite.

The guides of the early part of this period were, as a rule, sturdy and honest,—men who were thoroughly to be relied upon: but dash was unknown to them, and as a body they were entirely devoid of enterprise. They had, however, one firm conviction always before them, the full sense of the responsibility they were under for the safety of every one in their charge. If ever they erred on the side of magnifying their office, it was always with a view of putting themselves in a position to check foolhardy persons, who talked above a whisper while passing below séracs whose positions were suggestive of indifferent equilibrium. In looking at the coloured sketch of De Saussure and his son coming down from the Tacul, which hangs in the Alpine Club Rooms, I have always wondered at the boldness of that rosy-cheeked, smiling youth, who had the audacity to kneel down and drink great cupfuls of glacier water under the very eyes of some ten Chamonix guides.

We must not disparage the expeditions made when the century was still in its teens, for the glaciers were infinitely more difficult than they are at present. In going from the Montanvert to the Jardin, I fancy one had to pass over séracs not much less troublesome than those on the Géant when the col is in an easy condition. There were no maps in those days, and climbing appliances were of the rudest and most imperfect kind. When people started to make a new col, there was, in addition to the doubt as to whether its summit would be reached, a painful uncertainty as to when or where one would land on the other side of the range.

Nearly the whole of the mountaineering literature of this period consisted in narratives of ascents of Mont Blanc. The fireworks, cannon-firing, champagne, and bouquets, which throw a halo of temporary notoriety around the tourist of to-day at Chamonix, are as nothing compared with the honours which were heaped upon the 'ascensionists' (I will not call them mountaineers) at the beginning of the century. Mr. John Auldjo, who made the fourteenth ascent of Mont Blanc, tells us how on returning to the hôtel, "his room was thronged in a moment with gentlemen of all nations, every one of them desirous of assisting him." Those individuals who disport themselves in the main street of

Interlaken with ice-axes and ropes, borrowed for the occasion from their guides, would feel many a pang of envy were they to read the following passage from Mr. Auldjo's narrative. It should be explained that he had seen through his telescope from Les Bosses, a crowd of people who were waving their hats and handkerchiefs, and signalling to him. "I learnt that those ladies whom I had seen on the Brévent were principally fair countrywomen of my own, who by thus venturing up a very lofty mountain, the ascent of which in some places is very dangerous, had evinced great anxiety for the result of my undertaking. The Countess of Bertrand was one of the party, and had had a telescope carried up for her, by means of which she had watched our progress with the greatest interest, and was delighted on our arrival upon the summit." There was, too, a solemnity and importance about ascents of Mont Blanc in those days. "Many have made their wills before starting, and all left such directions regarding their property, as if they were persuaded that they never should return." When Captain Sherwill and Dr. Clarke climbed Mont Blanc in 1825, they wished to leave some record of their ascent near the summit. Any one who casually read their description of what took place, might imagine that the Captain and his friend had been assisting at the laying of the foundation-stone of St. Paul's or Westminster Abbey. "These (a few branches of olive) we had enclosed in a cylinder of glass, with the name of our king, and of his deservedly popular minister, subjoining the names of some of the remarkable persons of the age, whether high in honour as enlightened politicians, revered as sincere and eloquent theologians, admired as elegant poets, useful as laborious physicians, or adorning the walks of private life by the mingled charm of urbanity, gentleness, accomplishments, and beauty." This they "hermetically sealed down by an ice plug," with the reflection that "it may possibly remain unaltered for generations." They little thought at the time, that the monument which was intended, I fear, quite as much to perpetuate their own greatness in having ascended Mont Blanc, as that of their distinguished countrymen, was destined to last so short a time. But two years afterwards the glass was found by Mr. Auldjo, who wrote, "It had already perished, the bottle was half-filled with water, the paper was nearly destroyed, and the writing was entirely illegible."

These early narratives contain many interesting allusions to the guide-life of Chamonix. They give us a good idea of the feelings of terror with which the dangers of mountaineering were still regarded, and show us what a simple, good-hearted race the inhabitants of the valley must have been. Referring to his arrival at Chamonix in 1834, Dr. Barry wrote, "I met a guide who had ascended Mont Blanc once, but said he would never go again, and tried to dissuade me from making the attempt." In describing the preparations for his ascent, Mr. Auldjo says,—" Many of the guides who had desired to be chosen, in the event of my fulfilling my intention, now declined to proceed with me. The Chef des Guides fixed three o'clock for enrolling those who would volunteer; when that hour came, I could not fill up my list of six; many bringing for excuse that their wives would not allow them, others that their mothers, sisters, children, interfered; and I could only find four who were determined to accompany me. In the evening I made up the number; but again two of them changed their minds, and at ten o'clock only had I my six guides, certain of setting off in the morning." Then again,—" Six o'clock was the time fixed for starting, and every man was desired to be in attendance before that hour, but I could not get them together at that time, most of them had to part with their wives or relations; when they did join us, it was with a cortège, some crying, some upbraiding me with tempting those who formed their only support to sacrifice themselves to my curiosity and pleasure; many a bitter tear flowed, more than one heart waxed heavy on the morning of the 8th." When the start was actually made, things began to wear a more cheerful aspect. "No men could be in better spirits than my guides, laughing, singing, and joking, every one vied in giving amusement to the other." One is glad to know that this excessive hilarity did not lead to such carelessness as to cause fatal results. For, while they were glissading, Mr. Auldjo recalls how "when crevices were near the sides, or terminate the descent, it is dangerous, and no jokes are practised." Those who knew Mr. Auldjo when that genial, kind-hearted old gentleman was our Consul at Geneva, can well understand how it was that when he was leaving Chamonix, and shook hands with his guides for the last time, "every one of them wept."

It is interesting for those of us who have read the experiences of explorers in the Himálayas or the Andes, as to the rarefaction of the atmosphere, and upon other questions relating to mountaineering physiology; to hear the views expressed by the early pioneers of the Alps on similar subjects. For example, when De Saussure was discussing the possibility of reaching the summit of Mont Blanc, he was told by a Chamonix guide, that "it would be useless to take provisions, as he would be quite unable to eat, and recommended that he should provide himself with a light parasol and a bottle of scent." That distinguished scientist was of opinion, that "on the summit of Mont Blanc the firing of a pistol would make no more noise than a small cracker in a chamber." This ingenious theory was, however, triumphantly refuted some years later by Dr. Barry, who took a pistol with him when he made the ascent, and from the summit returned the salutes which were fired from the batteries at Chamonix. When Mr. Auldjo's party were approaching the Rochers Rouges, "they were seized with an oppression on the chest, and a slight difficulty in breathing; a quickness of pulsation soon followed, and a fulness in the veins of the head." Dr. Barry also, when somewhere in the neighbourhood of Les Bosses, "never found the flexors of the thigh and extensors of the leg so inadequate to the performance of their office as on that occasion, although he could not say that 700 feet lower down he had been conscious of the least fatigue." In the learned doctor's account of his ascent, he gives an "Abstract View of the Effects of Diminished Atmospheric Density on Respiration, and other Functions," which he experienced. The following may be taken as examples of what the good man suffered:—

At 12,000 feet.	Intense thirst. Incipient loss of appetite. Disinclination to eat continued, yet did not amount to nausea.
14,700 „	Loss of appetite complete.
15,500 „	A tendency to syncope. Utter indifference.

In his narrative he alludes to the last of these most unenviable conditions. "A degree of indifference came on, that deprived the highest point in Europe, though just within reach, of all its interest." During the descent he "could have imagined that he heard oxen lowing at a distance. It was the creaking noise produced by the points of the guides' bâtons in the hardened snow."

In the narrative of the ascent of the Wetterhorn, so frequently alluded to in these pages, the then junior Counsel writes, "I experienced what Balmat said he had always suffered from, three or four days after a great course, a raging and insatiable thirst; but this was the only uncomfortable effect left by the greatest and grandest expedition of my life." This last has been selected from among the many references to the physiology of mountaineering made by the writers of this period, as it is the only one of the scientific 'facts' they record, which I can corroborate from personal experience, though, it must be owned, I should not associate the symptom exclusively with high mountaineering ascents.

In 1821, the Société des Guides was founded at Chamonix. In many respects it differs essentially from other societies of guides in the various parts of the Oberland, as the Chamonix guides have received a sort of charter from their Government. Thus, any voyageur who in returning from an excursion refuses to pay the tariff, or otherwise infringes the Règlement, may be summoned before the Juge de Paix, and punished, it may be by fine, or, for aught I know, by imprisonment without the option of a fine. The records of the Société afford ample materials for an interesting sketch of its origin and growth. At first there were only forty guides on the list, and from 1845 to 1852 no Règlement was enforced. During these years the great revolution in Europe was taking place, thrones were tottering, tyrants were being overthrown, and people getting their rights, or perhaps more than their rights, all round, which naturally suggested to the younger guides that it was a most fitting time for them to protest against that monopoly of guiding, which the Règlement gave to the older and in some respects less capable members of the Société. Among those who took a prominent part in this movement was François Couttet ('Baguette'), and it is much to be regretted that at the present day none of the younger men in the district will come forward in the same way, to try to effect some alteration in a system which is only calculated to repress and put obstacles in the career of a guide who wishes to perfect himself in his craft, and to distinguish himself in his profession.

Thirty or forty years ago, the young guides seemed to have been possessed of much more energy and strength of character than those of the present day. When Professor Tyndall received a small grant from The Royal Society in order to ascend Mont Blanc, for the purpose of burying some self-registering thermometers on the summit, he applied to the Syndic and the Intendant of the Province to be allowed to dispense with the regulation number of guides and porters. His request was at once granted, notwithstanding the opposition of the Guide Chef, this functionary doing his best to bring the Professor's guides to 'justice' for disregarding the Règlement. "He sent a spy off after us," wrote one of the party, "who might bear witness that we were all safe on the chemin du Mont Blanc. This fellow overtook us not far from Pierre à l'Echelle, and we had some difficulty in restraining our young porters from inflicting a little wholesome chastisement upon him." On their return all the guides received a summons to appear before the Juge de Paix at Bonneville. The Intendant, however, very naturally considered it a piece of presumption on the part of the Guide Chef to dispute proceedings expressly authorized by himself. "The result was a great blow to the 'party of obstruction.' The summonses were dismissed, and the chief guide was packed off with a flea in his ear. He was told that what was wanted for the well-being of Chamonix was 'que les glaciers descenderaient un peu plus bas, et écraseraient quelques uns de ces gens si ignorants, si rétrogrades, afin que les autres pourraient marcher un peu mieux sans eux!' Our porters walked back in procession, with flowers in their hats, to Chamonix, and as they entered the village they caught sight of the unhappy chief guide; they pounced upon him, carried him to a neighbouring wine-shop, and inflicted upon him the ignominious punishment of making him hopelessly drunk, in which state they carried him through the streets in triumph." Let us hope that when this *custos* of the good manners of the Chamonix guides recovered from his vulgar carousal, he immediately imposed a fine upon himself. It was doubtless the purely technical point, that he was not seen in a state of intoxication while on a *course*, which prevented him from removing his own name from the roster of guides: for it was in the streets of Chamonix that he succumbed to the effects of his potations, and I am not aware that the elaborate Règlement provides for such an exceptional contingency.

Any one who takes the trouble to turn over the pages of the *Alpine Journal*, must notice that a visit to Chamonix by a member of the Alpine Club was generally attended with a considerable amount of excitement, and a delightful uncertainty as to what results might ensue. Out of all the numerous instances one could give, there is none more characteristic of the place than Mr. Whymper's narrative in 'Scrambles amongst the Alps,' of what occurred on his return to Chamonix after the first ascent of the Aiguille Verte. He re-entered the village 'amid firing of cannon and other demonstrations of satisfaction on the part of the hôtel-keepers. "One would have thought," he says, "that the ascent of this mountain, which had been frequently assailed before without success, would have afforded some gratification to a population whose chief support is derived from tourists, and that the prospect of the perennial flow of francs which might be expected to result from it, would have stifled the jealousy consequent on the success of foreigners. It was not so, Chamonix stood on its rights. A stranger had ignored their regulations, had imported two foreign guides, and furthermore, he had added injury to insult—he had not taken a single Chamonix guide. Chamonix would be revenged! It would bully the foreign guides; it would tell them they had lied,—that they had not made the ascent. Where were their proofs? Where was the flag upon the summit? Poor Almer and Biener were accordingly chivied from pillar to post, from one inn to another, and at length complained to me. Peter Perrn, the Zermatt guide, said on the night that we returned, that this was to happen, but the story seemed too absurd to be true. I now bade my men go out again, and followed them myself to see the sport. Chamonix was greatly excited. The *bureau* of the *guide chef* was thronged with clamouring men. Their ringleader—one Zacharie Cachat—a well-known guide, of no particular merit, but not a bad fellow, was haranguing the multitude. He met with more than his match. My friend Kennedy, who was on the spot, heard of the disturbance and rushed into the fray, confronted the burly guide, and thrust back his absurdities in his teeth. There were the materials for a very pretty riot; but they manage these things better in France than we do, and the gendarmes—three strong—came down and dispersed the crowd. The guides quailed before the cocked hats, and retired to cabarets to take little glasses of absinthe and other liquors more or less injurious to the human frame. Under the influence of these stimulants they conceived an idea which combined revenge with profit. 'You have ascended the Aiguille Verte, you say. *We* say we don't believe it. *We* say do it again! Take three of us with you, and we will bet you two thousand francs to one thousand, that you won't make the ascent!' This proposition was formally notified to me, but I declined it with thanks, and recommended Kennedy to go in and win."

Such continual controversies as to whether peaks had actually been ascended, whether their true summits had been gained or not, together with the petty annoyances and persecutions to which foreign guides are subjected, have naturally had the result of driving *bonâ fide* climbers away from the district. One cannot help regretting that the oldest regularly organized body of guides should have fallen into decay, and that what is perhaps the finest mountaineering centre in the Alps should have become practically deserted by mountaineers. Members of Alpine Clubs would certainly gain on the one hand by the abolition of the Société, but on the other they would lose an endless amount of very harmless enjoyment, afforded to them by the absurd vagaries of those who administer the still more ludicrous Règlement.

During the latter part of this period, the attention of the public was drawn towards the Alps by the numerous scientific articles on glacier movement and phenomena which were then being widely read. In 1843 Professor J. D. Forbes published his 'Travels through the Alps of Savoy'; during the summer of 1848, he visited Switzerland, and shortly afterwards wrote his charming work 'A Physician's Holiday.' In all the works of this class there is constant allusion to guides and mountaineering, although they were nearly always written from a scientific standpoint. But from a more popular point of view, with the exception of the publication of the first series of 'Peaks, Passes, and Glaciers,' some years later, probably no event in England has awakened so keen an interest in the Alps, as the entertainment which the late Albert Smith gave in the Egyptian Hall, descriptive of an ascent he made of Mont Blanc in 1851. This has been spoken of by his biographer as "that celebrated lecture which attracted hundreds of thousands to listen to it, and aroused the attention of Royalty itself." I have before me a little pamphlet, half programme, half souvenir of the entertainment. On one of the covers is an advertisement of the South Eastern Railway, giving the most direct route to all parts of the Continent; on the other side the United Service Life Assurance Company informs, in capital letters, the British public of their terms for life policies. There is also an advertisement of the 'Mont Blanc Quadrilles,' which we are informed, " have produced a perfect *furore* of delight at all the fashionable *soirées dansantes* of the season." If the scenes in Mr. Smith's panorama at all resembled the engravings in his book, or if the descriptions in that now out-of-print brochure are the same as those he gave in his lecture, I do not wonder that any Board of Insurance Directors should consider one of their advertisements most salutary and profitable reading for the audience, before the curtain rose. Mr. Smith made the ascent with *three* other Englishmen; and the following is an extract from their hotel bill for provisions :—

60 bottles of vin ordinaire.		20 loaves.	
3 ,, ,, Bordeaux.		10 small cheeses.	
10 ,, ,, St. Georges.		4 legs of mutton.	
15 ,, ,, St. Jean.		11 large and 35 small fowls.	

On their return they were charged fifty francs, 'for 103 bottles lost.' It is impossible to read Mr. Smith's descriptions of scenery, or in fact of any of the incidents of the ascent, without seeming to have a row of footlights, and a gentleman in dress clothes with a pointer in his hand before one. One recognizes the Showman in every page. For instance, when the party reached the valley on their return, " It was suggested that we should mount our mules to render our entry into Chamonix as imposing as possible." Then he goes on to say that they " heard the guns firing at Chamonix ever since we left the Pélerins; but as we entered the village we were greeted with a tremendous round of Alpine artillery."

As an antithesis to this vulgarity, if we turn over the table of contents in 'Wanderings among the High Alps' and Mr. Hinchliff's 'Summer Months among the Alps,' the first purely mountaineering books ever published, we shall have a very good idea of what glacier excursions were generally made towards the end of this period and the commencement of the next. In the Oberland the Tschingel and the Strahleck, and at Zermatt the Théodule Pass, seem to have been the height of the average mountaineer's ambition. In the Chamonix district the Col du Géant, the 'Grand Col' as the guides used to call it, was then very justly considered to be an expedition of great difficulty. The excursions most frequently made were the tours of Mont Blanc and of Monte Rosa, and cols of which the Gemmi may be cited as a fair example. The closing event of the 1788—1854 period, was the first ascent of the Wetterhorn from Grindelwald, referred to in the opening sentences of this sketch. For although many may claim that the commencement of systematic mountaineering dated from 1857, when the Finsteraarhorn was ascended by the Rev. J. F. Hardy's party, still we may fairly say that the iron *Flagge* which Ulrich Lauener planted on the summit of the Wetterhorn, was destined in more than one sense to become a landmark in the history of the Alps.

III. PERIOD 1855—1865.

This period has been called the 'great age of conquest' in the Alps, and it may also well be termed the 'golden age' in the history of mountaineering. During these ten years, a comparatively short space of time, the greatest, at all events the tallest, giants in the Alps were slain. The following list of the principal new expeditions which were made between 1855 and 1865, shows that these appellations are singularly appropriate for this period. It is also interesting to notice how in each successive year of this period the popularity of mountaineering steadily increased. As this work is limited to a record of the guides of the three great mountaineering headquarters, Grindelwald, Zermatt, and Chamonix, the ascents in these districts only have been given which were made during this period. Some claim that the 'great age of conquest' lasted till 1870, in which case the list would, of course, have been very much longer; but the ascent of the Matterhorn seemed to be such an important event in the history of mountaineering, that it has been preferred to select 1865, as the terminating year of this most remarkable period.

LIST OF THE PRINCIPAL NEW EXPEDITIONS DURING THE 'GOLDEN AGE.'

	Bernese Oberland.	Zermatt District.	Chamonix District.
1855		Monte Rosa.	
		Weissmies.	
1856		Allalinhorn.	
		Laquinhorn.	
1857	Mönch.		
	Klein Schreckhorn.		
1858	Eiger.	Dom.	Aig. du Miage.
			Col du Miage.
1859	Aletschhorn.	Rympfischhorn.	
	Bietschhorn.	Monte Leone.	
	Eigerjoch.	Col Durand.	
1860	Blümlis Alp.	Grand Combin.	
	Lauinenthor.	Château des Dames.	
		Alphubel.	
		Col de Valpelline	

GROWTH AND DEVELOPMENT OF MOUNTAINEERING
(1855—1865).

LIST OF THE PRINCIPAL NEW EXPEDITIONS DURING THE 'GOLDEN AGE'—*continued*.

	BERNESE OBERLAND.	ZERMATT DISTRICT.	CHAMONIX DISTRICT.
1861	Gr. Schreckhorn.	Nord End (of Monte Rosa). Lyskamm. Weisshorn. Castor. Mont Gelé. Felikjoch. Col de Sonadon. Col de Chermontane. Col de la Reuse de l'Arolla.	Col d'Argentière.
1862	Gr. Viescherhorn. Doldenhorn. Weissefrau. Jungfraujoch. Viescherjoch.	Täschhorn. Sesiajoch. Col delle Loccie. Mischabeljoch. Biesjoch. Col du Mont Brulé. Dent Blanche.	
1863	Silberhorn. Berglijoch. Studerjoch.	Parrotspitze. Dent d'Hérens. Diablons. Balferinhorn. Fletschjoch. Zwillinge Joch.	Col de la Tour Noire (sometimes called Col du Tour Noir).
1864	Balmhorn. Jungfrau, from the Rotthal. Gr. Wannehorn. Berglistock. Ochsenhorn. Studerhorn.	Pollux. Gd. Cornier. Rothhorn (Moming). Schallenjoch. Brunnegg Joch. Moming Pass. Col Tournanche. Laquinjoch.	Aig. d'Argentière. Aig. de Trélatête. Col de Trélatôte. Col du Triolet. Col du Dôme du Goûter. Col Dolent. Col du Chardonnet.
1865	Nesthorn. Lauterbrunnen Breithorn. Jungfrau, from the Wengern Alp. Gr. Grünhorn. Silberhorn (from N.).	Gabelhorn. Wellenkuppe. Ruinette. Pigne d'Arolla. Col de Bertol. Col de Bremay. MATTERHORN.	Mont Dolent. Aig. du Chardonnet. Aig. de Bionnassay. Mont Blanc, from Brenva Glacier. Grandes Jorasses (lower peak). Mont Blanc de Cheillon. Aiguille Verte. Col de Talèfre.

No better proof could be given of the energy and indomitable perseverance of the climbers of this period than the preceding record. Nowadays we can hardly realize the difficulties by which mountaineers were then surrounded. There were few guides who were competent to lead a new expedition, there were no Club-hütte, and the little mountain inns were without any of the comforts we find in them at present. Brown bread, cheese, salted mutton and very sour wine, formed the ordinary stock of provisions for a bivouac overnight, and the long ascent on the following day. Still, I can well believe that the climbers of the old school look back upon these days as some of the best and happiest of their lives. The names of the Englishmen who then climbed regularly every season in the Alps could be counted on the fingers of both hands. They all knew each other intimately; there was much good fellowship, and a Freemasonry among them, which those who remember the early days of climbing fondly imagine ought still to survive among the heterogeneous crowd of tourists who now flock to the mountains. Many lifelong friendships were formed during these years, and, as one turns over the pages of 'Peaks, Passes, and Glaciers,' or of the *Alpine Journal*, it is pleasant to notice how long many of the familiar combinations of names have remained unaltered. When those of the Old School who are left, drive up to some great staring hôtel, followed by a *queue* of smartly-dressed tourists with Saratogas and Gripsacks, how regretfully they must think of the little group of châlets they knew so well in days gone by, and how they must long for the perfect sense of freedom and complete repose they used to enjoy among them. How willingly they would dispense with the electric light, the spruce manager, and the row of white-vested waiters, could they but have the welcome of the old landlord in his high collars and homespun suit, and meet once more those friends who were always associated with the place.

It was not until the craze for mountaineering had fairly set in, that an ice-axe and a rope began to be regarded as the badges of that physical and social distinction which their ownership is now apparently held by some to confer. The travelling public previously considered that those who indulged in such an extraordinary pastime as that of climbing mountains were beyond the pale of criticism. They might in all other respects be of perfectly sound mind, and have many good and amiable qualities; but, like those notorious evil-doers who exist in every country village, they were their own worst enemies. By the risks they encountered their own lives were endangered, and not those of their compatriots at *tables d'hôte*, and as for the guides who were foolish enough to share their perils, they doubtless knew very well what they were about, like miners or the hands in a powder factory. We may feel certain that in the present day, any one of the aristocracy of Bond Street or the Linden who comes down to Chamonix from the Grands Mulets, finds himself a much greater object of popular admiration than Professor Tyndall or Mr. Leslie Stephen was, after descending to the valley after his first ascent of the Weisshorn or the Rothhorn. In the sixth edition of 'Murray,' who for so many years has been the philosopher and friend, as well as the guide of the travelling public, the Editor wrote in 1854,—"The ascent of Mont Blanc is attempted by a few. Those who are impelled by curiosity alone are hardly justified in risking the lives of the guides. It is a somewhat remarkable fact that a large proportion of those who have made the ascent have been persons of unsound mind."

It is interesting to notice how, during the first few years of the 'age of conquest,' guides seemed literally to spring into existence, although by no means in proportion to the increasing demand for them. In 1854 Melchior was *Knecht* of the Grimsel, and old Christian was looking after his sheep on the Zäsenberg, yet only five years afterwards each had laid the foundation of that great reputation which he was destined so soon to establish for himself. When we reflect on the vast amount of experience and skill which, according to our more modern ideas, a young guide must possess before he can hope to attain to the front rank of his profession, it may seem absurd to talk of Melchior and Christian blossoming out as guides, in such a short space of time. But no one would admit more readily than these two veterans, that guiding as it was understood and practised in those days could only be considered as a merely rudimentary form of that science into which it has since developed. As a rule the guides knew no district but their own, and that but indifferently well. Mr. Mathews tells us how, when he first made the Col du Mont Rouge, he sent for 'le premier chasseur de Bagnes,' to pilot them across it, notwithstanding the fact that Auguste Simond was of the party. It is worthy of notice that these chasseurs aided very largely in the exploration of the Alps; and, indeed, apart from the guides and chamois-hunters, the only other men who had any acquaintance with the glaciers at this time were the crystal-hunters and the smugglers. These, however, naturally looked with suspicion upon climbers when they began to invade what they considered to be their own peculiar preserves, and they cannot be said to have taken the smallest part in the mountain conquests.

There is one name belonging to this period without which no roll of the Pioneers of the Alps would be complete, JOHANN IMSENG, Curé of Saas, a man who was passionately fond of the mountains, and who was ever ready to do the honours of that native valley which he loved so well, to the strangers who came to explore it. It was from necessity, not from any inclination on his part, that he was forced to eke out his slender stipend by permitting travellers to lodge in his house. *La Cure* at Saas was, in reality, the Inn of the little village; but the host did not understand the mysteries of hotel-keeping. And Mr. Justice Wills has graphically described " a very wet afternoon which he once spent in the kitchen for the sake of the fire." " In the window-sill, which was small and dirty, were cups and saucers, eggs, and a large lump of butter, a can of milk cheek by jowl with filthy rags and clothes; a lot of dirty knives and forks, and the Lord knows what besides. Everything else was in the same style." This narrative gives us a most charming picture of the good old parish priest, and although one may never even have seen the Curé, the description of him and of the quiet, scholarly life he led, is so graphic, that one always looks upon him as an old acquaintance. " A more kind and hospitable man than the Curé it would be difficult to find," writes the Judge. " He is a good Latin scholar, and can talk Latin with an ease and fluency that would shame many a professed scholar, and he appears to be greatly beloved and respected by the inhabitants of his district. ' If they thought I was going to leave them,' he said one day, 'ils me déchireraient les culottes,' and I believe he did not at all overrate the estimation in which his parishioners held him. He knows something of the botany, and a great deal of the topography and history of the valley. He was the son of a peasant of Saas, and in his youth tended sheep and goats on the mountain sides, and thus acquired his great strength and activity. As a young man, and up to fifty, as he told me, he would mount without a moment's pause to the highest summits, and not 'a sob his toil confess;' now, he says, he must stop occasionally to admire the prospect. He has a dash of poetry in his composition, and loves the mountains almost passionately; but not so exclusively as to overlook even the little flowers of the Alps. There was a touch of deep feeling in the tone in which he spoke one day of their brief existence in these desolate spots,— ' Leur vie est très courte; elle est bientôt finie;' and the true lover of nature spoke out when he looked up at the great crags and the dazzling fields of snow above us, and said, while his eyes fired up like lightning, ' Oh, nous serons gais là haut.' " The first ascent of the Nadelhorn was made in 1858 by the Curé, but perhaps the best known of the excursions he made for the first time was the Adler Pass, from Saas to Zermatt. Mr. Justice Wills and Mr. R. C. Heath accompanied him in this expedition. Writing of it, the former says, " We took a reluctant leave of our friend, the Curé, whom we watched till an angle in the path concealed him from our sight. We learned afterwards that he reached St. Nicholas about eight, where he sat and slept for two hours, and starting again at ten, arrived at Saas about four next morning; at five he was at his post in the church, performing early mass, after which he went to bed and slept most of the day; but he was not a bit the worse for the expedition, a day's work which would have tired most younger men." The Curé was then considerably over sixty years of age. As a souvenir of the pleasant and successful expedition over the Adler, the two *voyageurs* presented their friend and guide with a snuffbox, bearing the following inscription,—

REVERENDO PATRI IMSENG,
EGREGII EJUS HOSPITII,
ITINERISQUE LONGI,
PER NIVES SEMPITERNAS ET RUPES TREMENDAS,
EO DUCE TUTE CONFECTI
MEMORES,
HOC MUNUSCULUM DEDERE
ALFREDUS WILLS ET RICARDUS CHILD HEATH.
MDCCCLIII.

An eagle's feather which they found on the summit of the Col, suggested the name 'Adler,' by which the pass has since been known. In the same way, some years later, a group of dead swallows suggested to Mons. Loppé and his party the singularly appropriate name 'Col des Hirondelles' for the passage they were then making for the first time.

I wish it were possible to quote all the references to the Curé, in 'Wanderings among the High Alps.' In reading them we can well understand how it is that his name is still remembered with so much affection and esteem, not only among his fellow-countrymen, but by the numberless strangers who received so many acts of kindness and courtesy from him.

This good, benevolent old man met with a sudden and most cruel death. His body was found one morning in the Mattmarksee, with marks of violence upon it, lying near the shore of the lake, where the water was so shallow that his upturned face was barely covered by it. It is said that an Italian who accidentally witnessed this cowardly and brutal murder, gave many years afterwards a clue, in his dying confession, to the names of the murderers.

It was in 1858 that the Alpine Club was founded. "To the various members of the Mathews family," the late Mr. William Longman wrote, "belongs unquestionably the honour of first putting forward the idea of the club; to Mr. E. S. Kennedy the merit of actively carrying that idea into execution. It is clear that the question was first seriously considered at 'The Leasowes' (the country seat of the late Mr. William Mathews, senior), on Friday, November 6th, 1857. The party consisted of the late Mr. William Mathews; his son, Mr. St. John Mathews; his nephews, Mr. W. and Mr. C. E. Mathews; and Mr. E. S. Kennedy." We can well understand that those who were interested in the same common pursuit, and who had enjoyed so much friendly intercourse abroad, should wish to establish some means of perpetuating and continuing their pleasant relationship at home. It was also thought that "many of those who had been engaged in similar undertakings would willingly avail themselves of occasional opportunities for meeting together, for communicating information as to past excursions, and for planning new achievements; and a hope was entertained that such an association might indirectly advance the general progress of knowledge, by directing the attention of men not professedly followers of science to particular points in which their assistance may contribute to valuable results." Circulars were sent out, bringing the proposed club under the notice of all the *habitués* of the Alps. A year, however, passed before the scheme was fully developed. It was not till the 22nd December, 1858, that the first meeting of the club was held. Mr. Longman gives the following account of what took place,—"One of the proposed rules was much canvassed, and had indeed been objected to by a large number of those who agreed to become members of the club, some of them going so far as to make their membership depend on its withdrawal. It was that 'a candidate shall not be eligible unless he shall have ascended to the top of a mountain 13,000 feet in height.' Some thought other qualifications than mere climbing should be recognized, others held that the height fixed was excessive, or pointed out that strollers up the Cima de Jazzi would be admitted, while a man who had ascended a peak like the Gross Glockner, or had been driven back by bad weather after nearly reaching the required height, would be excluded." Among the original members were: Mr. John Ball, Mr. Eustace Anderson, Mr. E. T. Coleman, the Rev. J. F. Hardy, Mr. Vaughan Hawkins, the Rev. J. B. Lightfoot (present Bishop of Durham), Mr. William Longman, Albert Smith, of Mont Blanc notoriety, the Rev. J. Taylor (present Master of St. John's College, Cambridge), Mr. G. V. Yule, the present Mr. Justice Wills, Professor F. J. A. Hort, Mr. T. W. Hinchliff, Mr. William Mathews, and his brother, Mr. C. E. Mathews. The following year Mr. John Ball wrote in the preface to 'Peaks, Passes, and Glaciers,'—"The expectations of the founders of the club have not been disappointed. It numbers at the present time nearly a hundred members, and it is hoped that the possession of a permanent place of meeting will materially further the object which it has proposed to itself." The names of the original members on the club list have now, alas! dwindled down to some fifteen names.

The meetings of the club were first held in Mr. Hinchliff's chambers, but suitable rooms were soon found in St. Martin's Place, where it has remained ever since. It is a curious coincidence that, as St. Martin is supposed in some parts of Switzerland to be the protector of all those who travel among the mountains, the members of the Alpine Club should have established themselves in a street bearing the name of the patron of our craft. In these rooms the club holds its meetings, where the achievements of the past season are dilated on, not wholly without those courteous platitudes which are the necessary concomitants of such discussions. Thus, during the past three years, speakers have frequently deemed it necessary to descant upon the fact that "the Alpine Club is one where, above everything else, good fellowship should predominate." The outward signs of "good fellowship," however, generally commence as soon as the meeting is over. Pipes are produced, and the members partake of what the present Secretary (with a truly British regard for propriety) styles in his balance-sheet for 1886, "Tea, &c." From the country cousin's point of view, these meetings, like the hunting-field, have one great charm: "One meets people one would not have the chance of seeing elsewhere."

During the first few years of its existence, the fact of being a member of the Alpine Club was justly considered equivalent to holding the blue ribbon of mountaineering. Nowadays all the prestige once associated with the club has sadly diminished. It was such men as Hinchliff, Moore, and Leslie Stephen who made the club, and who, by their pluck and perseverance, gained for it the respect of climbers of other nationalities, and that high reputation in the past upon which its present prestige is based. One great point of superiority over foreign clubs on which the Alpine Club have always prided themselves is, that a qualification is necessary for membership. I do not know precisely what the qualification is, nor, as far as I am aware, does any one else—it seems, if one may judge from a casual perusal of the candidates' book, to vary from time to time according to the views of the Committee.[1] It is, at any rate, but small evidence that the candidate is a climber in the real sense of the word. However, it serves its purpose, for members of foreign clubs have extremely vague and exaggerated ideas of the ordeal one is supposed to undergo before becoming duly qualified for election; and hence it is that the mountaineering capabilities of the average run of members are possibly overrated by those who are not actually members of the club. To be of any real value, a climbing test would require to be much more severe, and would necessarily include one or two excursions, say the Wetterhorn or some not over-difficult col, where the candidate had acted as guide, and done any of the step-cutting which might have been required with his own axe. It does not become me to speculate whether the membership of the club would be as large as it is at present, if such a high standard were enforced. I can only say that I can personally vouch that there is, at any rate, one member of the club who would never have belonged to it, if there had been an "entrance examination" of this sort when his name was put down. Had the authorities in the Alpine Club kept the qualification abreast of the rapid progress the science of mountaineering has made year by year, we might possibly still hold the high reputation (at all events, from a purely climbing point of view) which the club in its early days possessed.

It is a subject for regret that, with the exception of publishing their map of the Alps,[2] the club, as a body, has not sufficiently fulfilled its *raison d'être* in benefiting the general mountaineering world. Foreign clubs devote themselves to the well ordering of many details, which alike concern the interests of the climber and the well-being of the guide. The building and keeping up of their Club-hütte, the organization of insurance funds for the guides, and the examination of young guides, occupies a large share of their time and attention. They may not succeed, as many of us would wish, in exacting a sufficiently high standard from the candidates; but we are probably not aware of the difficulties which they may encounter in endeavouring to induce their Governments to assist them in the matter. What is done, is at all events in the right direction. The Alpine Club has expressed its disapproval of building huts, and, with one exception, has always stoutly refused to vote funds to aid in their erection or maintenance. Yet I have never heard of a member whose convictions on the subject took the practical form of pitching a tent for himself and his guides on the Stockje, or whose principles would not allow him when overtaken by bad weather, to seek shelter under the hospitable roof of the Schwarzegg or the Bergli Hütte. The two following sums, representing the total disbursement of the Alpine Club, and of the various foreign clubs towards mountain huts and refuges, have been furnished respectively by the present Secretary of the Alpine Club and Mr. Philip C. Gosset, who by the way has

---

[1] See Appendix.
[2] I find I am wrong in this statement. One of the contributors to the present book has been good enough to point out in the *Athenæum* that even this was not done by the Alpine Club, the requisite funds having been furnished by Mr. William Longman, the eminent Publisher of Paternoster Row, and by Mr. Stanford, the enterprising Map-seller and Stationer, 55, Charing Cross, S.W., the latter of whom was in no respect connected with the club.—C.D.C.

GROWTH AND DEVELOPMENT OF MOUNTAINEERING
(1855—1865).

drawn up a table which gives some most interesting statistics and information regarding the Club-hütte in the Alps, which it is hoped he may soon publish.

Total amount expended on Club-hütte by the Alpine Club £15
    „   „   „   Foreign Clubs £40,585

Members of the Alpine Club have never shrunk from frankly expressing their opinions on the shortcomings of these *cabanes* which are so generously and freely placed at our disposal. The first Editor of the *Alpine Journal* writes in one of the volumes, "The condition of this hut (Pierre à Beranger) is a disgrace to Chamonix." The above figures suggest a very practical way in which carping grumblers who are "compelled to sleep in such places" can individually contribute to their improvement and maintenance.

If we look over the proceedings published in the *Alpine Journal*, we shall see the class of business which, during the last four or five years, has principally occupied the attention of the club. The main discussions are of but small interest to the working members of the club, or to climbers abroad, as they do not in any way tend to the advancement of mountaineering. Their chief interest is probably confined to a number of the old members who have long since given up climbing, and have practically ceased to visit the Alps. From the fact of the Alpine Club taking no part in the various useful objects to which our brethren across the Channel devote themselves, but little is left for us to discuss of practical utility. And it naturally follows that the proceedings form a striking example of the truth of Dr. Watts' lines about "idle hands." What the future of the Alpine Club may be it is impossible to predict; but one cannot help feeling the keenest sympathy for those who founded the club, and to whom all its best traditions are due, when they see the old order changing and giving place to new.

The example of the founders of "The Alpine Club," as it is always called from its having been the first society of the kind to be established, was quickly followed by mountaineers in other countries. The following list is limited to those clubs which are concerned in the exploration of the Alps, and therefore the mountaineering societies in the Rockies, the Himálayas, the Pyrenees, and the Carpathians are not included.

	Founded.	No. of Members.
The Alpine Club ...	1857	475
Deutscher und Oesterreichischer Alpenverein, composed of a union in 1874 of the		
Oesterreichischer Alpenverein	1862	18,020
And the Deutscher Alpenverein ...	1869	
Schweizer Alpenclub	1863	2,607
Club Alpino Italiano	1863	3,669
Oesterreichischer Touristenclub ...	1869	9,020
Società degli Alpenisti Tridentini	1872	814
Club Alpin Français	1874	5,321
Société des Touristes du Dauphiné	1875	634
Oesterreichischer Alpenclub (originally called Alpenclub Oesterreich) ...	1878	859

These clubs have furnished many members distinguished either as men of science or art, or as well-known climbers who have taken an active and prominent share in the conquest of the Alps, and whose names have become household words to us.

In Switzerland, the brothers Bernard and Gottlieb Studer, Mr. Philip C.

Gosset, Herr E. von Fellenberg, Herr I. von Tschudi, Herr H. Dübi, Herren
F. and E. Burckhardt, Herr J. Weilenmann, Herr J. Beck, Herr R. Lindt,
Mons. F. A. Forel, Dr. A. Heim, Mons. E. Rambert, Mons. E. Javelle, Mons.
de Déchy. Nor can we forget the climbers of a somewhat earlier date, Ulrich
and Agassiz, Von Welden, &c. In France, Mons. C. Durier, Mons. G. Loppé,
Mons. Henri Cordier, the MM. Puiseux, Mons. P. Guillemin, Mons. A. Salvador
de Quatrefages, Mons. F. Perrin, Mons. H. Duhamel, Mons. H. Brulle, Mons.
J. Mathieu, Mons. Claude Verne, Mons. E. Boileau de Castelnau, Count Henry
Russell. In Italy, the Sella family, Dr. Martino Baretti, the Abbé Gorret, the
Chanoine Carrel, Signor L. Vaccarone, Mr. R. H. Budden, Signor A. Martelli,
Signor L. Nigra, Signor F. Giordano, Signor Ratti, Signor Bossoli. In
Germany, Dr. K. Schulz, Herr G. Euringer, the brothers Zsigmondy, Herr L.
Purtscheller, Herr A. Lorria, Herr G. Lammer, Herr J. Meurer, General K.
von Sonklar, Herr J. Studl, Herr K. Hoffmann, Herr P. Grohmann.

I have already pointed out how the peaks ascended in the Alps between
1387—1787, the 'prehistoric' period of mountaineering, were all climbed for
the first time by those who lived within sight of their summits. During the first
half of the present century, Englishmen can hardly be said to have taken any
part in the mountaineering conquests which were then made. In 1811 the
Jungfrau was first climbed by the Herren Meyer, the Finsteraarhorn by Meyer's
guides in 1812, and in 1842 by Herr Sulger, the Lauteraarhorn in 1842 by
Professor Escher von der Linth's party, and in 1820, Herr Zumstein made the

first ascent of that peak of the Monte
Rosa *massif*, which bears his name.
None are more ready than the members
of foreign clubs to recognize the large
share which Englishmen have taken in
the ultimate conquest of the great Alpine peaks, and those who have so large
a share of the spoils of final victory,
cannot fail to hold in honour the names
of those who dealt the first blows of
attack, when the great war against the
Alpine giants had just been declared.

One of the most important events in this period was the publication in
1859 of the first series of 'Peaks, Passes, and Glaciers.' Writing in 1880,
Mr. C. E. Mathews tells us that these volumes " intimated as much as created
the popularity of mountaineering; " and probably the first recognition of climbing
on the part of the press was the review of this book which appeared in the
Times, in an article entitled 'Alpine Travelling.' The writer after pointing out
that " an overwhelming influence not unlike that which inspires the pilgrimages
of a true believer, the dancing of a dervish and the swinging of a fakir, compels
our infatuated countrymen to keep moving over the earth as if they were
searching for the ends of it," goes on to say :—" Of this strange sect there is a
variety who have particularly devoted themselves to the climbing of mountains.
Fully to understand the nature of this pursuit, it must be remembered that
both in ancient and in modern times the ascent of great heights has always been
regarded as a severe punishment. According to the Greek idea, there could not
be a more awful punishment than that endured by Sisyphus, who was doomed
perpetually to ascend a high mountain, rolling up a stone, which no sooner reached
the summit than it rolled down again with a crash. So in Christian times,
when holy men sought various ways of purifying themselves from sin by under-

going penance in its severest forms, it was discovered that to be hoisted on to the top of a huge pillar was exceedingly efficacious; and from the fortitude with which he endured this species of torture, one well-known saint was called St. Simeon Stylites. If we turn to a more secular mode of existence—to the British Navy, for example—it will be found that one of the most common penalties there in force, is compelling the offender to mount to a considerable elevation; the contumacious midshipman is, in fact, mastheaded. From all which, and from many other instances that might be mentioned, it is quite evident that the wonderful ascents of high mountains of which we hear so much are a sort of penal discipline. It is true that our unhappy countrymen, who have to submit to this discipline, speak of it as being not unattended with pleasure—as in some cases indeed, producing the highest form of enjoyment which the human mind can conceive. For the most part, we believe that this talk is just as sincere as the shout of delight which mischievous boys give when they go into the sea on a bitterly cold day, and hope to lure their more cautious companions into the same misery. But if we may now and then accept the professed pleasure of our travellers in their mountaineering exploits as perfectly genuine, still the explanation is very simple; they have attained that state of feeling which the spirits who fell into bottomless perdition anticipated as their only chance of relief in the time to come, a state in which, to use the phrase of the poet, their torments became their elements. And the fact that one of the fiercest tortures of the Greek hell is regarded as one of the sublimest pleasures of an English holiday, is as fine a commentary as we could wish on the saying of the old chronicler, who declared that some among us take their pleasure very sadly—' ils s'amusaient tristement, selon la coutume de leur pays.' When we find a very clever man making an entertainment out of the ascent of Mont Blanc, and for thousands of nights compelling the laughter of myriads by the recital of his achievements, may we not well think of old Froissart's saying? When we find Mr. Leech in one of his most amusing sketches, depicting the exhaustion of a fat old lady who has made a three days' visit to London, and describes to her nieces the delights of the metropolis, in which, led by a mysterious influence that may excite our marvel but not our scorn, she ascended on the first day to the top of the Monument, on the second to the top of St. Paul's, and on the third to the summit of the Duke of York's column, who but must regret such unwonted irreverence in this most genial and refined satirist. To the prosaic Englishman all this climbing of hills and mounting of stairs is the merest superstition. We can understand what the poor villager does who climbs a greased pole for the sake of the leg of mutton or the flitch of bacon which is the prize stuck on the top. But to go sprawling up glaciers, to be mastheaded on the tops of Aiguilles, the whole thing is so incomprehensible and looks so very solemn that, though we cannot admire it, we would not on any account speak lightly of the performance."

Probably no works were ever written on any form of sport, which have afforded so much real enjoyment as these volumes have done. It is pleasant to think of the many tired and jaded folk, who, after a long weary day in the City or the Temple, have felt something almost akin to a breath of the glacier air, or a whiff of the pine-woods, while reading one of these spirited chapters. How often they have been the means of making the cares of the past day vanish, and of conjuring up many pleasant recollections of past seasons in the Alps, and hopes and prospects for the seasons that are to come. The narratives never lose their freshness, and though we may have long since become familiar with the scenes which are described, we never tire of reading them over and over again. The sketches are so graphically written, that the authors succeed in making us share all their difficulties, hopes, and triumphs. Collectors of works on the Alps are often accused of having a better acquaintance with the title-pages, than the contents of the volumes they hoard. But I doubt if there ever was an Alpine book-collector who was not thoroughly familiar with every chapter in 'Peaks and Passes,' and did not take some volume of the series from its shelf more frequently than any other in the whole of this collection. For it is by no means from the fact of 'very scarce' being marked on the booksellers' catalogue, that 'Peaks and Passes' always find an eager customer on any of those rare occasions when a complete set is in the market. It would be curious to know what sum an *uncut* copy would fetch among bibliomaniacs.

During this period many valuable additions were made to the literature of the Alps. Professor Tyndall's 'Glacier of the Alps' and 'Mountaineering in 1861' appeared, and Mr. John Ball commenced the publication of his valuable Guide Books in 1863. A tone of genuine sincerity pervades the early works on mountaineering, which is doubtless one of the great secrets of their lasting charm and interest. The writers spoke about the difficult places they came to, and the assistance they had from their guides; they did not even shrink from alluding to the fact that they were tired after a sixteen hours' climb. Here, for instance, is an example of that simplicity which cannot fail to charm,—"At the commencement of a long day," Professor Tyndall wrote, "I often find myself anxious if not timid." But now, after a lapse of twenty years, any one who compares the literature of the 'golden age' with that of the present period, must be struck with the enormous physical superiority of the amateurs of to-day, over the founders of the Alpine Club, if we may judge by the accounts they themselves give of their own performances.

In 1863, the Alpine Club resolved to establish a more permanent record of their achievements, and a quarterly magazine was accordingly set on foot under the appropriate title of *The Alpine Journal*. In the preface, the Editor (we presume) writes:—"It may perhaps be thought rather late to commence the publication of an Alpine Journal, when so many of the great peaks of Switzerland have been already climbed, and the successful expeditions described. But we can assure the most sceptical readers that the Alps are not nearly exhausted even by the many new ascents of last summer, of which we are now recording the first instalment." In this conflict with imaginary Alpine sceptics the Editor gives evidence of the possession of much sound common sense, foresight, and shrewd judgment. We are at the same time bound to say that he does not make quite so lucky a shot when he points out, in the following sentence, that "even if all other objects of interest in Switzerland should be exhausted, the Matterhorn remains (who shall say for how long?) unconquered and apparently invincible." It was successfully ascended from both the Swiss and Italian sides within the next two years, and we have taken it as the concluding event of the period, the ascent having been made on the 14th July, 1865.

Throughout the whole of the annals of mountain conquest, there is no narrative which possesses the same thrilling interest as Mr. Whymper's account in 'Scrambles amongst the Alps' of his successive onslaughts upon, and ultimate victory over this peak. Its wonderfully beautiful and apparently inaccessible form, together with the tragic and melancholy event connected with the first ascent, throw a halo of painful romance around this great stone beacon, such as no other mountain in the Alps, and one might almost say no peak in any range in the whole world possesses. It is not from feelings of mere idle curiosity that every tourist who arrives at Zermatt visits the graves of the Rev.

Charles Hudson, Mr. Hadow, and Michel Croz. It is a half-unconscious feeling of respect and sympathy, which draws men and women of every nationality round these granite slabs. The keen interest and excitement which the news of the accident awakened in the public mind, and which was rendered if possible more intense by a fatality on the Riffelhorn, and another on Monte Rosa which occurred almost at the same time, had not subsided, when a letter appeared in the *Times*, proposing that the event should be commemorated by building a suitable church in memory of those who had perished. The oak reading-desk in this, the Protestant chapel in Zermatt, was the gift of the Rev. Charles Hudson's widow; and the Bible which accompanied it was the one which her late husband used during the Crimean War, where he was serving as Chaplain to H.M.'s Forces. Let us hope that this relic may always be preserved as a memorial so characteristic of this good and brave man's life. Two other interesting mementos of the Matterhorn accident have been removed from Zermatt. One is the page of the Monte Rosa hôtel-book, on which Mr. Whymper wrote a short account of the dismal events immediately after their occurrence. This melancholy souvenir has perhaps now found a place in the scrap-album of some respectable householder in Brooklyn or Brompton; and can we not imagine its production among his less adventurous neighbours, to confirm his oft-repeated assertion, that he was within an ace of being asked to take part in the expedition. The other abstracted memorial, the whereabouts of part of which would not be so difficult to trace, is the rope which, for more than twenty years, indicated to every party on the Matterhorn the exact spot where the fatal slip took place. This cord was, to the lasting regret of his fellow-countrymen, taken possession of by an Englishman, who, while making the ascent with a friend, sent his guides to carry off the spoils. Never has the good feeling and courtesy of members of the Foreign Clubs been more conspicuously displayed than on this occasion. It is said that this relic was being distributed among his *table-d'hôte* acquaintances when the greater part of it was rescued through the courteous but firm remonstrances of Herr Josef Seiler. It is lamentable that such almost sacred mementos as these should be at the mercy of any sacrilegious curio-hunter who chances to prowl among the mountains.

Of all the sad records of Alpine accidents which we may have read, season after season in the newspaper columns, I do not remember a more touching one or a simpler statement of facts than the letter which the then English Chaplain at Zermatt wrote to the *Times*. Even now, after a lapse of twenty years, when we have almost come to look upon the Matterhorn accident as a historical event, one cannot read the musty thumb-marked file without realizing something of that thrill of horror which the news conveyed to every quarter of the globe. "After an arduous walk, in which we were exposed to much danger," the Rev. J. McCormick wrote, "we reached the snow-field on to which our friends had fallen. When we looked up at the 4000 feet above us, and observed how they must have bumped from rock to rock before they reached the bottom, we knew they could not be alive, and we feared they would be so awfully mangled that we should not be able to recognize them. Our worst fears were realized. We found no traces of Lord Francis Douglas, with the exception of some trifling articles of dress. His body must either have remained on some of the rocks above or been buried deeply in the snow. Croz lay near to Hadow. Hudson was some fifty yards from them. From the state of their remains the danger of the place (for it is exposed to showers of stones) and the very great difficulty of the way to it, we came to the conclusion that the best thing we could do would be to bury them in the snow. We drew them all to one spot, covered them with snow, read over the 90th Psalm from a Prayer-book taken from poor Hudson's pocket, repeated some prayers and a few words from the Burial Service and left them." The Swiss Government, however, decided that the remains should be removed from their quiet and lonely resting-place; and a few days later the three bodies which had been recovered were brought down to Zermatt, and interred near the village church. The efforts to recover the remains of Lord Francis Douglas proved fruitless, and, to quote Mr. Whymper's most appropriate and expressive words, "he lies where he fell, buried at the base of the grandest cliff of the most majestic mountain of the Alps." On the 27th of July an extremely able, and at the same time a most temperate leader upon the accident appeared in the *Times*, and during the month following not a day passed without several letters on the same subject being inserted. Never were the details of a great catastrophe discussed in the columns of a newspaper with a more earnest, one might almost say, a more reverent spirit. The effusions of such people as 'Senex' and 'Nemo,' who usually rush into print on such occasions, appear to have been ruthlessly suppressed by the *Times* editor. "There are occasions," says the *Times*, "on which a journal must brave certain unpopularity and ridicule, even in quarters where it may most wish to stand well. We desire the sympathies of the young, the courageous, the enterprising, and we can feel their taunts." Then referring to Lord Francis Douglas, the writer says:—"We believe he was the heir presumptive to one of our noblest titles, but far more than that, one of the best young fellows in the world." In conclusion he writes:—"But of course young men will go to Switzerland, they will ascend mountains, and they will feel a very natural and irresistible desire to do what everybody has done before, and still more, what nobody has done. It was the blue ribbon of the Alps that poor Lord Francis Douglas was trying for the other day. If it must be so, at all events the Alpine Club that has proclaimed this crusade, must manage the thing rather better, or it will soon be voted a nuisance. If the work is to be done, it must be done well. They must advise youngsters to practise, and make sure of their strength and endurance."

The Matterhorn was the last of the great peaks in the Monte Rosa district which remained unascended, it was the "blue ribbon" of the Alps, and hence it is that apart from any other reason, the date of its ascent may most fitly be taken to be the closing event in the "great age of conquest."

※※※※※※※※※※※※※※

IV. PERIOD 1866—1885.

During the commencement of this period, the "second generation of guides," as they have been called, came to the front; such men as Hans Jaun, Rubi, Lanier, the brothers Payot, Andreas Maurer, Emile Rey, and Ferdinand Imseng. By the end of the "golden age" the guides held very different opinions and ideas as to "what would go" or the practicability of certain routes, from those they had at the commencement. Above all, they had gained confidence in their own powers. Experience had taught them that the word "impossible" formed no part of the vocabulary of their craft. They had come to regard the most inaccessible-looking peaks as a regimental roughrider looks upon an unbroken colt; with the full and certain knowledge that human power and patience must eventually master it. The second generation of guides reaped the benefit of the ten or fifteen years' experience their elders had already gained. They learned in a few seasons many important axioms of guiding, which had taken the earlier generation years to determine. With the exception of the Meije, which was climbed in 1877, all the great peaks in the Alps were conquered by 1870. The most remarkable first ascents made during this period, were those of the Gspaltenhorn, the Aiguille de Blaitière, the two peaks of the Aiguille du Dru, and the Dent du Géant; though it should be remembered that artificial aid was used in this ascent to a far greater extent than had previously been the custom. Both peaks of the Aiguille de Charmoz were ascended in 1881 by Mr. Mummery, a gentleman whose name will always be associated with that of Alexander Burgener, as having performed the most remarkable of those *tours de force*, which brought that guide so prominently before the public. All that was now left for climbers who were ambitious of doing something absolutely new, was to make new routes up well-known mountains, or ascend peaks, which in the early days had been looked upon merely as the buttresses of the great piles of snow and ice of which they formed a part. I think it was Monsieur Loppé, who, in comparing this period with the previous one, and referring to some rather sensational ascents which had then just been made, said, that in order to climb nowadays, "il faut un gymnaste pour faire des escalades, un ingénieur pour faire des mines, et puis un jeune homme très-fort pour porter les sacs." As this period advanced, it gradually became more and more difficult to find anything new. After a mountain had been ascended, say from Zermatt and then from Zinal, the different points of the compass were by turns brought into play to describe the exact direction of the route taken, and to indicate whether it was by the "S.S.E." or "S.E. by E." arête that the ascent was made. The brains of the hunters after new routes were sorely taxed in trying to discover fresh variations of old tracks. If, however, they could only manage to strike a few feet to the north of Mr. So-and-So's route, or descend by the couloir when some *Herr* had kept to the rocks, they were thoroughly pleased and proud of their performance. In the next number of the journal of their club, they were sure to chronicle the particulars of these performances, to record the precise moment they "struck the moraine," and the exact time of duration of the expedition, "exclusive of halts." The descriptions of the muddles out of which their guides contrived to extricate the heroes of these narratives, are rather like parodies on those familiar incidents which gives so much life and zest to the pages of 'Peaks, Passes, and Glaciers.' One might as well try to gather pleasant pictures of mountaineering from Bunyan's description of the ascent of the Hill Difficulty, as from this class of Alpine narrative.

In the old days, when Mr. A. arrived at Grindelmatt in order to attack the Swaghorn, and found that it had been climbed the day before by Mr. B., he did not take his disappointment much to heart, he was comforted by the thought that after all the Swaggerhorn and half a score of other great peaks were left for him. But as the list of fresh possibilities began to diminish, there was much heart-burning and jealousy among the aspirants to these somewhat barren honours. An unpleasant state of matters often ensued, such as can only be understood by those who have stayed in the same hôtel with climbers, who suspect each other of having designs on the Col (which ought to be) *dit* Imbécile. It sometimes happened that the rivals met 'entirely by accident' on the glacier and after the manner of the representative 'Truthful James' of Saasthal, guides have been known to try and account for their presence on that particular spot by saying that they were going after chamois, utterly regardless of the fact that no one in the party possessed a gun. I doubt if in the whole of the columns of the *Field*, where disputed matters regarding sport are usually discussed with considerable asperity and vigour by gamekeepers and others, one would find a tithe of the envy, hatred, and all uncharitableness which pervades Alpine controversies. Matters of Alpine, as of any other controversy depend after all so much upon the point of view from which they are regarded. Take, for instance, the typical wrangle about the Dru. If photographs were taken from the Montanvert, and then again from the south, of the three great towers crowning the buttress which descends from the Aiguille Verte to the Mer de Glace (the Pic sans Nom and the two Drus), I doubt if any one who had not actually seen these peaks would believe that the photographs could possibly represent the same subject, even though he was told that they were taken from different points of view. Mr. Charlet, in conducting tourists across the Mer de Glace, had from boyhood upwards pointed out the nearest of the three obelisks as being the Dru, the one which ultimately proved to be much the more difficult of the two; and it was only natural he should do so, as the central one of the three buttresses cannot be seen from the Montanvert. Mr. C. T. Dent, in his popular and witty volume 'Above the Snow Line,' gives an illustration of that peak of the trio which he has appropriated, from a point of view which must give an entirely new idea of this great stone minaret to the majority of his readers. When Mr. Charlet in his turn gives the world a volume of his mountaineering experiences, which could not fail to make another most interesting work of the kind, he will doubtless preface the narrative of his hard-fought conquest with an illustration of the peak as it is seen from the Montanvert, where for years it has excited the admiration of every one of the thousands who visit Chamonix. The appearance of this line of flying buttresses when seen from various points of view, alters so completely and gives the pinnacles such an entirely different aspect, that they can be made to lend themselves in support of any theory regarding their relative importance. I have always wondered that one of the tribe of peak-baggers has not secured the Pic sans Nom, and I make them a present of the suggestion. It certainly overtops, and as seen, for instance, from near Les Tines, it entirely eclipses either the Pic Charlet or the Pic Dent.

During this period, several of the guides in the Alps were taken abroad for the exploration of mountain regions in other countries. The first guide to quit his native valley for this special class of work was François Dévouassoud, and to him belongs the honour, of which a less modest man might justly feel proud, of being the *doyen* of the pioneers who have set out at different times for the Caucasus, the Himálayas, New Zealand, or the Andes. He cannot now be considered to be *the* traveller guide as his performances have been eclipsed. It probably required considerably more strength of character than we perhaps appreciate for some of these guides to start for far-distant countries, where they vaguely imagined they might encounter adventures similar to those they may have read of during the long winter evenings in some popular Penny Dreadful book of travels.

François is a most remarkable man. He passed some years at a Jesuit Seminary with the view to entering the priesthood of that powerful body: he however abandoned the idea, returned to his native valley and joined the Société des Guides instead. He was in practice as a guide before the commencement of the "golden age" of climbing, but, as Mr. D. W. Freshfield's sketch in this volume shows, he has never done a single new expedition of any importance in his native district, or even ascended any one of the more difficult of the great Chamonix aiguilles; still no list of the Pioneers of the Alps would be complete without his name. He has the bump of locality in a marked degree, and few of the readers of Murray's Guide to Switzerland are probably aware how much they are indebted to François for the minute details regarding the by-ways in every district in the Alps. He is a great reader, a good linguist, and I believe that some of the pages of this work have been submitted in their original form to his judicious criticisms by a contributor. He is a charming companion—I know of no greater pleasure than having a long talk with François, he at once impresses one as a clever, intelligent man of the world who has seen much of it.

From all we can learn, the difficulties of the expeditions to the Caucasus have been unduly overrated and magnified; not by any means intentionally, but simply from the fact that none of the little band of early explorers had ever travelled in a really rough country. The small *contretemps* of travel they encountered were simply those such as any Englishman unacquainted with the habits of the people, the language, or unprovided with proper introductions, could not but fail to meet with, in any Russian territory which the Messrs Cook had not succeeded in opening up for the tourist. It is even said that one of these ingenuous explorers nearly brought about a serious diplomatic complication by attempting to photograph the fortifications of Sebastopol from his bedroom window! The height of the mountains in the Caucasus always conveys a most erroneous idea of their difficulty. Writing to me of the ascent of the "greatest mountain of the whole range," Mr. F. C. Grove says, "Elbruz was such a very tame and easy ascent—bar the fatigue. If Knubel had been the mightiest of guides, he could hardly have distinguished himself." That there are difficult peaks in the Caucasus no one can deny; but they are still unascended. The guides who have been taken from the Alps to this "great field for exploration," have usually been called upon to display those qualities we associate with a Dragoman.

The brothers François and Michel Dévouassoud have explored the Caucasus, a district which has been visited by Peter Knubel, and also by Alexander Burgener, who accompanied the now President and the present Secretary of the Alpine Club. This expedition has not only been naturally rich in photographic results, but has already afforded ample materials for at least two most enjoyable and improving evenings at the Alpine Club. J. A. Carrel and his son Louis have visited South America; Michel Payot has travelled in the northern part of that continent; and Edouard Cupelin has ascended Teneriffe. Hans Jaun, Josef Imboden, Kaspar Maurer, and Ulrich Kauffmann have visited the Himalayas, and the last-mentioned guide has taken part in the first ascent of Mount Cook in New Zealand. Without entering upon the question as to whether the natives of these districts will ever attempt, or are capable of undertaking, the further conquest of their own mountains, the reason for guides being selected from the Alps is a very obvious one: it is the only district in the whole world where men are to be found at the same time competent to act as guides in a region unknown to them, and possessed of a knowledge of difficult rock and ice work. The men chosen may, with scarcely a single exception, be considered to be those who had previously taken a degree with honours in their craft.

The closing event of this period may be considered to be the ascent of the Aiguille Blanche de Peuterot by Mr. H. S. King, C.I.E., with Emile Rey and two Valaisan guides, an event which is referred to in the sketch of Rey.

An illustration of this snow-pinnacle on one of the greatest buttresses of Mont Blanc, may be found in the eighth volume of the *Alpine Journal*. This was the peak on which Professor F. M. Balfour lost his life in 1882, while attempting to ascend it with only one guide. To Mr. King belongs what I am sure such an enthusiastic mountaineer as he is, must consider the melancholy distinction of scaling the last unascended peak in the Mont Blanc Range,—the last link in that long chain which it had taken exactly ninety-nine years to complete.

* * *

V. ALPINE ACCIDENTS.

THERE are probably few events which call forth more universal or genuine sympathy than an accident in the hunting-field, on the river, or among the Alps. Those who had never followed the hounds, or even seen one of the great snow-peaks, heard alike with real sorrow the news of the death of Whyte Melville or Francis Maitland Balfour. There is something inexpressibly sad in hearing of those who are in all the hey-day of sound health, at the very moment when they are enjoying to the full some of the best and most lasting pleasures nature can give, being suddenly struck down. The crosses and wreaths made of autumn leaves and berries gathered amid the gnarled roots on the Riffel-Alp, laid as they often are by unknown hands on the graves of those who have not been even passing acquaintances, are far more genuine tokens of sympathy than the most costly *immortelles*. It is only those who have stood at the door of a Swiss Inn, and watched all the familiar preparations for a long mountain expedition made by those who are destined, alas! never to return, that can understand how it is that when we wish our parting friends 'Good Speed,' the words are no mere conventional form of courtesy; and how we grasp their hand when we welcome their return as if we had not met for years. One cannot hear of an accident in the Alps without a crowd of grim and almost ghastly pictures coming to one's recollection. Some of us may remember the hours spent in anxious waiting when the fate of the missing party was not absolutely known; next, the muster of the guides, and the search party's return; then, perhaps, a funeral in the mountain churchyard —for what is more appropriate than that the soldier should be laid in the battlefield near the place where he fell. I can never forget the pathos with which Pfarrer Strasser of Grindelwald, the man whose real kindness has comforted more sorrow-stricken folk on these sad occasions than probably any other of his cloth, once pointed to a slab in his churchyard, and then to a great peak on which an accident had taken place, and said, "That is really the poor fellow's monument." And those who come afterwards to stand for a few moments by the grave, and thus pay a tribute to the memory of an old friend, will not find that the beautiful surroundings make their task more sorrowful. One prefers to think of the old comrade resting amid scenes he loved so well, than in the dreary grimness of a family vault. After an Alpine accident, the newspapers are generally flooded with correspondence on the subject. This may partly be accounted for by the fact that the silly season in the newspaper world happens to fall about the same time as the climbing season in the Alps. Apparently those whose experience of mountaineering is limited to a successful crossing of the Gorner Glacier, or whose ideas of the dangers of the Matterhorn are probably based on the difficulties they have undergone in passing another party on the Mauvais Pas, do not hesitate to rush into print and give the world the benefit of their ideas on the subject. "Criticism is good for all of us," Mr. C. E. Mathews wrote, "but it is only really valuable in proportion to the knowledge of the critic." I cannot help thinking that if "Clericus" and "A British Matron" happened to be staying at Cowes or in Leicestershire when an accident took place in the Solent or the hunting-field, they would feel some misgivings in addressing "Mr. Editor," lest they should inadvertently get out of their bearings on subjects about which they must feel themselves to be totally ignorant. But the science of mountaineering would seem to be different from that belonging to any other form of sport. It appears to be popularly believed that all its details and mysteries can be mastered in a single day's excursion. A Cook's tourist who happened to come into the *fumoir* of some hotel, and heard another of his fraternity describing the incidents of a trip to the Grands Mulets and back, might well be excused if he imagined that the hero of the evening was an old and seasoned mountaineer, from the decided and unhesitating way in which he invariably laid down the law as to the use of the rope, &c., and criticized the performances of his guides. A mountain ascent is generally made in private, so to speak. The audience, gathered round the telescope in front of an hôtel, is, as a rule, very charitably disposed. If the progress was slow, they are sure to say that the snow must be soft, and that the party is in reality going fast; but from the immense distance its movements appear to be slow. When we first begin to climb, we seldom have the opportunity of gauging our own powers with those of other amateurs, as would be the case with Tennis, Rowing, or in fact with almost any other form of sport. I remember well after my first glacier excursion I took to reading books of Alpine travel, and used to picture Mr. Leslie Stephen being hauled over the crevasses on the Eiger Joch exactly as I had been over those on the Théodule. Out of the whole mass of what has been written about Alpine accidents, and the perils and dangers of climbing, there is one paper in the *Alpine Journal* (vol. xi.), entitled "The Alpine Obituary," which for temperate expression of opinion, based upon careful investigation of facts ascertained during a long and varied mountaineering experience, stands by itself among the literature on this subject. The Alpine death-roll, upon which Mr. C. E. Mathews bases his remarks, is confined to purely mountaineering accidents which have befallen climbers at work on great peaks or glaciers. The many deaths which have taken place on beaten tracks below the snow-line, resulting from apoplexy or heart disease, or the mishaps of adventurous tourists who have slipped on grass slopes while endeavouring to get plants of Edelweiss, and which are always chronicled in the newspapers as "another Alpine accident," are naturally not alluded to. Neither has he referred to the deaths which have occurred on minor peaks, such as those round the upper end of the Lake of Geneva, which I regret to say have now reached a considerable number. I do not personally vouch for the fact, but I have often been told by several Swiss friends that more accidents have taken place on the Dent du Jaman than any other mountain in the whole of the Alps. In most cases the victims have been young Englishmen living with crammers at Vevey or Montreux, who start for the ascent without proper equipment, and while endeavouring to take a short cut make the fatal slip. The Britisher of the age at which he aspires to Woolwich or to Sandhurst, usually forms his estimate of the intelligence of the inhabitants of those foreign countries in which he finds himself temporarily compelled to reside, by their proficiency in Cricket or Football. Hence it is that he has the utmost contempt for the well-meant counsels of the old pasteur in whose house he boards, or the friendly warnings of the country folk he meets on the upper pastures. It has often happened that a melancholy element of romance has been thrown around these rash and utterly indefensible escapades, by the plucky and almost heroic way in which the survivors have risked their own lives in attempting to save that of their comrade. And in after-life these lads will at least have the satisfaction of feeling that they tried to act as brave, true-hearted men should do, on that day which they will always look back upon, as the one on which they first knew what it was to meet with a great sorrow. Mr. Mathews's paper is thoroughly characteristic of the writer, it is practical, straightforward, and to the point. There is an impartiality and temperate tone about his words which make one almost imagine that we are listening to the summing up of a judge, coming as they do from one of the founders of the Alpine Club, who for more than thirty years has scarcely missed a season in the Alps, and has been a most popular and unanimously elected President of the Club, and one of the most distinguished and successful climbers among its Members. Even those who are as firmly convinced in their own minds that climbers go up mountains in order to swagger about their own performances, as that the members of the Oriental Club suffer much secret agony from partaking of large helpings of chutnee, must admit that in his paper he has endeavoured to avoid all exaggeration, and succeeded in his aim, to "nothing extenuate, nor set down aught in malice." "Although we must ever mourn for the brave men," he writes, "who have rendered good service to the Club, and whose loss marks a gap that will not easily be filled, it is none the less our duty to see that the responsibility is put upon the right shoulders, and that our pursuit should not be held up to unmerited obloquy because some sanguine men persist in neglecting the ordinary safeguards which alone make that pursuit justifiable." By Mr. Mathews's kind permission I am able to give the table appended to his paper, which shows the names of the *Herren* and their guides who perished on great peaks or glaciers between 1856—1882, together with the cause of each accident. There are forty-six accidents, resulting in a total loss of eighty-seven lives, forty-nine of the victims being *Herren*, and thirty-eight being guides or porters. In the Journal of one of the foreign clubs, some additions were made at the time to Mr. Mathews's melancholy list. I prefer, however, to give the table as it appeared in the *Alpine Journal*:—

FATAL ACCIDENTS IN THE HIGH ALPS, 1856—1882.

Date.	Travellers.	Guides.	Where Accident Occurred.	Remarks.
1856, July.	E. de la Grotte.		Findelen (Glacier Zermatt).	Fall in crevasse; party insufficiently roped.
1860, August 15.	Mr. J. M. Rochester, Mr. F. Vavassour, Mr. B. Fuller.	F. Tairraz.	Col du Géant.	Avalanche of fresh snow; party insufficiently roped.
1863, August 7.		Porter, name not recorded (with F. W. Jacomb and Chater).	Saasside of Fletschjoch.	Fall in crevasse; insufficiently roped.
1864, February 28.	M. Boissonet.	J. J. Bennen.	Haut de Cry.	Avalanche; ignorance of the state of winter snow.

ACCIDENTS.

FATAL ACCIDENTS IN THE HIGH ALPS, 1856--1882 (*continued*).

Date.	Travellers.	Guides.	Where Accident Occurred.	Remarks.
1864, August 9.		Ambroise Couttet (with 2 Austrian gentlemen).	Mont Blanc (Grand Plateau).	Fall in crevasse; unroped.
1865, July 14.	Lord F. Douglas, Rev. Chas. Hudson, Mr. D. Hadow.	Michel Croz.	Matterhorn.	Slip on rocks.
„ July 18.	Mr. Knyvett Wilson.		Riffelhorn.	Fall on rocks; traveller alone.
„ July 27.		Porter, name not recorded (with H. J. and J. F. Bailey).	Monte Rosa.	Avalanche.
„ August 23.	Herr Hüpner.	Eugène Imfanger.	Titlis.	Slip on snow; party consisted of two persons only.
„ August 31.	Herr Hüsch.		Gross Venediger.	Fall in crevasse; no rope.
„ „	Mr. W. G. Watson.		Windacher Ferner (Tyrol).	Fall in crevasse; no rope.
1866, August 23.	Mr. Bulkeley Young.		Mont Blanc.	Slip on snow; no guides.
„ October 13.	Captain Arkwright.	Michel Simond, François Tournier, Joseph Tournier.	Mont Blanc (Ancien Passage).	Avalanche; bad guiding.
1868, July 27.	Colonel Pringle.	...	Creux d'Enfer, near Bex.	Slip on rocks; alone.
„ August 29.	Count Louis de Cambacérès.		Glacier du Trient.	Unroped; two persons only.
1869, July 27.	Rev. J. M. Elliot.		Schreckhorn.	Fall on rocks; no rope.
„ Sept. 15.	Mr. Chester.		Lyskamm.	Fall on ice; probably unroped.
1870, August 2.	Mrs. Geo. Marke.	Olivier Gay.	Mont Blanc.	Fall in crevasse; unroped.
„ Sept. 6.	Mr. Randall, Mr. MacCorkendale, Mr. Beane.	Jean Balmat, Joseph Breton, Edouard Simond, Auguste Couttet, Auguste Cachat, Ferdinand Tairraz, Alphonse Balmat, Johann Graf.	Mont Blanc (Mur de la Côte).	Furious storm; climbing in bad weather, probably bad guiding.
1871 (?)	Herr F. Bodmer.		Piz Tschierva.	Fall in crevasse; traveller alone.
1872, July 24.	Herr Von Allmen.	Johann Bischoff.	Jungfrau (Roththal Sattel).	Avalanche.
1873, June.	Rev. B. Marriott.		Near Pontresina.	Fall on rocks; traveller alone.

D

FATAL ACCIDENTS IN THE HIGH ALPS, 1856—1882 (*continued*).

DATE.	TRAVELLERS.	GUIDES.	WHERE ACCIDENT OCCURRED.	REMARKS.
1873, Sept. 14.	Professor Fedchenko.		Col du Géant.	Exposure; incompetence of guides.
1874, August 31.	Mr. J. A. G. Marshall.	Johann Fischer.	Mont Blanc (Bronillard Glacier).	Fall in Schrund; midnight.
1875, August.		Antille.	Triftjoch.	Slip on rock; unroped.
„ Sept. 2.	M. Brunker.		Upper Grindelwald Glacier.	Slip on ice; alone.
1876, August 28.	Mr. Johnson, Mr. Hayman.	Franz Sarbach.	Felik Joch.	Avalanche and exposure; climbing in a fog.
1877, June 7.	M. Henri Cordier.		Near Glacier du Plaret (Dauphiné).	Fall in torrent under snow; unroped.
„ August 20		Porter, name not recorded.	Col de Miage.	Avalanche; unroped.
„ Sept. 6.	Mr. W. A. Lewis, Mr. Noel H. Patterson.	Niklaus Knubel, Peter J. Knubel, Johann Knubel.	Lyskamm.	Fall from cornice.
1878, July 29.	Herr Reuter.		Salève (?) near Coire.	Slip on rock; two travellers only.
„ August 18.	Dr. Sachs, Herr Heinitz.	Jos. Reinstadtler, Züschg.	Monte Cevedale.	Slip on snow, and fall in crevasse.
1879, August 14.	Dr. W. O. Moseley.		Matterhorn.	Fall on rocks; unroped.
„ August 15.		Jos. Brantschen.	Matterhorn.	Exposure (?)
„ August 18.	Mr. Forrester.		Diablerets.	Fall on ice; no guide.
„	Dr. Carl Foeltz.		Taufig (Styrian Alps).	Fall on rocks; alone.
„ Sept. 14.	M. Melley.		Gantcrist.	Fall on rocks; alone.
1880, July 18.	Dr. A. Haller.	Peter Rubi, F. Roth.	Lauteraarjoch.	Fall in Bergschrund.
„ July 25.	Herr Welter.		Neveser Ferner.	Fall in crevasse; unroped.
1881, August 8.	Signor D. Marinelli.	F. Imseng, B. Pedranzini.	Monte Rosa (Macugnaga side).	Avalanche.
„ August 18.	Mdlle. Dupré.		Glacier du Mont Lans (Dauphiné).	Climbing in bad weather; cold and exposure.
„ Sept. 4.	Mr. H. Latham.		Bussalp (Grindelwald).	Avalanche; alone.
1882, July 19.	Professor F. M. Balfour. F.R.S.	Johann Petrus.	Mont Blanc (Aiguille Blanche de Peuteret).	Slip on rocks; two persons only in expedition.

FATAL ACCIDENTS IN THE HIGH ALPS, 1856—1882, (continued).

DATE.	TRAVELLERS.	GUIDES.	WHERE ACCIDENT OCCURRED.	REMARKS.
1882, August 3.	Mr. W. Penhall.	And. Maurer.	Wetterhorn.	Avalanche; two persons only in expedition.
„ August 12.	Mr. W. E. Gabbett.	J. M. Lochmatter. — Lochmatter.	Dent Blanche.	Slip on rocks.
„ August 15.	Herr von Rütte.		Dündengrat (Blümlis Alp).	Slip on rocks; two persons only in the expedition; no guides.

"What then are the conclusions to be drawn?" Mr. Mathews asks in concluding his paper. "Surely my readers will already have done so for themselves. Mountaineering is extremely dangerous in the case of incapable, of imprudent, of thoughtless men. But I venture to state that of all the accidents in our sad obituary, there is hardly one which need have happened, there is hardly one which could not have been easily prevented by proper caution and proper care. Men get careless and too confident. This does not matter or the other does not matter. The fact is, that everything matters; precautions should not only be ample, but excessive. Mountaineering is not dangerous provided that the climber knows his business and takes the necessary precautions—all within his own control—to make danger impossible. The prudent climber will recollect what he owes to his family and to his friends. He will also recollect that he owes something to the Alps, and will scorn to bring them into disrepute. He will not go on a glacier without a rope. He will not climb alone or with a single companion. He will treat a great mountain with the respect it deserves, and not try to rush a dangerous peak with inadequate guiding power. He will turn his back steadfastly upon mist and storm. He will not go where avalanches are in the habit of falling after fresh snow, or wander about beneath an overhanging glacier in the heat of a summer afternoon. Above all, if he loves the mountains for their own sake, for the lesson they can teach and the happiness they can bring, he will do nothing that can discredit his manly pursuit or bring down the ridicule of the undiscerning upon the noblest pastime in the world."

To those who climb it may, and does, alas! happen, that a choice has to be made between apparent self-preservation and our duty to our comrades. We can only hope that should it ever be our fate to be so tested, we may act with loyalty to our friends, and be faithful to the old traditions of our race. "All being ready," as old Mr. Auldjo wrote nearly sixty years ago, "we bade adieu to those who were to return, and shaking each other by the hand, swore to keep faithful, and not to desert each other in danger or difficulty, declaring that all distinction of person should cease,—that we would be brethren in this enterprise." The old man's words are well worthy of being written in letters of gold in every mountain inn in the Alps. This is the true spirit in which all mountaineering expeditions should be undertaken. Although guides hold certificates from the Swiss Government, and are therefore theoretically qualified to conduct a party on any mountain in that district, this qualification is one which no one could possibly admit to hold good in practice. I do not suppose that any one who required to undergo a critical operation, would rush off to the first house where he remembered having seen a red glazed lamp or "M.R.C.S." attached to a name on a brass plate, to undergo it, although the occupier would be doubtless technically authorized to use the contents of his surgical instrument case as he thought desirable. It is much to be regretted that an accident on a great peak does not have the effect of making people pause for a moment, before they rush on places where in the old days "angels feared to tread." As a rule the travelling public do not seem to take to heart any of the lessons which an Alpine accident teaches to all of us. Instead of deterring tourists from exposing their own lives and those of their guides, a horrible catastrophe only seems to throw a glamour of notoriety around the mountain, part of which these so-called mountaineers fondly imagine will be reflected on the persons of all those who afterwards are dragged by their guides to the summit. There were far fewer ascents made of the Lyskamm, than there have been in recent years, since the name of that mountain was brought before the public by the tragic death of the brothers Knubel. During the climbing season there are always old hands to be found in the mountain inns, who as a rule are only too ready to give a new-comer the benefit of their experience or knowledge of the district; if for no other reason, from the recollection of the difficulties they themselves encountered when it was the sole object of their ambition to be able to say they had done Mont Blanc or the Breithorn. Any one who has read the fascinating account which Professor Tyndall gives of his long struggle with the Matterhorn, or Mr. Whymper's narrative of his hard-fought conquest, must pause to take breath when they read the reasons which have been given for attempting such a peak as this. In the newspaper columns we read, "We had ascended the Titlis, and made other excursions among the hills. We knew that ladies had made the ascent, and youths; and the mountain had besides been climbed by friends of ours whose physical strength, to say the least, was not superior to our own. It was the regular thing to go up the Matterhorn, and we accordingly determined to make the ascent." *The regular thing to go up the Matterhorn!* I suppose he is right, and that it has actually come to this pass. If it was not from the fear of making a misquotation, there are one or two passages which occur to one's mind as being singularly appropriate to the downfall of such a mighty peak as this. Times are indeed changed in Zermatt since it was frequented by the group of climbers portrayed in Mr. Whymper's engraving of the imaginary "Club House" of the place. Some of those whose portraits are in it have passed away, but I wonder what their feelings would be if they could return once more, and stroll down the little village street, and see how the surroundings have altered. It is difficult to picture the pioneers of the "age of conquest" period, being asked at every turn if they "want a guide for the Matterhorn, Sir?" or to have the cards of those same so-called guides "autorisés par le gouvernement" thrust into their hand with that irrepressible persistency only to be equalled by the manner in which the velveteen-coated gentry of Naples pester us to buy sponges and tortoise-shell combs.

Year after year the swarms of tourists who come out to the Alps, become larger, every year the facilities for travelling become easier. It was only last year that one of Messrs. T. Cook and Sons most experienced and trusted colleagues explained to me at great length the reasons which prevented the firm with which he was connected from issuing tickets for the ascent of Mont Blanc. I presume, of course, that it was the intention of the Messrs. Cook only to issue return tickets to the summit and back. As the idea becomes more and more firmly fixed in the minds of the travelling public, that it is "the regular thing to go up the Matterhorn," it will indeed be a marvel if the entries on the Alpine death-roll become less frequent. "Climb if you will," wrote Mr. Whymper, "but remember that courage and strength are nought without prudence, and that a momentary negligence may destroy the happiness of a lifetime. Do nothing in haste, look well to each step; and from the beginning think well what may be the end."

* * *

VI. MOUNTAINEERING WITHOUT GUIDES.

SINCE the commencement of systematic mountaineering many very remarkable feats have been performed by amateurs without guides. So early as 1856, "Where there's a will, there's a way" was published by Mr. E. S. Kennedy, and the Rev. Charles Hudson, who was killed nine years afterwards on the Matterhorn, describing several glacier excursions their party made without guides, including the first ascent of Mont Blanc from St. Gervais. This was a most remarkable performance for amateurs, taking into account the period at which this feat was achieved, as any one must admit who refers to the table of first ascents in the "golden age," and notices how the science of mountaineering had then barely commenced. "We had all perfect confidence in each other," the authors write, "we had all more than ordinary experience in mountain difficulties, we had all crossed glacier passes without guides; and we had made some of the more difficult ascents. By examining maps and models we had made ourselves as nearly masters of the route as possible, continued training had put us into capital condition, so that we could have sustained very prolonged exertion, and we knew the nature of the difficulties to be overcome, and were consequently enabled to guard against danger. It was after this preparation that we started upon our enterprise, and we maintain that the risk of serious accident was but little greater than incurred by the pedestrians in the streets of London." Then the writers go on to say that they wished to put the ascent of Mont Blanc, "within the reach of all who, like ourselves, are inclined to say,—

'Fain would I climb, but that I fear to pay.'"

Of these early attempts without guides one of the most remarkable (it is mentioned by Mr. Whymper in his work, but no more detailed account of it seems to have been published) appears to have been made by the Messrs. Parker on the Matterhorn in 1860. In 1870, 'The High Alps without Guides,' by the Rev. A. G. Girdlestone, appeared. In the first chapter the author says "that among the many excursions in the Alps with which the writer is acquainted, he can only record two which have not disappointed him by their ease as compared with the descriptions of them in Alpine Club or private publications." "It is well," he says, "to bear this in mind." He goes on to speak of the defects of guides, and certainly there is no wonder that any one who had the misfortune to meet with the same experiences as Mr. Girdlestone in his dealings with them, should wish to dispense with their services altogether. He would not "have commenced a campaign against guides, had it not been for their domineering disposition and their exorbitant tariffs. The guides consider glacier excursions as feast-days," and "the provisions of the luckless traveller having been plentifully ordered, are to be fully and constantly enjoyed. To resist their attempts to halt and feed even at intervals of two hours, if so minded, is apt to produce sulkiness and consequent probable failure in an expedition, or may be unavailing. I believe that I shall be borne out by most mountaineers in saying that the necessity of keeping one's guides in good humour involves a very unpleasant amount of subjection to them." Trying to provide small-talk for my guides during the monotony of a steep snow slope, or otherwise attempting to keep them in good humour, are social duties connected with mountaineering in which I, for my own part, have been sorely remiss.

It is always instructive, however, to hear two sides of any subject discussed. In spite of these most unpleasant defects of character, which Mr. Girdlestone observed among the guides, he admits that, "there are occasions when the arduous step-cutting in hard ice has to be undertaken during long periods. For such work, as well as for sureness of foot, and ease in awkward places, a guide, even a second or third-rate one, used to the mountains, and often engaged in muscular labour, has an immense advantage over any amateur, however skilful." In recent years the most notable expeditions made by amateurs without guides, have been by the brothers Zsigmondy, one of whom lost his life on the Meije, and by the brothers C. and L. Pilkington, and Mr. F. Gardiner. In 1881 the three last-named gentlemen ascended the Matterhorn from Zermatt in one day, climbed the Wetterhorn from Rosenlaui, crossed the Finsteraarjoch, ascended the Gross Nesthorn and the Ecrins, traversed the Rothhorn (Moming), crossed the Mönchjoch and ascended the Jungfrau from the Wengern Alp. In recording these feats in the *Alpine Journal*, the present editor says, that he believes them to be "without parallel in Alpine history." This same party, among other first-class expeditions, also made the ascent of the highest summit of the Meije. In referring to the second ascent of this peak, which he made with that tried and experienced veteran Christian Almer, the Rev. W. A. B. Coolidge speaks of it as being one of the two "most difficult" expeditions he ever made with his old friend and guide, while describing the success of both as being "wholly due to Almer's indomitable pluck and skill." In 1876 the Matterhorn was ascended by Mr. Cust and a party of amateurs; Mont Blanc has been climbed by that distinguished mountaineer Mr. Morshead, who, in spite of the dangers which he of all others knew so well that he was liable to incur, ventured by himself to the summit as a protest against the stringent rules of the Société des Guides, to which reference has already been made. There is also, by the way, a legend of some Scotch gentleman, who is said to have reached the summit without guides, but whether this escapade was undertaken from a praiseworthy wish to save the "saxpences" and half-francs in his own pockets, and not from any desire to break down an intolerable system, "deponent sayeth not." He reached the Dôme de Goûter from the summit, where his movements seemed to indicate an inability to descend further, as he was observed to be circling round and round. It was rightly concluded that he must be suffering from snow-blindness, and Christian Lauener and a party of guides most disinterestedly hastened to his aid. Professor Tyndall, as we have already stated, made the ascent of Monte Rosa, without companions, in 1858; but probably the greatest feat of this description ever performed, having regard to all its attendant circumstances, was Jacques Balmat's first attempt to ascend Mont Blanc.

In commenting upon ascents without guides, Professor Tyndall's remarks on the subject are well worthy of our attention. Writing in *Macmillan's Magazine* with reference to the performances of the author of 'The High Alps without Guides,' he says, "He (Mr. Girdlestone) deems guides, and rightly so, very expensive, and he also feels pleasure in trying his own powers. I would admonish him that he may go too far in this direction, and probably his own experience has by this time forestalled the admonition. Still there is much in his feeling which challenges sympathy; for if skill, courage, and strength are things to be cultivated in the Alps, they are, within certain limits, best exercised and developed in the absence of guides. And if the real climbers are ever to be differentiated from the crowd, it is only to be done by dispensing with professional assistance. But no man without natural aptitude and due training would be justified in undertaking anything of this kind, and it is an error to suppose that the necessary knowledge can be obtained in one or two summers in the Alps. Climbing is an art, and those who wish to cultivate it on their own account ought to give themselves sufficient previous practice in the company of first-rate guides. But whatever be the amount of preparation, real climbers must still remain select men. Here, as in every other sphere of human action, whether intellectual or physical, as indeed among the guides themselves, real eminence falls only to the lot of few."

VII. MOUNTAINEERING IN WINTER.

THE first winter expedition made in the Alps after the commencement of systematic mountaineering was in 1862, when Mr. T. S. Kennedy, with old Peter Taugwalder and Peter Perrn attempted to ascend the Matterhorn. In 1866 Mr. Horace Walker, and the late Mr. A. W. Moore, crossed the Strahleck and Finsteraarjoch, accompanied by Melchior Anderegg, Christian Almer, and 'Peterli' Bobren. The following winter Mr. Moore crossed the Brêche de la Meije, and subsequently, with his friend Mr. Walker, he made a winter tour among the Dolomites. Mr. Coolidge, in his interesting sketch of Almer, says, "To him too (Almer) is due the fashion of winter mountaineering," and threatened to withdraw his paper if the sentence was altered. Most mountaineers, however, will prefer to give to the two *Herren* of the party, the distinction of being the first to prove to amateurs the possibility of finding enjoyment in mountaineering at that season of the year. Like his two companions, old Christian had doubtless done a good deal of chamois-hunting during the winter months, but it is highly improbable that any one of that distinguished trio of guides would have dreamed of going over the Strahleck *comme distraction* at that or, in fact, at any other season of the year, had Messrs. Moore and Walker not engaged them for the expedition. They would doubtless otherwise have been in their own homes, engaged in those particular occupations, which apart from guiding, have usually been associated with the name of each. Mr. T. S. Kennedy's attempt on the Matterhorn was not undertaken so much with the object of exploring the beauties of the Alps in their winter garb, as with that of attacking a mountain under different conditions from those which prevail during the summer months.

"I hope," Mr. A. W. Moore wrote in the *Alpine Journal*, "that the success of our expedition will induce others to follow our example. I am sure that no one who may be favoured with reasonably good weather will return disappointed. A full moon is desirable, and indeed in consequence of the shortness of the days essential, suppose any high expeditions are contemplated. As regards the prudence of attempting such, our experience goes to show that snow and glacier excursions, under favourable circumstances, may be made with less actual difficulty than in summer." Most of the great peaks in the Alps have now been ascended in winter. The Wetterhorn, the Gross Schreckhorn, and the Jungfrau, have been climbed by Mr. Coolidge, and the first of these peaks was also scaled by Mr. Eccles, who, with the exception of M. Loppé has probably made more winter expeditions in the Alps than any other amateur. Monte Viso was successfully ascended by Signor L. Barale. The Piz Bernina, the Gross Glockner, the Mönch, the Finsteraarhorn, and several of the Dolomites have also been conquered in winter. On the 31st of January, 1876, Mont Blanc was ascended by an English lady who has since made her home near Argentière.

In the winter of 1882, which was noted for a most exceptionally long spell of continued fine weather during January and February, the present writer crossed the Col du Géant, ascended the Aiguilles du Tour and du Tacul for the first time at that season, and also made an ascent of the Buet. The following winter, 1883, a well-known English lady ascended the Aiguille du Midi, and made a number of other excursions, which she has recorded in 'The High Alps in Winter.' But none of those who have visited the Alps during the winter months can show such a splendid record of achievements as the Signori Sella. It includes the ascent of the Matterhorn in 1882, and in more recent years, Monte Rosa (Dufour-spitze), the Grand Paradis, the Lyskamm, and the passage of the Lys Joch, combined with the ascent of the Signal Kuppe. During the winter of 1888 the Lauteraarhorn and the Gross Veischerhorn were ascended, the summit of the Jungfrau was crossed from the Bergli hut to the Wengern Alp, and the third winter ascent of Mont Blanc and first from the side of Italy was made by the Signori Sella, who, with their guides, started from the *cabane* of the Aiguilles Grises, and crossed over to Chamonix.

The great drawback to making winter ascents is the extreme shortness of the days; one cannot start much before 6 a.m., owing to the cold, and by 5 p.m. it is quite dark. It is a somewhat costly amusement, as, when one is compelled to sleep in the club-hut, porters must be sent in advance with blankets, wood, &c. Once fairly on the glacier, the going is in many aspects easier and safer than it is in summer, as the snow-bridges are more solid, and there is not the same risk of falling séracs. The most toilsome part of the *course* consists in wading through the snow-covered rhododendron bushes, on the lower slopes, or scrambling over the moraine where the spaces between the great boulders are generally concealed by the half-frozen snow. The cold is not nearly so intense as might be imagined. Mr. Coolidge found the summit of the Schreckhorn on the 27th of January, 1879, "deliciously warm." In describing the second winter ascent of Mont Blanc, which took place on the 30th of January, 1882 (the first having been on the 31st of the same month, six years before), I wrote at the time, of the change we experienced after our three hours' step-cutting from the 'Corridor,' on reaching the top, where we could almost have imagined ourselves

to be "going into a greenhouse on a winter's day." The appearance of the landscape is vastly different in winter from what it is in summer. If one looked down upon the valley of Chamonix from the Brevent or the Pierre Pointue, we should best describe the scene by comparing it to a picture, the lower half of which was in black and white, and the upper part filled in with colours. The winter sun throws a deep shadow across the valley, making the châlets, pine-trees, and dark patches of cliff appear to stand out as sharply against the snow as if they had been drawn on a white ground with the blackest of pencils. Above, everything is seen in colour, light, and brilliancy, and never does the sky appear so wonderfully transparent and beautiful, as when seen in winter from an Alpine valley. The views from the summits are simply marvellous. The most distant peaks stand out against the horizon as clearly as those in the panoramas in Baedeker. Not a vestige of mist is to be seen; there is a sharp, almost harsh line where the sky and earth meet. The air is so perfectly clear, and there is such a lack of atmosphere in these landscapes, that if it were possible to reproduce the scene on canvas all idea of distance would be lost. And, therefore, if one of our friends in the Belle Arti were to see the picture, he would most certainly say that it reminded him of some early master's first style, before he had thrown off somebody else's influence.

After my third visit to the Alps in winter, I thus attempted to describe their aspect at that season of the year. "During the last few years much has been written on the difference of the Alps in summer and in winter time. The characteristics of the two seasons can practically be summed up in a couple of sentences. Contrasts of rich colouring, produced by the snow-peaks, blue sky, and the many-coloured foreground of dark pines, meadow-land, and rock: *versus* the wide expanse of pure snow, the huge icicles on the cliffs, the frozen waterfalls, the leafless stems of the trees encrusted with hoar frost, and the wonderfully clear bracing atmosphere. Nature has a different garb for every season of the year—the fresh young shoots and flowers of spring, the dark reds and golden browns of autumn, or the beautiful forms of snow and ice. To decide which garb best becomes her would indeed be difficult. But the oftener one goes to the upper valleys in winter, the more one notices the entire absence of colouring; the more one feels the monotony of the wide expanse of snow, which never changes till the setting sun throws a rich glow over the landscape; a prospect somewhat marred by the thought of the number of hours which must elapse between 4.30 and the time for 'turning in.' Even

the most prosaic peasant must feel a certain amount of pleasure when he first sees the perce-neige appear through the snow, apart from any association the flower may have in his mind with the advent of the tourist. And *àpropos* of the tourist, nothing contributes more to the dreariness and desolation of the surroundings of the Swiss inn in winter than the objects which are associated in our minds with the travelling public. A snow-covered 'Ici on marque les bâtons' signboard is not a pleasing object; and no amount of snow and ice can make a pile of green-painted tables and garden-benches look picturesque. If we take the trouble to read between the lines what has been written about the Alps in winter, we shall see how often the purely physical side of enjoyment is brought to the front. The sleighing, the pleasure of taking exercise in an atmosphere so keen and bracing that fatigue is almost an impossibility. Then, again, the novelty of seeing old friends under an entirely new aspect. Were it possible to reverse the seasons, and transform July and August into January and February, I doubt very much if one would see the same faces year after year in the great mountaineering centres. When we think of our favourite peaks and valleys, it is always in their summer garb they come to our imagination."

VIII. ICE-AXE AND ROPE.

THE form of ice-axe in use at the end of last and the beginning of the present century was practically the same as that of the shipwright's adze. The chamois-hunter employed the same tool for step-cutting when he crossed a glacier, as his son used for chopping up the firewood for his châlet. The handle was some two feet in length, and could be conveniently stuck in one's belt. The guide who is depicted on the cloth cover of the volumes of the *Alpine Journal* is represented with an axe of this kind. While talking with Christian Almer about the ice-axes of his early days, he produced from an outhouse of his châlet a pick which he said was used throughout the Oberland previous to 1854, when systematic mountaineering may be said to have commenced. The "butt" or unpointed end served to batter steps in *néré*, and the pick was employed for scratching footholds in hard ice. Figure 1 is taken from a sketch of old Christian's quaint-looking *Pickel*, which is an interesting memento of the early days of climbing in the Alps. Reference is made to the Oberland ice-axes in 'Wanderings among the High Alps,' in connexion with the first ascent of the Wetterhorn from Grindelwald. "The sticks the Oberland men carried were admirably suited for their work," writes the able author; "they were stout pieces of undressed wood, with the bark and knots still upon them, about four feet long, short with an iron point at one end, and fixed at the other into a heavy iron head, about four inches long each way, one arm being a sharp spike, with which to hew out the ice when needed, the other, wrought into a flat blade with a broad point, something like a glazier's knife. This part of the instrument was extremely useful in climbing rocks. It ran into clefts and fissures too high to be accessible, or too small to admit the hand, and once well planted formed a sure and certain support. This kind of alpenstock is hardly ever seen at Chamonix. Our ice-hatchet on the Col du Géant and the Col Imseng was perfectly different, though better adapted to the mere ice work we had then to perform, and its great utility called forth repeated expressions from the Chamonix men, to whom it was new." Figure 2 represents the axe used at Chamonix in the old days. In the well-known print of De Saussure going up the Glacier du Tacul some of the party are represented carrying *piolets* of this sort, and most of the old guides, in the now half-faded photographs taken some twenty years ago at Chamonix, hold these formidable-looking weapons in their hands. They are highly suggestive of the sham battle-axes which are carried by the High Sheriff's javelin-men when that important county functionary is in attendance upon H.M.'s judges at the assizes, or on other "state" occasions. The form of the head is precisely

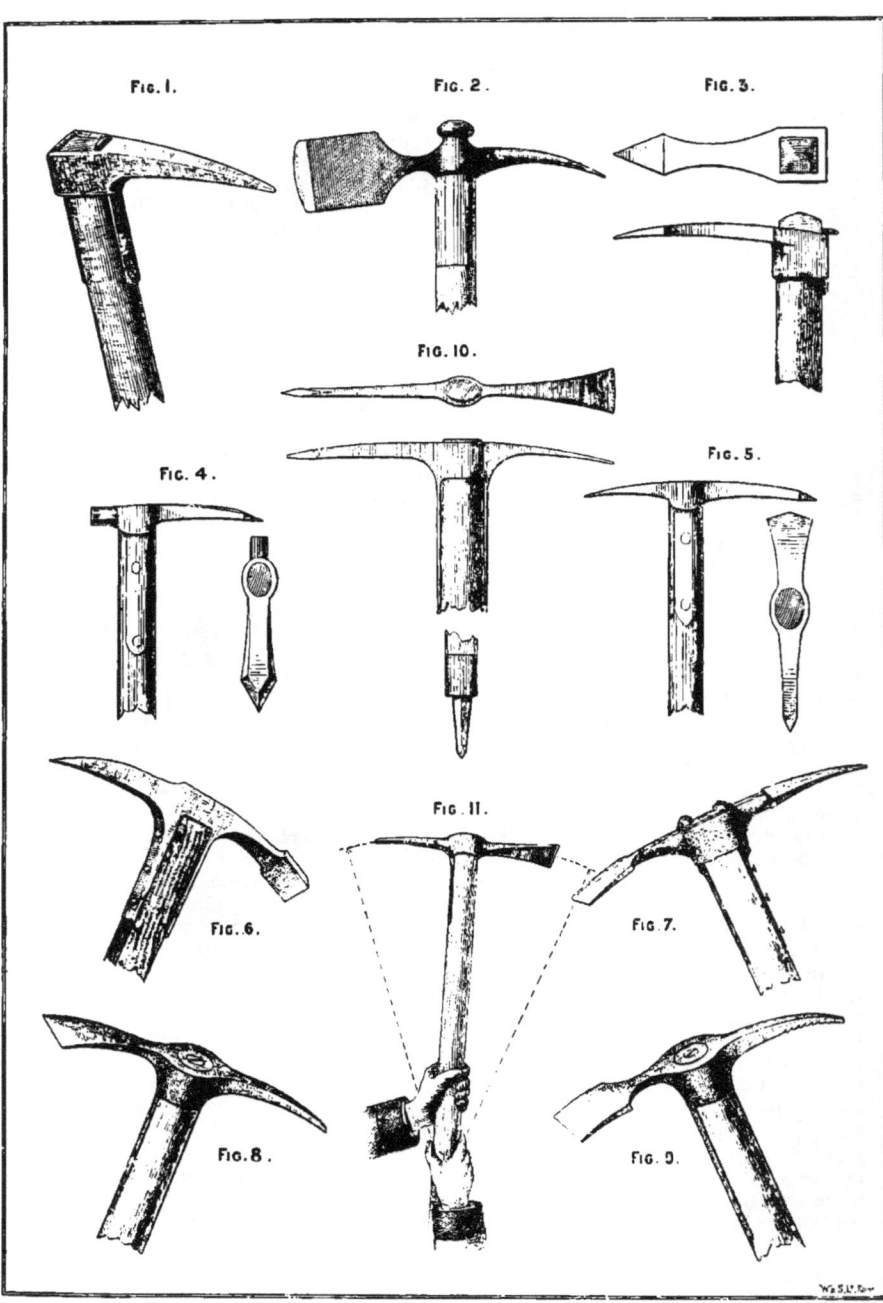

the same as the hatchets for chopping wood one often sees in country towns in France. The shafts of these axes were always of a most unwieldy length.

In 1864 the Alpine Club attempted to determine upon some instrument which should be at once the most practical and most useful form of ice-axe. The question appears to have been raised by Mr. Leslie Stephen, who sent a "note" to the *Alpine Journal* on the best forms of alpenstock for the High Alps. "There seems to be a great variety of opinion amongst Alpine travellers," he wrote, "as to the best form of ice-axe. Every man is, of course, attached to his own theory, and it is as dangerous to criticize a man's alpenstock as his sonnet. I venture, however, to make a few remarks in a dogmatic spirit, with the hope of calling forth, if not criticism, at least flat contradiction. In my opinion then, for walks of the Gemmi and Rigi order, the best thing is a walking-stick. Where more effort is required the alpenstock, which is properly a two-handed walking-stick, becomes useful. In high snow expeditions, the axe may sometimes be called for. I must here take the liberty of observing that I do not myself ever cut steps when I can get a guide to do it for me, first, because a guide can do it very much better, and secondly, because he is paid to do it. Consequently I only wish for an axe capable of being used occasionally, as in a walk to the Jardin or a stroll over the Aletsch glacier, and not one fit for cutting an elaborate staircase up the Eigerjoch." Then Mr. Stephen goes on to say, "I have seen many friends of mine, first-rate mountaineers, who carry alpenstocks six feet long, with an axe at the end heavy and big enough for the 'headsman' of historical novels. I can only state my own opinion, that they have utterly spoilt their alpenstock without getting a good axe. Their implement, considered as an alpenstock, is hopelessly clumsy, for it requires a greater muscular effort to bring it from left to right in case of a sudden emergency. As an axe, the length of its handle makes it unwieldy and awkward. I should prefer carrying a lighter alpenstock and allowing my guide to carry an axe." The shape of ice-axe which Mr. Leslie Stephen goes on to describe is given in figure 3. The following May the Committee of the Alpine Club invited the members to send to the club-rooms, "any specimens of axes and ropes, which they might think worthy of notice." A large number of axes were sent for exhibition, and it is much to be regretted that the working drawings have not been preserved, even although some of the men of genius who designed these weapons may now secretly rejoice that there is no record of their fearful and wonderful inventions. A committee of six members of the club, including Mr. F. C. Grove and the Rev. H. B. George, was specially appointed to discover by experiment the kind of rope best suited for Alpine purposes, and to "consider in detail all the conditions to be fulfilled in the construction of an ice-axe." Their report was read and adopted by the club, on the 5th of July, 1864. The opinion of the committee would have carried much more weight had they tested in some practical manner the different ice-axes. Five minutes' ice work on a glacier would have been more satisfactory than any amount of imaginary step cutting in No. 8, St. Martin's Place, W.C., where we may presume the trials were conducted, even although all the conditions to be fulfilled were considered "in detail." We fear that the decision of the committee cannot have been arrived at without much risk and danger not only to the walls and furniture, but to their own lives, when, for example, one of the most stalwart among them showed how he could knock away a piece of ice-cornice from the level of the mantel-shelf. The report is an exhaustive one, and may still be considered an interesting and instructive document, although the majority of the recommendations the committee then made have now been proved to be practically worthless. Probably the only one of their conclusions respecting axes which would at the present time be generally admitted as sound is,—that they should not have movable heads. The committee first lay down the law on the subject of ropes, and then proceed to discuss the question of ice-axes. With regard to ice-axes they say their task was less easy. "There is," the report says, "no subject on which the members of the Alpine Club seem to have such divergent opinions," and they pointed out that there is no case on record of any one having met in Switzerland two members of the Alpine Club armed with the same kind of weapon. The two forms they recommend are given in figures 4 and 5; figures 6, 7, 8, and 9 represent different models which their designers claim to possess some distinctive superiority. Figure 7 is known as the "Kennedy," figure 6 as the "Coolidge," figures 8 and 9 the "Nixon" and the "Carfrae." Up to the present time by far the most perfect form of axe we have, is the one designed by Mr. Charles Pilkington, which bears his name. It has taken years to perfect, and when, as in this case, the object of the craftsman has been to make every detail in his design aid in carrying out the purpose which his model is intended to fulfil, the result is pretty certain to be an artistic one. The maxim, "Where use is banished beauty scorns to dwell," is as equally true of an ice-axe as it is of a racing yacht, a violin, or a racquet. Our illustration of the "Pilkington" (figure 10) is too small to give any idea of its graceful lines and perfect proportions. Few climbers are in the habit of doing step-cutting themselves for any continued length of time, hence they do not realize the immense difference which exists between a couple of axes. One may be so perfectly balanced that it can be used for an hour with comparatively little fatigue, another will tire the strongest arm in less than half the time. Mr. Pilkington always succeeds in getting the point of percussion at the right place, that is, just where one would naturally take hold of the axe if one were going to use it. He sends me the following interesting details: "The axe is forged in a solid block of iron, not of steel, and is tipped with steel, and then cut out by machinery. The balance is difficult to get, as every man insists on having a different handle, and the least extra weight or length alters it. I always have the handles finished by degrees, feel the swing of the axe, taking off more or less as required. The main point as to cutting well is to have the centre line of pick and adze on a radius from the spot where the lowest hand grips the axe-handle when cutting with a full swing (see figure 11). I have had about twelve axes made under my own personal superintendence, and none of them have failed, though —— thinks, and many others, that a heavy and splendidly made spike at the bottom is necessary; it utterly ruins them for step-cutting. There is more 'anchor' on the adze end, as it is only for scraping and holding on with. The pick end must be much straighter. I have found the best test for the bend of the spike end to be,—Hold the axe with the lowest hand only (as when cutting), and let the head fall with its own weight pick end downwards on to hard wood. If it goes in sweetly without jarring it is all right. The spike can be bent to the right spot if it is not right." Mr. Pilkington's axe has no teeth cut in the spike end. For perfection of finish, the ice-axes made by Messrs. Hill and Son are vastly superior to those of any other professional maker in England. They cost, including "wrist strap" and leather covers for the head and spike in the handle, about £2. The great diversity of opinion among amateurs regarding their ice-axes is very well illustrated by a visit to the Messrs Hill's wareroom in the Haymarket, who, although they possess a very large stock including all the well-known patterns, almost invariably make axes to order, from the fact of each customer having some individual fad regarding the weight or shape of the blade. Those who make ice-axes would seem to be even more sorely tried than the makers of guns, golf clubs, bats, racquets, or in fact those who turn out the equipments for almost any other form of sport. At Zweilütschinen and at Chamonix there are blacksmiths from whom one can order most excellent reproductions of the well-known models for about twenty francs.

The village smithy in an Alpine village is as favourite a place of resort among the guides, as it is in the Midlands among the farm-labourers. The smith himself probably knows something of step-cutting from his winter experiences in chamois shooting. And one can well imagine that much practical criticism is expended on each axe before it leaves the forge. Although the blades of these "home-made" axes do not possess the smoothness and finish of some of those of English make, still as a rule their balance is perfect. They give unmistakable evidence of honest and skilled workmanship, and form a striking example of some of Mr. Ruskin's theories as to what the aims of the artisan ought to be.

A leather band is often fixed to the shaft below the head, and is found to be of great use in bad weather by preventing the fingers from being frost-bitten. Some years ago a clever little device occurred to that genial climber, the Rev. H. B. George, who found that by putting on the shaft a few of the indiarubber rings which are generally used for keeping the ribs of an umbrella round the handle, one is able to grasp the axe much more firmly during a storm of snow or rain, when the "grip" is slippery.

One of the earliest references to ropes being used as means of assistance in crossing glaciers is by Simler (A.D. 1574). The Rev. F. T. Wethered has kindly furnished me with the following translation from that writer's pithy chapter, which is styled by the author, "De itinerum Alpinorum difficultatibus, et quomodo hæc superari possint."—"Moreover, the old (*vetus*) surface of the glacier (*glacies*), over which not seldom a way has to be made, presents deep apertures (*hiatus*) of three, four, or even more feet in width: into which, if any one should fall, without doubt he must perish. But on occasion these apertures are covered over with fresh fallen or with drifted snow, and therefore those who at such times travel through the Alps are wont to hire guides to precede them. They tie a rope around these men, and several of those who follow attach themselves to it. The leading guide pioneers the way with a long pole (*pertica*), and carefully searches for these apertures in the snow, but if by chance a person unawares falls into one of them, he is held up and drawn out by his companions who are fastened together by the same rope."

No mention of the rope is made by Windham and Pococke in their account of their visit to the Mer de Glace, and Mr. F. F. Tuckett points out to me that its use is only twice referred to by De Saussure in the description of his ascent of Mont Blanc in 1787. At that time a long pole was often used instead of the rope, guides held each end, and the *voyageur* walked between them, using it as a sort of balustrade. This most unsatisfactory method is depicted in that scarce print of De Saussure going up the Glacier du Tacul, to which reference has so frequently been made in this work. Placidus à

Spescha (1762 to 1834) was in the habit of using the rope in his mountaineering excursions. A cord made of silk is occasionally used, and is considered by some to be lighter and stronger than a hempen rope; but it has never found any great popularity among amateurs. A rope of this description is understood to have been used during the sensational, though somewhat unsportsmanlike descent of the Eiger arête.

The chief requisite for rope which is to be used for mountaineering excursions is, that it should be able to bear a *sudden* shock, nearly every other sort of rope is made with the view of standing a long and continued strain. The Alpine Club committee on ropes and axes say, in their report, " Most of the good light rope sold in London will support a dead weight far greater than any which it is ever likely to sustain in the Alps; but in estimating its strength it is always assumed that the strain will be gradually applied. The Alpine traveller's rope, on the contrary, if tried at all will have to resist a sudden jerk which may be a very violent one: and it is against this danger that the most careful precautions should be taken, as some lamentable accidents clearly show."

The rope approved by the committee of the Alpine Club can be obtained from the well-known firm of rope-makers, the Messrs. Buckingham, Bloomsbury, London, W.C. It is distinguished by a red thread which runs through the centre. From being made of the very finest Manilla hemp, which is extremely elastic in texture, it does not become hard and unpliable after being exposed to wet weather for any length of time. It bears a sudden strain of sixteen stone. Whatever differences of opinion may exist among amateurs as to the various parts of a climbing kit, all unite in praising the Messrs. Buckingham's admirable work. Artificial aids to climbing have always been discountenanced by the majority of amateurs.

In 'Scrambles amongst the Alps' (page 110) Mr. Whymper describes an ingenious claw or grapnel which he employed in difficult places where there was no hold within arm's length, but where there were cracks or ledges some distance higher. The claw could be stuck on the end of the alpenstock and dropped into such places, or, on extreme occasions, flung up until it attached itself to something. *Crampons*, which I presume a "mountaineering purist" would look upon as "artificial aids," are never used in the Oberland, and are only seen in the Tyrol. One of the most indispensable aids for winter excursions are *cercles* for fixing to the soles of one's boots. They may be described as miniature Canadian snow-shoes, round in form, which enable one to cross a plateau of the softest snow without breaking the crust, and in doing so sinking well over the knees. The mountaineering tent designed by Mr. Whymper is the one which is almost invariably selected by amateurs. There seems to be as great a difference of opinion among amateurs regarding sleeping bags as there is about ice-axes; whether they should be made of sheep-skins, blanketing, or blanketing covered with indiarubber, exercises the minds of all those who adopt that most comfortable of all ways to "sleep out" for a peak.

The Oberland sacks, with pockets on each side, have now completely superseded the complicated English-made knapsacks. Circular wine-tins are not so much used as they formerly were; the little wooden *tonneaux* made in Valais, or the chamois-skin wine-bags with the hair inside, are generally admitted to keep their contents in better condition and be less liable to be damaged than any other. *Rücksacks* are considered by many practical mountaineers, among whom we may mention Mr. F. F. Tuckett, as being beyond all comparison the best form of carrying-bag. One of the most useful additions a climber can make to his kit is a large folding-up leather cup, not altogether unlike the shape of a Glengarry cap, which holds upwards of a quart. They are most useful when one has to send the guide from the bivouac any distance in search of water. One of them was christened a "*Dampfschiff*" by Melchior Anderegg, to distinguish it from the small pocket drinking-cups of the same form and material. This is the only instance where a slang term has been applied to any of the "fixings" of mountaineering.

IX. GUIDECRAFT.

THE following sentences were written some years ago about the death of one of the great guides in the Alps:—"One should not esteem lightly the loss of a valiant and courteous guide who will never wield ice-axe more. These, I know, are the terms of old romance, associated with pageants, and great solemnities, and companies of stately men and fair women. It may seem incongruous to apply them to people who wear hob-nailed boots and clothes of the roughest homespun, and talk in an uncouth highland dialect of German. But if valour and courtesy are not the fitting words for the character of the best Swiss guides, I know not what other to find. They are ever ready to perform what they have undertaken, or at least carry the attempt to the uttermost of man's power, not as the bare fulfilment of a bargain, but joyfully and as an honourable achievement. They are ever watchful, not merely for the safety of the travellers they have taken in their charge, but for their ease and comfort in everything; and all this they do as if it were pure pleasure to them, and the most natural thing in the world." No truer words were ever written than these. In the latter part of the same article, Mr. F. Pollock goes on to say:—"These men, though they live away from cities, and read and write but little, are neither uninstructed nor incurious. You may converse with them of most things except books, and find them willing hearers and sensible speakers. Their duties as citizens are few and simple, as a rule, but when once and again such a matter comes home to them as a revision of the Federal Constitution, their votes are at least as intelligent as the average British elector's—if, indeed, after the disclosures we are now reading every day, that is anything to say. They all have taken their turn at soldiering too, and may have to take to it again. Of the average Swiss troops I know nothing; but I conceive that the Oberland contingent must be difficult to surpass anywhere in physique and intelligence." On our sea-coast, or among our moors, there are many true-hearted and brave men, who possess those qualities which can only be gained in Nature's somewhat hard school, but we are not brought into such close intimacy with them as we are with our guides, nor have we the same uninterrupted opportunities of forming an estimate of their character, and of earning their friendship. I doubt if there is any other class of men who aid us in our various sports with whom we are thrown so much in contact; with whom it so often happens that we share our only blanket, and have in many ways in a most literal sense "all things in common."

It would take many a long cruise to give us the same associations with our skipper, as we have with our guide; though the seasons we have passed with him in the Alps may have been but short ones. Even the most boastful of all those who sometimes speak of their guides as being unnecessary adjuncts in their mountain conquests, must recollect at least one occasion when they remembered having paused for a moment to speculate what the result would have been, if their brave leader had swerved, or if his strong arm had failed him. Apart from the many qualities which are brought into play in the exercise of their profession, none are more associated with the guides than their perfect truthfulness and sincerity, and the loyalty they show to their *Herren*. It is indeed a rare test of a man's honour and sense of good-feeling to be able to serve more than one master, and to hear the confidences and hopes of each for future conquests, and yet never to betray the most inadvertent or hasty expression which could possibly pain a rival. Not a week passes during the climbing season without our knowing that some guide refused Mr. So-and-So's offer to go up some difficult peak, because the English gentleman with whom he had been earning his eight francs for the last two days intended to postpone his departure for twenty-four hours, in order to go to the Zäsenberg and back. Judging only from the casual knowledge of the morality of other professions, which may be gained from the reports of the Law Courts in the daily papers, we may doubt if there be any other craft where virtues of this kind are more constantly practised. Even the most injudicious partisan of a candidate for some Alpine Club who attempted to prove that his *protégé* had made an ascent which was a fiction, would find it difficult to induce the most impecunious of guides to lend himself to the deception. And *àpropos* of this subject, if Mrs. Opie had dined regularly at the *table-d'hôte* of one of the mountaineering inns for three months, she would have overheard ample materials for another most racy chapter to her instructive work. But to return to the guides,—the straws on the surface of the stream indicate its direction. And if we take any of these small incidents which we hear chaffingly told about the sayings or doings of the more eminent guides and their peculiar idiosyncrasies, as for instance, A.'s dislike of going sailing-excursions on the Lake of Thun, B.'s rooted objection to hôtel *ascenseurs*, or C.'s aversion to snakes, one cannot but remark in them the entire absence of any criticisms which could possibly detract from their character as upright and good men.

During the climbing season a guide is indirectly brought into contact with many different sorts and conditions of men. He is a much keener judge of human nature, and probably has had a far greater and more varied experience of it than any of the Oxford or Cambridge undergraduates, who are good enough to give him a little reflected glory gained from their achievements among the mountains. Whether he happens to be engaged by a Bishop or a sporting Stockbroker, he is equally guiltless of attempting to adapt himself to what he may suppose to be their peculiar fads. To each he expresses, without the slightest *arrière pensée*, his views and opinions as to the wickedness of making ascents on Sunday, his ideas on the Federal Game Laws, or relates his last "unpleasantness" (shall we call it) with the Garde Chasse, all with the same perfectly unconscious, unaffected simplicity. No matter what the circumstances or surroundings may be under which we meet, those true sons of the mountain never change. They are

E

always the same, whether we chance to be spending an evening in a club-hut, planning an expedition with them on the balcony after *table-d'hôte*, or when they come to stay with us in our English homes. It is very rarely that we find among guides any of those qualities which are popularly supposed to be requisite for a diplomatist. "I'm not going well to-day," said one of the best-known amateurs in the Alps to his guide. "No, *Herr*, you are not," was the reply; "I have been noticing that for some time." And often have I told this *Herr* that he was simply fishing for a small compliment, in order to make the snow seem less heavy on his first training-walk of the season, and that he secretly hoped his guide would tell him that he was going like a chamois or a bird, or (greatest triumph of all) "So wie Herr Stephen oder Herr Hartley geht." Unfortunately for the ordinary run of the general public, it is impossible for them to have more than a mere casual acquaintance with the great guides, as it is a very remote chance if they do not have a long engagement with some old patron, and consequently their services are rarely to be obtained for a single excursion. And what I have said must therefore seem to be an ideal of perfection, which some of my readers—whose ideas of guides' morality and capacity are derived from the loafers who sit outside the Mont Cervin, or the unit whose number happened to be first on the roster when they entered the Bureau at Chamonix—may imagine to be an impossible one. One can well believe that they would only sneer at us, if we told them that we valued the friendship of our guide as one of the best possessions and memories of the long seasons we have spent in the Alps. That there are bad guides, sometimes very bad ones, as well as the good men, no one would for one moment dream of denying. But my claim for the craft is, that those many good qualities I have referred to are very generally to be found among guides of the first rank, and are most typically characteristic of them. Even in the lives of those guides who are still a long way from the top of their profession, an element of romance is to be discovered which does not exist among those belonging to almost any other craft.

The Alps, those districts which the pioneers whose names we are recording have opened out to us, have an individuality and a peculiar charm of their own, which I doubt if any other mountain ranges in the whole world possess. Those of us whose fate it has been to run to and fro upon the earth, never visit a mountain district which is new to us, without mentally comparing it with the Alps. Whether we have been looking at Mount Everest from Sinchel, or watching the shadow of Adam's Peak as it gradually reaches the horizon, or while in camp among the Rockies or the Sierra Nevadas, the Alps always remain the criterion of our ideal of what is beautiful, and form the basis from which we regard what are perhaps vaster and more imposing ranges. Nothing takes a more prominent place in our recollection of the Alps than all the signs of mountain life in the valleys at the foot of the great Peaks. It will be long before climbers have the same feeling towards the dark-skinned Bhoteas, with their suggestive-looking kukeries stuck in their belts, or even the cheery Japs who may have saluted us on the slopes of Fuji, as we have with the sturdy Oberläuder who greet us with *Grüss üch* on the familiar mountain-paths by Meiringen. The sunburnt faces of a group of Swiss guides as represented in the first attempts of an amateur photographer, have much more of what is *gemüthlich* about them than the long-robed men of Gebi in the "Frosty Caucasus." As time passes on, and as rum, missionaries, and British Vice-Consuls gradually prepare these now somewhat uncivilized districts for the climbing Britisher, we may perhaps hear of some Wili Ali who is regarded as a sort of Melchior by the explorers of these parts. But, until the advent of this happy epoch, we must always own that it is a double debt we owe to the pioneers of the Alps and their kinsfolk, who have not only opened out the great mountain highways for us, but beautified the valleys which lead up to them, and whose many friendly acts afford us such a number of pleasant recollections and associations with their districts. It is only when we are among some far distant range, that the absence of the châlets with their little gardens, the cow-bells, the cattle, and the tiny patches of cultivation reminds us how much these things contribute to beautify and enhance their surroundings.

Climbers whose ambition it is to achieve something new must go further afield than the Alps; but with the ever-increasing facilities we have for travel, the journey to Tiflis is much less fatiguing and scarcely longer than going from Paris to Geneva, before the railway was opened. Those of our friends who spend the winter in Calcutta in order to escape the London fog, or who make a run across to Canada for six weeks' salmon fishing, have very different ideas as to the distance these places are from England to what we had at one period of our lives. Whether the same number of climbers will continue to go every year to the Alps now that there are nothing but already-trodden peaks left for them to scale, the future alone can reveal. But, to the majority of men of every nationality, the Alps must always remain that "playground of Europe," where one may best "renew our lease of life, and restore the balance between mind and body, which the purely intellectual discipline of London is calculated to destroy."

There are no periods of our life which have given us a greater number of memories than the seasons we have spent in the Alps; some of them are sad, but there are many which we like to look back upon. It is pleasant as the years roll on, to think what our hopes and ambitions once were, and to recall our failures as well as our successes, to remember the great good-fellowship and *bonne camaraderie* we have enjoyed, such as can only exist among those who are engaged together in one common sport, not wholly unattended with danger. Nor can we ever forget those sad days, happily few and far between, when a deep gloom has seemed to cloud the great peaks, in spite of all the sunshine and brightness of the summer morning, and when *Herr* and *Führer* have alike mourned the loss of a friend. Such days may never come back to us, but the recollection of them must always remain one of our most enduring possessions, and can indeed only pass away with life itself.

C. D. C.

The Training of Mountaineers.

SOME years ago, when I was staying at a well-known mountain inn in Switzerland, a young gentleman, aged sixteen, came thither, accompanied by his tutor, who, having run him through from England by day and night unresting, led him the very next morning over a first-rate pass.

The boy was no doubt a school athlete of some pretensions for his age, but I need scarcely say that this treatment knocked him up utterly, and he was of no more use for that season. Happily, whatever harm it may have done to his constitution, the freak did not break his neck, as some freaks do. Now this is no unfair nor uncommon instance of the folly of Alpine travellers and the delusion of climbing enthusiasts. Like M. Tartarin, they regard, or seem to regard, the Alps as a put-up thing, and expect the administration to see them through. A man who would not dream of entering himself or his friend untrained for a polo or a football match, thinks that mountain-climbing comes by nature, and is outside of practice or of physiology. I speak of football or polo because in them, unlike tennis or cricket, a tiro may rush his way through the game, however clumsily, and at whatever risk to himself. But surely he could not pretend to make Hurlingham, Kennington Oval, or the Queen's Club the scene of his endeavours.

It is not beside the physiological aspect of climbing to remind the reader that this sport, like others, has to be learned. Useful, nay necessary, as a good general athletic training may be, yet specific skill in many new muscular adaptations is no less necessary, and this time and practice can alone impart. Time and practice so organize our habits of work that, if gradually and carefully instructed, we, through them, attain to an *automatic efficiency* which makes labour and achievement easy and mechanical. An inexperienced person, on the other hand, clever as he may be, if he go through the task, does it at a constant strain of attention and conscious effort which is most exhausting. Now few men are clever in new exercises, and many exceptionally strong men are almost equally clumsy. Again, besides the fatal accidents which have darkened, and, I fear, will darken their pages, there is a tale untold in Alpine records, though partly told to physicians at home, of men seeking and needing holiday, who return from ill-directed mountaineering dejected and enfeebled, or, at best, unrefreshed and disheartened, although under proper leading they could have returned cheered and recreated. Even a practised climber, unless he be in regular work, needs eight or ten days of graduated walking in Switzerland before he is fit for the heavier excursions, and I think no man in his first season should aim at such excursions at all. He may well find his way with a good guide through the increasing difficulties of shorter efforts, such as the Riffelhorn by its various sides and the passage of the Col du Géant, the Alphubel, or the Strahlegg, but until he attains some considerable measure of *automatic* efficiency he should not strain his powers and his attention on the longer excursions. A proficient in athletic games is doubtless inured to work in itself as hard as the ascent, let us say, of the Matterhorn, and hence may rashly conceive himself to be at once fit for that achievement. But if unpractised in this special pursuit, he has not gained the requisite automatic efficiency, so that the constant attention to every detail of a new exercise will exhaust his nervous energy, and his reserve force will become quickly expended. The middle of the second season is quite early enough for a young climber to enter upon excursions of the first class. But as unconscious imitation is a potent means of instruction, it is most desirable that the beginner should, so far as he can, attach himself from the first to the best guides and to amateurs better than himself, so that he may closely watch and imitate their style and accept their counsels.

The townsman should, if possible, enter upon some training before his departure for the Alps, nor should he throughout the year fail to keep up some out-door exercise. Over-training or false training, on the other hand, is even worse than over-exertion; at any rate I have seen far more evil effects resulting from it. Repeated endeavours to fine down below the normal bodily weight often end in organic disease in middle life, and incessant calls on the full activities of the body are no less dangerous. Men often forget that the bread-winning work of the day, work often wearing, often anxious, may be as much as the nervous system can well provide for while at home, and most Alpine climbers are engaged in professional life. Neither at home nor abroad does nature intend us to work constantly up to our indicated horse-power. We are built with a large reserve, but this reserve is to meet emergencies, and if we insist on regarding it, not as a reserve or factor of safety, but as a regular working store, we shall suffer for it. Like carnivorous animals, we should alternate our times of great activity with times of repose. Unfortunately, however, the restless mind of man refuses to be governed by the promptings of the more natural instincts. A practised climber has watched himself, and will do as he finds best, but tiros must begin tentatively, and learn the sport gradually. This, however, they too often will not do, and consequently we see men grow stale before their time, and after a season or two drop away in their work or shirk the Alps altogether. But really if Alpine climbing be pursued sensibly, it is not a hard sport, and it is one which may be pursued for many more years than most men give to it. It is a matter for much regret that too often when climbers have grown to be mature and seasoned hands, they give up the sport, believing, I think, that it is too hard a sport for middle life. Now this I conceive to be a mistake. Climbing indeed has this great advantage for older men, that it requires endurance rather than speed. Moreover, it banishes those brooding or anxious thoughts which too often beset middle-aged men to their mischief. The measured tramp on the hillside seems to lull the wits into a kind of monotony, and the work on ice and rock diverts nervous energy to the hand and the eye, while the background of the mind and perceptions is occupied by the more or less present consciousness of strange and splendid scenes. This is the very medicine for men whose main life is the life of great cities.

One may wonder that men who have once found strength and joy in Alpine climbing, and who have known the glory of the Alps, do so commonly fall off from the sport before middle life, and that very few pursue it in their later years. It is said that men are dissuaded from climbing by their wives, a grave and incredible imputation upon those mothers of heroes. It is more credible that men who grow idle learn to excuse themselves under such a plea. Too often no doubt family ties and family expenses forbid Alpine sport as they forbid other enjoyments, but, fishing excepted, Alpine climbing is still the cheapest of all outdoor sports as it is the best. Speaking as a physician, I find that yachting and Alpine climbing are the two sports which above all others restore life and vigour to hard-worked men, and if such men can afford any recreation at all, a month in Switzerland is an economical outlay. In the pace and quality of the eleven months' work it repays itself many-fold. Others are perhaps deterred, and herein I confess a common weakness, by the midnight call, the hard damp boots, and the stumbling over moraine in the dusk after an *ignis fatuus* ahead, with a candle in a broken bottle. For who has the assurance to deny the thankfulness with which he has, occasionally let us say, heard at 2.0 a.m. the news of a wet morning. Seriously, however, I believe that the majority of men are under the impression that Alpine climbing is a pursuit for youth only, and is too trying for maturer years. I admit that such was my own impression as a young man, and I used then to feel some misgiving in deserting other sports for one which I thought could only be the enjoyment of very early manhood. It is true that no man in any sport retains his best activity after about thirty-six years of age, but as I have said, Alpine climbing is rather a matter of endurance which men of natural vigour may retain to a very much later age. As Alpine climbing is a new sport, we had not until lately the means of judging of its effects upon older men. But the time has now come when we may say, *Si argumentum quæris circumspice.* In one way or another, a great deal of medical experience among Alpine men has fallen to my share, and yet I have no recollection of any one case in which I have had to advise a sound man to give up Alpine climbing altogether, either on account of his age or of any other condition. On the other hand, omitting as exceptional persons, those older guides, whose memoirs fill this book, let us turn to the list of members of the Alpine Club and see what some of its oldest members are still doing or have done. The late Mr. Frank Walker was in his sixty-fourth year when he ascended the Matterhorn in 1871, a different feat from its ascent in 1888. A gentleman, not personally known to me, and whose name I therefore cannot publish, in his eightieth year ascended the Schwarzhorn at Davos, and accomplished some of the easier peaks in the Dolomites in his eighty-first year. Mr. Horace Walker was certainly climbing in 1858, if not before, and is still doing good work. After ascending the Gspaltenhorn two years ago, he said that he could climb with even less fatigue than formerly, seeing that he did so with greater judgment. In 1886 I happen to know that among other things he ascended the Dent d'Hérens from the Stockje, returning by the Col de Valpelline. Mr. C. E. Mathews began to climb in 1856, and has made thirty-two seasons, and Mr. Morshead has probably a like record. In 1887, when we were at the Riffel together, these gentlemen started from the Col d'Ollen and took the Vincent Pyramide, Schwarzhorn, Balmenhorn, Ludwigshöhe, and Signal Kuppe in one day, returning to the Lysjoch hut in sixteen hours, only regretting they had not taken the Zumstein Spitze and the Parrot Spitze in the same day. I also know that in 1885, leaving the Fée Alp, Mr. Mathews and Melchior climbed to the Riedpass and took the Ulrichshorn and the Balferinhorn, descending to S. Niklaus in eighteen and a half hours, and the same year, camping out Auf der Blatte, they climbed to the Silber Sattel of Monte Rosa and took the Höchste Spitze and the Nord End, right and left.

Again, Mr. T. S. Kennedy, who was besieging the Matterhorn in 1862, walked with a knapsack last year from Aosta over the Col de Collon to Arolla in thirteen and a half hours, and the same year started for Mont Blanc from Couttet's Inn, reached the summit through deep snow from the Little Plateau, and was back at Couttet's to *table-d'hôte* in eighteen and a half hours from the start.

Another veteran climber well-known to most of us, seems to me to have fallen off in no respect from his early vigour. He was certainly climbing in 1857, and would then be about twenty-three years of age. For the last twenty years he cannot have missed a single season. Of some of his seasons I have personal knowledge, and I will take 1877, when he had reached middle age. This climber in that year ascended eight of the principal peaks in the Ortler district on eight successive days, sleeping every night in a hotel, and his score that season was twenty-one peaks and twenty-two passes in forty-four days. At the age of forty-five the same gentleman, between August 28th and September 4th, ascended the Wetterhorn, Schreckhorn, Mönch, Jungfrau, and Eiger, and crossed the Jungfraujoch from the Scheideck to the Æggischhorn Hotel, the Mönch and the Jungfrau being combined on one day.

To show that after fifty years of age cold and exposure may be borne as well as in earlier years, this mountaineer, on August 17th, 1886, the day of the much-discussed death on the Matterhorn, had started at 2.10 a.m. from the Pavilion Dollfuss, and reached the summit of the Lauteraarhorn at 10.10. Then the snow began to fall so heavily that progress became very difficult. The party crossed the Strahlegg unable to see a yard before them, and reached Grindelwald at 7.20 p.m., having been more than seventeen hours out, and wet to the skin for most of the time of the descent. As I have personal knowledge of these details, I venture to use them thus fully, and no doubt, of several other veterans, like records could be given by their friends. But I have said enough to show that mountaineering is a sport which may be pursued into later life with safety and pleasure. As men grow older it is, however, more and more important that they should approach hard work gradually until thoroughly fit, and as years increase this time of probation should be increased. Unhappily, many men, like myself, grow too heavy, and therewith too clumsy on their feet for difficult places, but we also may spend our days with heart and lungs as good as ever on passes and the easier peaks in the enjoyment of an air, the life-giving quality of which no other climate can rival. Not only may men who began the sport early carry it on with due care to middle and later life with impunity, but I believe that in so doing they will find a rare medicine for wind and limb. Whatever cobwebs may be gathering in the lungs, whatever fatty particles may be settling in the heart, these may be dissipated, and the vitality of the blood renewed by the forced expansion of the lungs under the influence of deep draughts of Alpine air.

Nay, farther, I have latterly, under the teaching of Prof. Oertel, sent patients with hearts actually degenerate to undergo graduated courses of Alpine climbing with remarkably good results. One gentleman I sent for this purpose to Switzerland, who, on his departure, could hardly walk up the street, yet before his return he had ascended the Niesen with ease and pleasure. Of the marvellous restorations to life and health which the Alps may work in cases of consumption I need not speak in detail. It is well known that in a large and increasing percentage of cases it has reversed our forecasts of despair to those of confident hope.

On the other hand, I remember no single instance in which mountaineering, undertaken with any sort of reason, has done the least damage to the internal organs of any man. Even low Alpine temperature seems not to cause the colds or rheumatisms one might have expected, seeing that exposure and fatigue may be so great. In one instance certainly I remember the heart was damaged by a most foolish overstrain in a young man whose frame was immature, and in a few more cases of very young men I have seen a state of irritable heart persist for a time after unwise exertion.

Of women my experience is somewhat different. I am told that some women climb year after year, doing their own work, and keeping good form. But, on the other hand, I know of too many instances in which serious harm has been done to women by relative over-exertion on the hills—Alpine and other. Women have less reserve of nervo-muscular endurance than men, and at the same time no less courage. Hence the temptation to them to do as the men do, and to measure themselves with men. The result only too often is that they break down, not at the time, perhaps, but after the excitement is over. Too many instances have come before me of this kind, cases in which no local disorder has followed, but rather a chronic exhaustion. The sufferers cannot imagine what is the matter with them; they are invalided, listless, and soon wearied. I have traced the cause and effect too often, I think, to be mistaken about it, and have seen, to my surprise, how long they take to recover. Restoration seems slow and fluctuating, and to need the care of years for its completion. It seems as if the nervous system became sapped in some way and to a degree which does not admit of entire amendment for a long time, if at all. I cannot too strongly urge upon women who are not of exceptional "physique" to engage in mountaineering with much caution, and not to mistake courage for capacity.

Let us compare Alpine climbing with other games. Tennis, if it does not greatly fatigue the body, yet unless a man begin young and thus become automatic, brings on that fatigue of attention to which I have already referred. My old friend and fellow-voyager, Mr. T. S. Kennedy, tells me that neither tennis nor polo fatigue him much, but that no sport tires him so little as climbing in the Alps. He says, "I think Alpine climbing requires one to be most fit, but to me it is the least tiring, and on returning home I always find myself at my heaviest. At the same time the dry air and the surroundings make it undoubtedly easier in Switzerland than it would be in Scotland. I do not recollect to have been ever put off my feed or made sleepless by the heaviest day in the Alps. Shooting tries me as much as anything, carrying a gun, tramping through heather or turnips and quartering ground in zigzags. And one always eats and drinks too much in a shooting lodge. Some of my hardest days were done in going after burrell sheep in the Himálayas, carrying a 10 lb. rifle over awkward ground at high elevations where rarefied air tells. On the whole, I should put fox-hunting as the most fatiguing thing I do; shooting next. These two sports take it out of me most, though I follow them perseveringly. After these come the games, if Alpine climbing may be called a game."

Next as regards diet. No traditions have been more rigorous or more senseless than the dietaries of trainers with their raw, monotonous and unpalatable foods and wearisome routines. But the training of men, like the training of hunters, has now been revolutionized and reconstructed on a sensible basis. The athlete who aims at vigour and activity, and not directly at the somewhat dangerous purpose of fining down his weight, should not only be allowed but should be encouraged to take a varied diet, and this of fresh, well-cooked foods. Vigorous men may eat, doubtless do eat, too much when in Switzerland, and it is well to advise some moderation in this respect. Still, I am more afraid of failure in the small than in the large eaters. Some men naturally eat but little, yet are wiry and enduring; still a small eater will do well to watch himself rather closely, and if he be also dyspeptic he should always keep his work within moderate limits. On the tramp no man should eat heavily. A large meal only loads the stomach, and should be followed by longer rest than can be spared. Frequent snacks are much better. Coffee and a roll on starting; breakfast before facing the serious labour of the day, say three hours after starting; and light refections thereafter as occasion may serve, are a common and good practice. Again I think marching meals should consist of light food, remembering that the chief expenditure is of starches, sugars and fats. Slabs of cold meat, the normal "proviant" of the tourist, are nauseous to me on the glacier, and I take them for the guides or on the chance of being belated. In default of light meats, such as chicken, or duck, that tastiest of morsels above the snow-line, I turn to eggs, thin sandwiches, sardines, bread and butter, cheese, light cakes and fruits ; and a handful of chocolate or preserved fruits should always lurk in the pockets. *Dulce est desipere in loco* and a most scientific lunch I once took part in near the Findelen Glacier of truffled larks and greengages lives in my palate to this day; light, sapid food, not deficient in fats and sugars, is the best provision for the working hours.

Next comes the great drink question. I once told a bilious acquaintance that his drink should be water. "Water?" said he in a thoughtful tone; "water? Do you mean what one washes with?" Yes, after many years' wanderings in Europe with all sorts of companions I still say "Water, and plenty of it." The old trainers put a foolish restriction on fluids, a piece of sheer nonsense. To load the stomach *suddenly* with a great bulk of liquid, or of anything else, is unwise, but let the traveller drink *gradually* as much fluid as he likes, the more the better if he enjoys it and perspires freely. Thus the adits and exits of the body are flushed, and the tendency to deposit fat is prevented. The addition of alcohol while on the march is a mistake. Native red wines well watered down may contain so little alcohol as to be practically harmless, but a man may easily take more even of them than is good for him. One of the best men I ever walked with, with whom I ascended several of the easier peaks without guides, declared to me that bottles of red wine suited him finely while on the march. He thought so because he liked it. As a matter of fact about the middle of our tour he grew worse on his legs, and after I left him I am told he fell to pieces altogether. Indeed, apart from the alcohol in them, I think those sour common wines must tend to derange any stomach, as Gladstone's clarets do at home. Cold tea is perhaps the best drink for climbers, or milk for those who can digest it. Milk suits me well as meat and drink, and has the advantage of combining both within itself. But, as a rule, I carry my own drink in three or four lemons, which, with a handful of loaf-sugar, take up little room in the pocket, and furnish a lemon squash wherever cold water is. After the day's work the use of a different dietary comes in. If one is happy enough to get in about four or five o'clock, how delicious is the cup of coffee and the cigar, with possibly forty winks during its progress, and thereafter a warm soap and water sponging, and change of dress for dinner. For mountain days I consider this warm wash to be more convenient, more cleanly, and more healthy than the cold morning tub. After this rest any reasonable dinner may be indulged in, and therewith a pint of Dry Bouvier or of sound malt liquor, which is as useful after as it is baneful during work.

But it is not given to the wayfarer always to get in so early. He will often arrive weary and late, in which case he will do well not to dine, not to load his exhausted body with a meal he has not energy to digest, but to drink slowly a bowl of warm soup with, it may be, a dash of cognac in it, and then to bed. He will sleep soundly, wake early with a clean tongue, and will breakfast like a wolf. But speaking generally, a young man who has any care for his health should never touch spirits, which are "as vitriol to steel," just sheer mischief. But are not spirits useful in case of fatigue on the tramp? This is a very important question. A little good cognac has travelled with me on most occasions, but, so far as I remember, no drop of it was ever needed or over drunk by me. Still, illness, such as faintness or diarrhœa, might attack some one of the party, or, illness apart, a little spirit might be invaluable on a pinch.

But it is a two-edged weapon and must be kept for special and rare cases. Now the unregenerate man is tempted to use spirit in the two cases for which it is most improper and indeed most injurious, namely "to keep the cold out" and to "keep a man up" when fatigued. To take the latter case first: he who works on alcohol works on borrowed funds. It spurs the strength out, but puts no strength in. The loan may be very precious on a pinch, but it is renewed at a terrible rate of interest. If the weary traveller have a long way before him, let him trudge on, avoiding spirits as he would avoid poison. They will cheat him into a seeming vigour for a brief while, only to plunge him into deeper exhaustion thereafter. If warmth can be maintained, a rest with some concentrated food, heated if possible, is the best means of counteracting weariness. The pot or skin of meat essence now carried by many travellers is excellent for such emergencies.

If, however, the traveller having lost more nerve than strength "funks" a trying passage which is not too long, then a dram may do good momentary service. Or again, if he be done up within sight of home, the same means may bridge over the difficulty. The rule is to use but little, and to use that little when the effort is likely to be completed before the benefits evaporate. The other blunder—to use spirits to ward off cold—has, I fear, more than once been a fatal error. Alcohol creates no warmth, but gives warmth to the surface by dilating the superficial blood-vessels. Into these the blood then rapidly flows at low pressure, and gives a sense of comfort to the nerves of sensation in the skin. But at what cost? At this; that this same blood thus spread out on the surface is chilled in its turn and courses back to the heart colder and colder on each circuit. Thus to give a dram to a man exposed to external cold is indirectly to chill his vitals, and to give him one more good chance of death.

The use of a dram comes in when the chilled man is at home, and when his surface can be kept warm by fires or blankets. Then the spirit will arouse the latent forces of the heart, and may be a precious means of restoration or even of rescue from death. But he who gives alcohol to a weary man when leaving him on a cold mountain side to go in search of aid, hastens by his very act the footsteps of death.[1]

The power of resisting cold varies much in different persons and in the same person at different ages. Each one must therefore estimate his own equation in this respect. Nevertheless, the most warm-blooded man will do well to guard his animal heat against such winds as that which Mr. Stephen discovered at the top of the Rothhorn.[2] At the low temperatures of the high mountains a wind or even a breeze abstracts heat with great rapidity. In still air very low temperatures may be borne well, but even on fine days there is often a shrewd and nipping breeze on the heights, and such breezes become very chilling if the weather change. A thick suit of all wool fabric should be worn and a woollen shirt under it, and I rarely omit to take with me a light woollen plaid or shawl. The coat having plenty of buttoning power on the pockets, can be taken off at will and easily carried in a back-strap or by the guide, while the shawl is an unnoticed addition to the pack till the Rothhorn wind comes, or a cold stone offers itself as a dining-stool, or an evening halt has to be made till the moon rises. Then the shawl-owner begins to score. Another advantage of clothing and under-clothing made of all wool is that they do not admit of a very rapid extraction of heat even when wet, so that the wearer may not feel very cold even if wet through.

Alpine boots are now too well made to need correction from me. But if the voyager do not wish to tramp down the Allée Blanche with a damaged boot on one foot and a dress-shoe on the other, I would advise him to go to the expense of a first-rate London maker. There never was so much rotten leather in the market as at present, and he should try to be sure that he gets bark-tanned leather if possible. A few makers in London make boots which will last for two hard seasons, but too many boots break up before the end of one. Let them be cut straight on the inner line so as not to press the great toe outwards, and let the welts be wide enough to protect the foot from stones, but not so wide as to be a little too broad for small cracks in rock-climbing; the heels should be low, should fall straight from the back line of the boot, and not slope forwards thence, and should be carried well under the foot. For a high instep it is well to insert a steel spring in the waist. Boot-makers will not allow for an adequate thickness of stocking, so that this duty must be especially enforced upon them. It is well, too, to have them to open well down on the foot, so that the boot may slip on easily when it is hard or damp, or the feet are swollen. Tender-footed men should soap the inside of the stocking about the balls of the feet for the first week or two, and every night should wash the feet with warm water and well rub in Lanoline ointment

---

[1] I am happy to be able to appeal to the high authority of Dr. W. Marcet, F.R.S., on the questions of the use of meat and alcohol on the march. *Vide* his papers in the *Alpine Journal*, vol. xiii. part i. Also Mr. Grove's paper, *Alpine Journal*, vol. xii. *Vide* also my own paper on the "Health of Mountaineers," *Alpine Journal*, vol. viii.

[2] "Playground of Europe," p. 99.

before going to bed. If callous skin form in places, let it be soaked in hot water and soda, rubbed down a little with the files sold for corns, and Lanoline ointment well rubbed in. After cutting corns let a soft rag covered with the same ointment be carefully tied round them for the next day's work. The stockings should of course be of the thickest and best all wool yarn, hand-knitted by a good knitter. A bad knitter makes them too hard. Old women in Scotland and Ireland are the best hands. If blisters form, they must be pricked carefully at the edges with a lancet or sharp penknife, and allowed slowly to drain themselves; if the secretion be pent up it tends to injure the new skin below. After the drainage they should be plastered up with surgical plaister in cross strips. The Heftband or "First-Aid" sent out by Hutchinson and Co. is very compact, and adheres well without heat or moisture. A traveller whose feet are tender should never carry weight. If a sprain occur, let the part receive frequent hot fomentations till the heat is subdued, and thereafter have rest enough, the limb being elevated somewhat. The stiffness which may follow should be subdued by hand-rubbing rather than by taking exercise. Arnica is of no value, and is not without some dangers of its own.

Dr. Leslie Ogilvie, Surgeon to the London Scottish Rifle Volunteers, has given attention to the subject of blisters on the feet, at the Easter, Whitsuntide, and other marches of the regiment. These were marches of from twenty to thirty miles a day, undertaken in all weathers, and the men have usually been out of condition and unused to walking, and have used no special precautions as regards boots, the majority marching in their ordinary town boots or shoes. He found that the timely use of boracic acid ointment prevents blisters, and its application after their formation has enabled men to continue long marches of more than twenty miles without much discomfort. The boracic acid is an antiseptic application, and also has healing qualities. He directs that the feet should be bathed in hot water at night, and then rubbed with the ointment, which is allowed to remain in contact all night by sleeping in socks. Next morning the bathing is repeated and the stockings are "soaped" with the ointment. Boracic acid seems also to check the excessive acid perspiration from which certain people suffer, and which, I believe, causes the rawness which is even more uncomfortable than a blister. Blisters were more common when the march was along dry, dusty roads, and those who had used soap or the boracic ointment suffered little, as the hard grains of sand had not such an irritating effect as when the feet were dry. Blisters were much less common during wet weather. In the German army salicylic acid is used in the treatment of blistered feet, but Dr. Ogilvie, after an extended trial of both, found the boracic acid superior.

Mountain sickness is a very curious affection. I never felt any degree of it, but it is real enough to many men, and not unknown even to guides. Its causes are obscure, and it may occur at moderate elevations. There is no certain cure for it except turning back, a remedy unpopular with Englishmen; but a short halt and a doze of five minutes, if possible, may remove the disagreeable sensation.

Frostbite is a hideous risk to the mountaineer, but happily does not occur very often. I shall never forget the terrible injuries which befell an unhappy English traveller who was benighted on the Felik Joch, and who fell under my professional charge at the Riffel. His hands and feet became gangrenous, and after long days of suffering he succumbed. Christian Almer in 1885 barely escaped the worse results of frostbite at the cost of all the toes of one foot. During a bad day on Mont Blanc, I was touched on one heel by the frost, and although no ultimate harm was done, I suffered excruciating pain for some days thereafter. Small degrees of frostbite, in which the skin becomes red or livid and tender, are common enough, especially on the fingers if unprotected. In the next stage the part becomes hard, white and insensitive, and in the third stage the part is killed outright, and perishes by dry gangrene, unless it blisters and moistens under too rapid an application of warmth. Thick warm woollen gloves should be carried, of course, by every mountaineer, and the boots should be removed as soon as possible after prolonged exposure. The treatment of frostbite applied by the guides is good, namely, persistent friction with snow or with sponges dipped in iced water. As the skin becomes warmer and the colour improves, the part may be wrapped in dry flannel. Scores of cases of frostbite are cured by these means. The great secret is to let the return of warmth be as gradual as possible. It is impossible, of course, in this place to indicate the treatment of the graver class of cases.

Snow blindness is a term which seems to cover two or three distinct affections, the nature of which is not yet quite fully made out. All people exposed to snow, and especially to snow with the sun on it, have learned to protect the eyes. Esquimaux and Laplanders wear horn spectacles or wooden covers with horizontal slits in them. Indians, for the same purpose, wear a protection of buffalo skin. Mr. Brudenel Carter tells me that the commonest form of snow blindness is a gradual or an acuter darkening of the field of vision, sometimes to the point of complete blindness, which disappears sooner or later when this influence of the snow is cut off. But, he adds, there are two other kinds of snow blindness, one consisting of a hyperæsthesia of the retina to light, so that the affection is worse by day, and the other in a diminution of retinal sensibility, so that vision is present by day but is quickly lost as dusk comes on—the so-called "night blindness." To this, of course, must be added the indirect blindness due to scorching of the outer coat of the eye, which is to be regarded in this respect as a part of the skin of the face.

Sunburn has been studied with care by Dr. Bowles of Folkestone, who will shortly publish his observations. Dr. Bowles reminds us that sunburn comes from sun on the snow, and not from sun on white rocks and so forth, which is remarkable when we consider that much of the heat rays must be occupied in melting the snow and thus made latent. On the other hand, we see no marked "sunburn" in glass or metal workers, and others who are exposed to a heat of four or five hundred degrees. To lie on the back with face to the sun may cause far less sunburn than a much shorter exposure to radiation from freshly fallen snow. Dr. Tyndall, on the other hand, was a good deal "sunburnt" while experimenting with the electric light at the North Foreland. Dr. Bowles has also noticed that the dark colour of the chälets is largely due to "sunburn" and "gradations of the colour" may be seen which correspond to planes of radiation from banks of snow. Snow blindness, at any rate in certain forms, Dr. Bowles attributes to the same cause, which is not mere heat, for, as he says, sunstroke is not common in the Alps, nor indeed especially so in the tropics. He attributes "sunburn" to the action of the actinic—violet and ultra-violet—rays reflected from the snow, this reflected light not being necessarily of the same quality as that which is incident. Dr. Bowles thinks a light brown wash, simulating the colour of the cheeks of the Engadiners, may prevent sunburn, but his experiments in this direction are incomplete. Captain Abney has made many experiments with the electric light, and with sunlight at high altitudes, and in both the ultra-violet rays are in great excess over those found in sunlight on the plains. Captain Abney has published these facts in various lectures and papers, and has attributed sunburn to these rays, and shown how it can be avoided by using washes containing fluorescent substances. The only method of relief, and this an inadequate one, is to sponge the burnt face lightly in water in which a small quantity of strong ammonia has been dissolved.

T. C. A.

The Portraits.

It is scarcely necessary to say much regarding the portraits, or the other photographs which are interspersed throughout this volume.

When my colleague proposed that we should undertake this work, I was, from force of habit, imbued with what may be termed the "proper ideas," believing that no effective portraiture would be undertaken without the aid of a studio-light and the necessary accessories. But after further turning the matter over, however, the portable studio was discarded, and the artificial "background" was placed "in limbo." Common sense suggested that the *Führer* should not be posed in a drawing-room, nor portrayed in a light in which they were never seen, nor was it desirable that they should be made to appear better-looking than they really were.

A word or two of explanation must be given as to the costumes of those who have been good enough to "sit" for their portraits. We were obliged, by force of circumstances, to secure them as we found them. Some few came in the stiffly-starched collar and newly-purchased coats of *fête*-day attire, while others arrived in their ordinary mountaineering dress. Experience showed us that a whisper of our object invariably procured us the former costumes, which, though suitable for record in the family album, were not in character with their occupation as guides. When it was found impracticable to get the necessary changes of garment effected, we endeavoured to make such modifications as we could. For instance, in one portrait, to sit for which the guide came over from Meiringen to Berne, the Sunday garb, which would have made the sitter look more like a *Pfarrer* than a *Führer*, was discounted by an artifice which it is hoped is not too transparent.

That the rate of progress in securing these likenesses was slow, will be evident when it is said that it took an absence of five weeks last autumn from England to get photographic shots at twenty guides. The remainder were inaccessible, and had to be tracked home this spring.

It may be that the *Herren* who have been led to the summit of some peak by these guides, or who even have passed season after season in their company, are not specialists in the *quasi*-science of physiognomy. A general impression of what is pleasing in the guides, no doubt, presents itself to their minds, but it is probable that they would be at a loss to see how the subtle markings of light and shade, of bump and furrow, added together, give rise to the impression. In this respect the photographer, though his victim may be the acquaintance of an hour (humbly following in the wake of the artist), has an advantage if he has followed his art, be it as an amusement or as a profession, with knowledge; and further, he should be able, as far as his means allow, like the engraver, to give his photograph both the impression of colour and of chiaroscuro.

When I began photography, twenty-seven years ago, such a rendering of colour would have been impossible, and even in more recent times it would have been difficult to translate the splendid bronze complexions of the guides into delicate black and white shades. The newest of all processes came, however, to our help, giving in photographic monochrome the true values of colours more correctly than the older methods could effect.

The faces, if not the figures of the guides who are portrayed in this work have a sort of undefined charm, not from anything strikingly good-looking in them, but from the general expression of rugged determination and quiet self-reliance which may be traced in all. It has been whilst relating some mountain experience, or whilst talking over the trivial duties of the village life, that we have endeavoured to secure their portraits. In no case did they absolutely know when their photographs were being taken, and they were usually surprised to find the operation over before they thought it had begun.

Open-air portraiture at the best of times is difficult. It is rarely satisfactory to take a portrait in sunlight, since, though contrary to all usual acceptation, photography is not truthful. The rendering of very bright high lights in juxtaposition to very deep shadows is at the best of times difficult in a photograph. For this reason it was determined that, as a rule, the portraits should be taken in the shade, using all legitimate means to gain the impression of relief which is so much required, and which is so often absent in them.

Now as to the negatives themselves I would say a word. Not a single touch, beyond what light placed there, has been allowed to be added to face or figure. The object in view was not to produce marble-like imitations of our pioneers, with all the soul taken from them by "re-touching" the negatives. This "artistic improvement" destroys characteristic crow's-feet and wrinkles, and softens asperities which should be seen if the characters of the men themselves are to be recognized. I leave such re-touching to those who are bound to obey the behests of their customers, and who, like the unjust steward, endeavour to halve the debts which the latter owe to time, making a Venus out of a Sarah Gamp, or an Adonis out of a Major Pendennis. As for the surroundings which cannot be excluded from a photograph, and which the painter can adapt to suit his subject, some very slight modifications have been made in some of the plates from which the portraits were printed; though the majority remain of exactly the same tone as the original negative would give. This is, however, exactly the contrary manner to that in which the "studio photographer" would proceed. He can change his background, lighten or darken it at will without difficulty, as indeed he can the face itself; but whilst he leaves the former very much as it is impressed on the photograph, he uses his discretion in "improving" the latter; and I believe that the large majority of my professional brethren agree with me in condemning this practice in principle, but, as one said, "What can we do? The public will be made beautiful, and if we won't do it, they will go to some one who will."

It is a matter of congratulation, to ourselves at all events, that the scope of this work does not require one to be a party to a conspiracy to perpetrate such pictorial untruths, and which might almost be said to be a violation of the Decalogue. I wonder how it would strike any of those who know old Ulrich Lauener, had he been rejuvenated by the illegitimate recourse to the pencil on the photograph, or had Melchior Anderegg been deprived of those brow-markings which are his characteristics?

As to the purely technical part of the work I need say little. Regarding the apparatus, none of those fantastically and ingeniously constructed cameras which abound in different "movements," and to which it is ruin to strain a hinge or displace a screw, were employed. A good old-fashioned but light camera by Meagher, which has stood the wear and tear of nine campaigns in the lower Alps and still remains as serviceable as ever, was brought into requisition. One thing special there was, and that was a longer focussed lens than usual, viz. about 13-inch focus. This was used to prevent as far as possible the distortion in perspective that is so often imagined when lenses of short focus are employed. It is not that the perspective is faulty in reality, but the impression that it is so arises from the fact that to give the idea of truth every photograph should be examined with the eyes at the same distance from the print as that of the focus of the lens. Now it is impossible to scrutinize a picture at a distance of from 8 inches or less, a foot being the smallest distance to which the ordinary eye can accommodate itself. For this reason the choice was made of this lens. Those who are photographers will appreciate the fact that the lens employed was 2 inches in diameter, and would be used with the full aperture, thus allowing great rapidity of exposure. So much for the photographic outfit. The portrait negatives were placed in the hands of Messrs. Annan and Swan for reproduction by their photo-engraving process. The advantage of this method of printing is the absolute intensity of permanency, and a great uniformity in each individual print. The small mountaineering pictures which are interspersed here and there are also permanent, and serve admirably to show the strides which have been made in rendering photography subservient to the production of blocks which can be set up and printed with type. Some of the pleasantest memories of our tours are those in which the subjects of the latter are associated.

In our journeyings to Grindelwald, Zermatt, and Chamonix, and during our stay at these places, we were fortunate enough to secure the services of Melchior Anderegg. It would ill become us to forget the aid which he so willingly gave in our camera wanderings, and the zeal with which he hunted up those guides who for the time were not *zu Hause*. "Whatever he does, he does well," may be said of him; he even took an interest and aided me in some experiments I made at Zermatt on sunlight, and which were undertaken, at least so it was solemnly affirmed by "those who know" beneath my balcony at the Riffel-Alp Hotel, to search for glaciers in the sun. After a quarter of an hour's instruction, Melchior was *au fait* at what I wished him to undertake, a heliostat then to him became an entity, and a beam of sunlight an object worthy of all respect. In fact he paid as great attention to the spectroscope as he did to the details of travel. W. DE W. A.

Melchior Anderegg.

MELCHIOR ANDEREGG was born at Zaun near Meiringen, in the year 1828. As a lad he helped his father to tend cattle in the neighbourhood of his native village, and at the age of eighteen he taught himself the art of woodcarving, in which he has attained extraordinary skill. He became in early life an excellent chamois hunter, and the knowledge of crag and glacier so gained enabled him to take a foremost place as a professional guide, at the moment when the craze for Alpine adventure set in. At twenty years of age and for some time afterwards, he assisted his cousin, Johann Frutiger, in the management of the Inn at the Grimsel. The first glacier expedition he made in the capacity of guide was with an English gentleman, Mr. Robert Fowler; but up to the year 1859, when he was thirty-one, there is but little record of his achievements, for his guide's book had been stolen by some man who assumed his name, and who for a short time traded upon his reputation. The first entry in the book now before me, which contains the testimony of some of our best climbers to his capacity, his courage and his high personal qualities, bears date the 18th of July, 1859, and is signed with the honoured name of Frank Walker. The last entry is dated the 10th of September, 1872, and is signed by M. Albert Millot of Paris. It states " that any recommendation of Melchior Anderegg is unnecessary," and the statement was literally true, for by that time the name of Melchior was as well known as those of the great Mountains he loved so well, and to the summits of which he had conducted so many climbers with such unerring skill, prudence, and success.

The first reference to Melchior in Alpine literature is to be found in 'Summer Months amongst the Alps.' In that charming book the late Mr. Hinchliff describes his introduction at the Grimsel, in 1855, "to two guides, named Melchior Anderegg and Johann Höckler, both of whom looked very promising fellows." With these guides Mr. Hinchliff made the passage of the Strahlegg to Grindelwald. We hear little of Höckler, except that he carried the cellar. Melchior, as usual, took all the honours of the day.

Some time later, in the same year, Mr. Hinchliff again met his guide of the Strahlegg, "with his apron of green baize," exhibiting his woodcarving to some travellers at the Schwarenbach, and at once engaged him for an ascent of the Altels; after which, says Mr. Hinchliff, "I parted with him with great regret, considering him a most excellent and trustworthy fellow, one of those true and stout hearts with whom it is always a pleasure to be associated." From that time to this Melchior Anderegg has been at the very head of his profession. Climbers not unnaturally think most highly of the guides they know best. Those who have not actually worked with Melchior and know him only by reputation, may have a preference for Almer or for Lauener, for Dévouassoud or for Rey. But ask them whom they would place second, and the verdict would be unanimous in favour of Melchior Anderegg. The men who could equal Melchior in his best days as a pathfinder or as a cragsman may be counted upon the fingers of one hand, whilst for the combination of qualities which make a guide first rate—capacity, boldness, true prudence, unvarying courtesy, and sweetness of disposition—there is a

consensus of opinion among competent judges that there has been no superior to the subject of this memoir.

His first ascents were important, though not very numerous. He led the late Charles Hudson in his ascent of Mont Blanc by Les Bosses du Dromadaire in 1859, and Messrs. Frank and Horace Walker, A. W. Moore and G. S. Mathews in their memorable first passage over the same mountain from Courmayeur to Chamonix by the Brenva Glacier in 1865. In company with Mr. Leslie Stephen he made the first ascent of the Rympfischhorn in 1859, and of the Alphubel, the Oberaarhorn, and the Blümlis Alp in 1860. With Mr. Stephen and Mr. E. S. Kennedy he conquered the Monte Della Disgrazia in 1862. With Mr. Stephen and Mr F. C. Grove he first climbed the Rothhorn from Zinal in 1864. He found a new way to the top of the Jungfrau by the Roththalsattel with Mr. Stephen and Mr. R. S. Macdonald in the same year, and in later days, in company with Mr. Stephen and M. G. Loppé, he first reached the summit of the Mont Mallet. He was the first on the Dent d'Hereus, with Messrs. R. S. Macdonald, M. Woodmass, and F. C. Grove, in 1863, first on the Balmhorn with Mr. and Miss Walker [1] in 1864, and first on the highest peak of the Grandes Jorasses with Mr. Horace Walker in 1868.

Melchior is a guide who possesses an irresistible personality. Quiet, grave, sometimes almost taciturn, he, like all really good guides, is seen to the best advantage in critical situations and when real emergencies arise. He is never at fault, he always knows what to do and does it. None of his *Herrschaft* ever dreamed of questioning his decisions or disputing his authority. It is only those who have served under his command, as Sir William Napier so well puts it, who really know "why the soldiers of the tenth legion were attached to Cæsar." His real superiority is only manifested when those who have worked with him have the comparative misfortune to be guided by a less competent man. In the case of all other guides I have known, however eminent they may have been, there has been some drawback, some self-assertion, some want of courtesy, some defect of temper, some lack of consideration for the feelings of others. No one ever could or ever did find fault with Melchior Anderegg. Melchior achieved his reputation in the early, almost in the prehistoric, days of mountaineering.

It is sad to notice, in looking through the various testimonies to his worth recorded in the book to which I have referred, how many of his former employers are amongst us no more, but "Litera scripta manet." The Rev. Charles Hudson, who perished on the Matterhorn, writes of him "that for difficult ascents, he is incomparably the best guide I ever met with." And Mr. Hinchliff writes that "on all occasions he proved himself perfect, both as a friend and a companion." Mr. Frank Walker bears frequent testimony to his "courage, skill, honesty, and true gentlemanly feeling." Mr. Adams-Reilly describes how on one occasion, when ascending Mont Blanc under Melchior's guidance in company with another party led by two eminent Chamonix guides, "he and Melchior had crossed the couloir on the Aiguille du Gouté and smoked a pipe on the opposite side before the other guides had finished consulting as to how the couloir was to be attacked." Mr. R. S. Macdonald writes that the "praises lavished upon him were justly deserved;" Mr. A. W. Moore that "praise would be superfluous," while the encomiums of living climbers, E. S.

[1] Miss Walker was the first lady to climb regularly, season after season, in the Alps. In company with her father and brother she has ascended most of the great peaks.—C. D. C.

Kennedy, Horace Walker, Leslie Stephen, F. Crawford Grove, F. Tuckett, F. Morshead, and others are hearty and unanimous.

Melchior may be said to have founded a school of Oberland guides. He initiated into the mysteries of the craft such men as Hans Jaun, Andreas Maurer, von Bergen, and others of less note, and his influence is distinctly to be recognized in their method of guiding. Jaun, who has since won so eminent a place in the highest rank of his profession, was first introduced to me by Melchior as a promising young porter. Like all Melchior's pupils he had an almost idolatrous veneration for his master. The cause was easy to understand. I remember on one occasion when Melchior was leading in a position of great difficulty, calling Jaun's attention not only to the confidence which Melchior exhibited, but to the wonderful grace and ease of his movements. "Yes," said Jaun, "but he is the king of guides." To see him at work is both a

picture and a lesson. There is no slovenly step-cutting when he leads. In this respect he has had no superior, indeed it may be doubted if he has ever quite been equalled. No Red Indian chief ever found his way through primeval forests more deftly than Melchior finds his pathway in the most difficult séracs, with his active axe held like a racquet in one hand, and his keen eye instantly fixing upon the right foothold. However intently he may be occupied, he always knows what each member of the party behind him is doing, as many a Chamonix porter has found out to his cost when, in a moment of forgetfulness, he has made a careless use of the rope.

Melchior is one of those guides who combine the virtues both of prudence and of courage. He knows when it is right to go on and when it is the truest bravery to turn back. "Es geht, Melchior," said a fine climber once in my hearing when we came to a dangerous spot. "Ja," replied Melchior, "Es geht, aber ich gehe nicht." The result has been that under his guidance, accidents of any kind have been few and far between. Indeed I know of two only. He led the party over the Col de Miage in 1861, when Mr. Birkbeck fell more than 1700 feet; but the accident happened when that gentleman had unroped, and left his companions, and it was due purely to misadventure. In the year 1883 he led Mr. J. T. Wills and myself up the Dent d'Hérens, and in descending, Ulrich Almer, who was our second guide, was struck by a falling stone and severely hurt. After many hours of labour and anxiety, we succeeded in getting our wounded guide on to the Col de Valpelline at nine in the evening, and had no alternative but to sit out and wait for dawn. The care with which Melchior looked after his injured comrade, and the tenderness which induced him to take off his own coat that his friend might be the better protected, while he himself braved the night cold in his shirt-sleeves, will not easily fade from my recollection.

Melchior's motto is "thorough," and he acts up to it consistently. No detail seems to escape him. Of this faculty, exercised under very novel circumstances, I venture to give the following illustration. Five and twenty years ago he came to England on a winter visit to some of his old friends. He arrived at the London Bridge Station in the middle of a genuine London fog. He was met by Mr. Stephen and Mr. Hinchliff, who accompanied him on foot to the rooms of the latter gentleman in Lincoln's Inn Fields. A day or two later the same party found themselves at the same station on their return from Woolwich. "Now, Melchior," said Mr. Hinchliff, "you will lead us back home." Instantly the skilful guide, who had never seen a larger town than Berne, accepted the situation and found his way straight back without difficulty, pausing for consideration only once, as if to examine the landmarks, at the foot of Chancery Lane.

On the occasion of his visit to England I thought it would be an amusing change for him to take him down a deep coal-pit. The interest he showed in the working was extraordinary. I can see him now, clad in a miner's jacket, holding a dip candle stuck into a lump of clay, and watching the colliers at work with the grave earnestness which is his distinguishing characteristic.

Under no circumstances does Melchior forget what he believes to be the interest of his employers. On one occasion Mr. Morshead and myself were at Pontresina, preparing for an ascent of the Bernina. We thought it prudent to retain the services of the chief guide of the district, who not only demanded an enormous fee, but also that we should engage a comrade of his own on similar terms. Melchior was indignant, his sense of honour was touched, and he offered to take us, and did take us, to the summit of the Bernina without local aid. Just and fair in all his own relations with his employers, he resents any attempt at imposition by others.

The qualities that win the esteem of men are not always those that women most admire. In Melchior, however, there is such a combination, that while some of our best climbers are proud to attribute their successes to his genius and his courage, there are also some of the gentler sex who can never forget what they owe to his unswerving courtesy, gentleness, and kindness of heart.

I shall have written to little purpose if I have not conveyed the impression that Melchior is more than a mere guide. Few men are held in such esteem by their neighbours and their friends. His temper is so even and his judgment so sound, that in disputes amongst his own people his decision has often been sought and accepted as final, with perfect satisfaction by men who, but for him, would have gone to law against each other.

He is a genuine artist. In many a London drawing-room or on the table of many a University Don are to be found specimens of his art, which are valued no less for their intrinsic worth than from their being souvenirs of a valued friend. Some years ago the late Mr. Adams-Reilly sent him photographs of the fighting stags, two well-known pictures by Landseer. In a few months there came back two excellent pieces of carving, which I am happy to have in my possession, executed with vigour and freedom, and not only in exact accordance with the photographs, but in themselves admirable as works of art. It is amazing that a man who was entirely self-taught should not only have been able to turn out such work, but should also have been able to carve life-like statuettes of his friends, which have been found worthy of exhibition in a London Gallery.

He is a keen lover of nature. In too many cases, as Mr. Ruskin has truly observed of the Swiss peasant, "the wild goats that leap along those rocks have as much passion of joy in all that fair work of God, as the men that toil among them—perhaps more. The sun is known only as a warmth—the wind as a chill—the Mountains as a danger." There are guides who regard a gigantic precipice or a lofty aiguille from no other point of view than that raised by the question of whether one can go up or down. Melchior is not of this kind. He understands the lessons which the mountains teach and the glories they reveal. I have many remembrances of scenes of beauty never to be forgotten when, following the cold grey of the early morning, the sun has smitten the great peaks one after another with a crimson flash, or when at sunset the whole western horizon has been one vast flame, and as they recur to me I can recall Melchior's face lit up with genuine enthusiasm as he exclaimed, "Schön! Schön!"

In 1864 Melchior married Marguerite Metzener, a girl who at that time had charge of the woodcarving in the Hôtel at the foot of the Rhone Glacier. They have had a numerous family, eight sons and four daughters. The eldest son, also named Melchior, was trained for a guide; he inherited his father's charming disposition and much of his skill, though not his strength, and it was thought better that he should become a woodcarver only. The second son, Andreas, is a rising guide of great promise, and is likely to succeed to something of his father's fame.

Melchior Anderegg has always preserved a keen attachment for his early patrons. They always had the first claim upon him. If his services at any particular time were not required by Stephen or Walker or Morshead or myself, then, and then only, was he open to fresh engagements, but he always looked forward with the warmest interest to new work with old friends. I am conscious that it is difficult to set down undoubted facts about such a guide as Melchior Anderegg, and yet to avoid altogether the charge of exaggeration. Those who have known this famous guide will make no such charge against me, and if those to whom he is a stranger will look well at the admirable portrait placed opposite this memoir, they will not fail to read in that the record of a noble life. The fine face has more furrows than when I first knew it nearly thirty years ago, and the once jet-black hair is now silvered by the advancing years, but as yet the eye is not dim nor the natural force abated. To say that I owe him a debt impossible to repay is not to say much. He first taught me how to climb. For more than twenty seasons he has led me—in success and in failure—in sunshine and in storm. He has rejoiced with me in happy times; he has nursed me when suffering from accident with a charming devotion. Year after year I have met him with a keener pleasure. Year after year I have parted from him with a deeper regret. He cannot expect to continue for many more years in active occupation, but the recollection of his splendid and faithful services is a priceless possession to those who have known and loved him; and in the green old age which troops of friends so heartily desire for him, he can look back with content and satisfaction upon a prosperous and brilliant career.

C. E. M.

Johann von Bergen.

JOHANN VON BERGEN, or "Hans" as he is always called, was born in 1836 at Meiringen, a village which can claim to have produced a greater number of guides of the first rank than any other in the Oberland, one might almost say than any other in the whole of the Alps. Hans belongs to what has been felicitously termed the "Melchior school" of guides. Although he does not display that grace and perfect ease of movement which are so characteristic of Melchior, and of one or two of the guides who have been trained by him,

he has many of those other qualities which we associate with such names as Jaun and Maurer. His force and skill as a cragsman, his wonderful power of making short cuts through a maze of séracs, and his knowledge of the varying conditions of snow and ice are alike unsurpassed.

As a rock climber he is pre-eminently in the first rank. Very tall and spare, and with legs and arms moreover long out of proportion to the rest of his body, he is of a build admirably adapted for going up difficult rocks. Without the slightest effort he can reach to a ledge of rock far above his head, and swing himself up to it, in a way which would be impossible for a shorter man, and would puzzle most of equal stature. Any one who for the first time sees von Bergen on a peak, must be struck with his enormous stride. On steep rocks his "reach of leg," if one may be allowed to coin an expression, is almost as remarkable as his reach of arm. Once on an "off day" at the Montanvert some one suggested to the guides that they should try how far they could clamber up the wall of the Hôtel, by the rough-hewn projecting stones at its corners. The two Jauns, Rey, and von Bergen were of the party. And no one who saw that friendly contest can forget how von Bergen walked up to the wall, and placed his foot in a space between two of the stones which was almost on a level with his chin.

In winter Hans is a *Holzhauer*. He lives in a picturesque cottage, in the little hamlet of Willigen, just where the mule-path to Rosenlaui and the Great Scheideck diverges from the main road, a cottage which for neatness and comfort may be considered to be the *beau idéal* of an Oberland châlet. By thrift and good management he is, from a guide's standpoint, in very comfortable circumstances. He has a little herd of cows in which he takes much honest pride, and when camping out at the Kastenstein, or similar places where one would have supposed that there was little in the surroundings to suggest reflections on the management of a dairy, the conversation almost invariably turns upon agriculture when Hans is one of the party.

He is related to Melchior Anderegg, and has not only the most unbounded admiration for his kinsman's powers as a guide, but the greatest reverence and respect for him as a man. And, indeed, if one did not know that this esteem was genuine it might almost seem to be somewhat ludicrous. No schoolboy was ever prouder of a big brother's achievements in the Eleven or in the Football field, or more jealous of his reputation, and convinced of the absolute infallibility of all his opinions, than von Bergen is of the position the "King of Guides" holds in his craft. Mr. C. D. Cunningham, who has known Hans for several years, writes, "Once when von Bergen was at the Montanvert he was taken somewhat seriously ill. I do not remember what the exact nature of the malady was from which he was suffering; but, at all events, the united contents of all the travelling medicine-chests in the Hôtel were powerless to effect a successful cure, such as was accomplished some ten days later by the Meiringen doctor. Hans spent the greater part of the day lying on a couple of benches in the Guide's room, where he was carefully tended by Melchior. And it was indeed pleasant to see not only the perfect feeling of confidence, and sense of repose which Melchior's presence evidently gave the sick man, but to watch the tender, almost womanly way old Melchior watched over his friend and kinsman. That von Bergen was very far from well there could be no doubt. For when he started in a downpour of rain to walk down to Chamonix, the sturdy Oberlander consented (although under strong protest) to take an umbrella and a waterproof."

Previous to 1871, when I first met Hans and engaged him at Melchior's strong recommendation, he had been acting as guide for some years, but had never enjoyed the opportunity of engagements of any great length. Since then he has acted regularly as my guide every season for thirteen years. My having monopolized him so much, accounts for the fact that he has comparatively fewer names of well-known climbers in his book than most men of the same rank as guide. The members of the Alpine Club who have had the best opportunities of judging of his powers are, Mr. E. Hulton, Mr. J. Walker Hartley, and Mr. W. E. Davidson, who writes in Hans's *Führerbuch* in 1880, "He still possesses in the fullest degree all those remarkable powers as a guide and excellent qualities as a man which gained for him the very high position he occupies amongst the leading guides of the Alps."

No accident has ever happened to any one under von Bergen's care. On one occasion, when making the ascent of the Eiger, he was the means of saving the life of an Englishman as he was literally falling over the precipice, under circumstances similar to those by which Mr. Birkbeck so nearly lost his life on the Col du Miage. Hans, in the most gallant and plucky manner, and without a single thought of the risk he himself was running, sprang forward just in time to seize the falling *Herr*. Both rolled down some feet, and had it not been for a projecting ledge of rock both must inevitably have been dashed to pieces on the pitiless crags of those tremendous cliffs.

Perhaps von Bergen's consummate skill as a cragsman was never more notably displayed than on the Aiguille de Blaitière in September, 1875, when from the col close to the summit of the Aiguille, he led a party of three down a new and very difficult way on to the Mer de Glace. The rocks in the couloir were extremely steep, and there was much ice in places; return would have been impossible without a ladder, and bad weather came on, but von Bergen's iron determination and skill were never for one moment at fault. He had in several places to lower the other two members of the party from ledge to ledge, and it was here that his great "reach of leg," and his remarkable power of availing himself of it, as well as of his great reach of arm, to its fullest extent was most perfectly exemplified. The rocks at the bottom of the couloir were cut off from the glacier by a huge bergschrund, which would have puzzled a chamois, and was totally unprovided with a bridge, but von Bergen was equal to the occasion, and the gigantic leap with which, after safely lowering his two companions, he landed himself on to the Mer de Glace, was not the least remarkable of his many great feats that day. In 1876 von Bergen made the first ascent from the Urbachthal of the principal peak of the Engelhörner, and in 1877 the second recorded ascent of the Finsteraarhorn by the south-eastern arête, where, thanks to Hans' unerring instinct in discovering the exact route up steep rocks, some of the difficulties met with in the first ascent of the mountain by the same route would seem to have been avoided. The season of 1878 was marked by the first ascent of Mont Maudit, led by von Bergen and Jaun. The party quitted the Grands Mulets at 2 a.m., ascended *via*

the Corridor to the summit of Mont Maudit, descended thence to the Corridor again, and so *via* the Mur de la Côte and the Rochers Rouges to the summit of Mont Blanc. The descent was made by the Bosses, and Chamonix regained about five the same evening. In 1879 von Bergen was leading guide in the ascent of the Gabelhorn from the Arben Joch, and in September of the same year, finding himself alone with one Herr on the summit of the Blümlis Alphorn at a very early hour of the morning, he made the passage from the summit of that peak to the adjoining summit of the Weisse Frau. This little climb cost the two three and a half hours of the very hardest work, and on completing it, Hans contented himself with looking back and remarking, "Nur Einmals ist genug," but he still speaks of it as a "dummheit," of which, for fear of its repetition, but little notice should be taken.

Hans has a grave, earnest, wistful face. Like many men whom the average run of people would say had few pretensions to be considered good-looking, his features light up with a singularly kindly expression when he meets a friend. No heartier or truer welcome awaits one in the Alps than his, and there is an unmistakable ring of sincerity about his voice as he grasps your hand and says, "Till next year." Many a painter would consider himself fortunate if Hans would consent to sit as a model for a Huguenot. For not only has he much of the outward appearance, but many of the characteristics of those good and brave people. Although a man of a retiring disposition, he does not hesitate boldly to express his opinion when any question arises, as to what he considers to mark the line between right and wrong. It is even said that on one occasion he respectfully but very firmly expressed his disapproval of the language employed by a certain Scotch gentleman, who, on long and soft snow slopes has been heard to vent his feelings in what his friends always supposed to be some Gaelic dialect; but which von Bergen's quick and watchful ear at once detected to be German, none the less expressive because it was ungrammatical.

In 1882, after one of the worst seasons on record, the following note appears in his *Führerbuch*, "We have now travelled together eleven seasons, and it is only with pleasure that I look forward to many more, which, when one is with Hans, the very worst weather cannot spoil." The writer could claim then to speak with some authority of a friend and companion whose fidelity had been as unfaltering as were his powers of endurance on many an Alpine peak and pass, and it has been a pleasant duty to him now, in response to the request of the Editor of this work, once more to bear his testimony to a tried and trusty comrade.

H. S. H.

Johann Jaun.

AFTER a ten years' separation from the Alps and their Pioneers, I am asked to give my recollections of my guide JOHANN JAUN. Beyond the pages of the *Alpine Journal*, I have found nothing but a few ragged pencil notes to help me. The mistakes and shortcomings of my testimony must be put down to my memory, which, though grateful, is, with the rust of a decade, very fallible. And, moreover, the finest passages in a climber's experience are just those that are least capable of record. Only one instance to the contrary occurs to me, namely, the wonderfully vivid description of his "Race for Life," which is narrated by Mr. Tuckett in volume v. of the *Alpine Journal*. After emerging from the spray of an avalanche that wanted but a few feet of sweeping the whole party to the moraine above the Wengern Alp, Mr. Tuckett straightway proceeded to measure the avalanche, and to calculate its weight in tons. Now I have neither the pen of a Tuckett, nor his stores of carefully recorded observation to help me, yet my duty to Jaun forbids my silence. He was my constant guide; to him I owe whatever expeditions worthy of note I may have done; by him I have been brought scatheless through many risks and some grave dangers; through him more than any one else, was the great pleasure I have gained from the Alps secured. I propose, then, first to give my opinion of Jaun as a guide, and next to illustrate this opinion by personal notes from my experience.

Jaun was born near Meiringen in 1843, and had the inestimable advantage of an apprenticeship under Melchior Anderegg, who as a guide is admitted to have no superior, and as a teacher no equal. A pupil of such a man is taught the right style; he has nothing to unlearn, and after a few seasons he can, so to speak, complete for himself his education. Jaun was Melchior's favourite pupil. This relation between the two men has been maintained, though extended by the fact that the master has now, for many a year, regarded his old pupil as a valued ally; and of all the distinguished guides of the present day, it may safely be said that there is no one for whose opinion on questions relating to mountaineering Melchior has so much respect. Hans is generally called "Hänserli" by his friends, to distinguish him from Hans von Bergen, yet another distinguished Meiringen guide who owes much of his success to Melchior's training.

In what for a better term may be called the "mechanical qualities" of a guide, as an ice-man and a cragsman, Jaun, when I first engaged him in 1869, had nothing to learn. A very rapid step-cutter, he yet invariably graduated each step exactly to the inclination of the ice slope as well as to the skill of the climber, and, however slight and crude the step might be, it was always absolutely right as far as it went. On rocks I never saw so quick a climber, and when their feasibility had to be tested, Jaun would nearly always be chosen as the pioneer; and then, unroped, I have seen him, in going from one point of vantage to another, do more in ten minutes than an ordinary climber would do in an hour. And yet, with all his speed, there was no slovenliness; no stone would be loosened to fall on those below. His skill on ice he doubtless learnt from his master Melchior. In his cragsman's craft he was self-taught, as every Meiringen *Jäger* is, on those most treacherous and difficult of all rocks in the Oberland, the Engelhörner. And to learn the true cragsman's art there is no school to compare with that of the chamois-hunter—for stalking throws one entirely on one's own resources, and neither rope, axe, nor stock can be used, without risking scaring the quarry. Jaun possesses all that wonderful neatness and grace of movement which is so characteristic of his master, and in these respects he may fairly be said to have never been equalled by any other guide. If a young amateur could only see Hänserli on a difficult piece of rock work, he would learn more by watching him for ten minutes than in a whole season's work with a couple of ordinary guides. No matter how steep and smooth the *pente* may be, or how small the hold he sees he must grasp above him, Jaun always proceeds to work with the same ease and apparent certainty of success with which a trained gymnast walks up to his trapèze.

There are some guides who, on coming to places of great difficulty on a rock arête, at once proceed to apostrophise the gendarme who bars the route, they probably call him a "mauvais diable" (if indeed no stronger expression be used), and in trying to circumvent him they tighten the rope, turn up the collar of their coat, and attack the intervening rocks with a sort of "knock you down" air. No matter what difficulties Häuserli may have to face, he encounters them all with the same imperturbable command, and, above all, he always knows when to turn back. It is a picture to see him at work; for, in addition to being an unsurpassed cragsman, it would be difficult to find a more perfectly made man, or one more finely proportioned.

Coming now to the intellectual qualities of a guide, by which I especially mean those of a path-finder, Jaun from the first showed excellent powers of observation, which, under Melchior's training, enabled him at a glance to gauge the feasibility of a route, or in the case of alternative routes, to determine which was the more practicable. His experience as a chamois-hunter in the detection and approach of his quarry were no doubt in this respect invaluable to him. But it was on ice that Jaun's great intellectual powers were most plainly seen. Again and again when we have seemed hopelessly lost in a maze of séracs has he led the party through the difficulties with a masterly ease, as if the ground-plan of the glacier were under his eyes, and where with us there was confusion and doubt, with him there was clearness and unfaltering decision. Mr. J. O. Maund recalls one occasion on which Jaun displayed this quality in a most wonderful manner. They were crossing the Mönchjoch together in bad weather, nearly half a foot of fresh snow had fallen, and for the moment they were brought to a complete stand-still, and were unable to find the route. Jaun suddenly began to scoop away the snow from the ice "like a truffle-dog," to use Mr. Maund's own most expressive phrase, and almost immediately exclaimed, "Here are the tracks of the last party."

Lastly, in regard to the moral qualities of a guide, Jaun has in the very highest degree the two great essentials of courage and of absolutely unqualified loyalty. He is further generous, unselfish, without a trace of vanity, and with unfailing good-humour. His "*bonne camaraderie*" has made him popular in his own district, and gained him outside it hearty friendships amongst both French and Italian guides with whom he has travelled. Throughout the whole of his career he has shown such a perfect disinterestedness regarding money-matters, as almost to verge upon improvidence. However distinguished his fellow-guides, he would always be welcomed as their leader; however ordinary their rank, he would never seem to lead. His whole disposition is a most loveable one, and there is a delightful simplicity about him. He will confide his "mishaps" (shall we call them?) with the *garde-chasse*, or any of the small incidents which impede the progress of the work in his woodcarving atelier, to those *Herren* whom he has learned to look on as his old friends, with the same frankness as if they were his elder brothers.

It was in 1869, that I first met Jaun. I had started with a companion for the Alps, under the belief that climbing was an "*a priori* instinct," and relying on the maxim that all guides were equal. The Titlis settled my companion, and the incompetence shown by my guide on our second ice journey on the Aletsch glacier decided me to start alone for the Saas Valley, determined out of sheer mulishness to do something though my guiding axiom had been shattered. At the entrance to the valley, I was met by Messrs.

C. E. Mathews and Morshead with Jaun carrying their traps. They kindly relieved him of these, and allowed him to shoulder mine. He was thereupon changed from porter to guide, and began his eventful career. Infamous weather forced us back from the easiest passes, and at length drove us over the Théodule Pass to Courmayeur. Jaun knew that I was a greenhorn, and had taken him, then a comparatively unknown porter, for my guide. He proposed, therefore, that as a matter of mutual confidence we should go over the Col du Géant by ourselves. I joyfully assented. Chancing, however, to meet two Courmayeur guides, our project was rejected in favour of their plan to ascend Mont Blanc from the *cabane* on the Aiguille du Midi. We found the hut choked with ice, and so tried to sleep outside with a blanket apiece. We started next day without breakfast, which after a night spent without sleep or warmth, brought us by the time we were three parts up Mout Maudit, to so sad a plight that one of the Courmayeur men advised our return, and that our bottle of champagne should be drunk. I agreed, of course claiming my right as "Sommelier." As I was in the act of smashing the bottle with significant deliberation, Jaun stopped my arm, and motioned the party to move forward. We reached the top with little further difficulty, and got to Chamonix none the worse for our hardships. Jaun and I then swore an alliance, and climbing after that without him, would have been hardly climbing at all.

In the following year (1870) Jaun was called out on frontier service during the Franco-German war, so he did not join me until 1871. We did plenty of hard work, but nothing that was new. Two incidents, however, are worthy of record. Mr. Wallroth with Peter Knubel had joined us for a few days. We were descending the ridge of the Lyskamm in a storm, when my foot slipped. As I glided down the ice wall, I was too busy in getting my axe to bite to think of shouting to the others. Consequently the rope becoming taut, Jaun who was leading, and Wallroth who was behind me, were capsized, and in their turn gave me a fresh impetus. I shall never forget Jaun's startled look and shouted directions to us, whilst like an automaton he turned face downwards, with legs apart, and with hands, weight, and momentum turned his axe into an ice plough. Knubel being the last on the rope had sprung to the Italian side and held us safely, whilst we, I fancy, must have looked something like the papers on the tail of a kite. Had it not been for Knubel, our situation would have been one of undoubted danger, but even so I think that Jaun's coolness in directing us, whilst he was acting as brakesman, would in any case have brought us to the ridge once more in safety.

Later on in the same season, having successfully ascended the two peaks of the Grandes Jorasses, I was returning leisurely with Jaun (the second man having been sent forward to collect our things from our *gîte*) and began to cross the last ice slope before taking to the rocks. The ice fall was steep, and as a slip would have been dangerous, Jaun had roped me, and was cutting steps. The night came on apace, and my feet getting numbed Jaun had to cut hand-holes above. By the time my hands had lost sensation, twilight had deepened into night, and as Jaun informed me that he could not hold me if I slipped, I asked to be unroped. Jaun point-blank refused, but promised to tell me as soon as a slip would do no harm. I passed a time of indescribable nervous torture until I heard the welcome leave to go as I pleased, when I slid down a few yards of ice, carrying Jaun with me into a deep snowdrift. He had shared the terrible tension, and, forgetting everything in the sense of present safety, he warmly embraced me.

In the year 1872, I joined forces with Mr. F. Gardiner and my brother, who took respectively Peter Knubel and Jean Joseph Maquignaz as guides. I will refer to only one expedition out of many in a most successful tour—our passage of the Matterhorn from Zermatt to Breuil. Jaun had never ascended the peak, which was in those days almost unknown except to local talent, but the two other guides had already accomplished the ascent. Maquignaz had done so several times, and his excellence as a rock-climber is universally admitted. Alongside of these men, my faith in Jaun as a marvellous cragsman, and as a born leader, was no longer simply the estimate of affectionate enthusiasm, but took the rank of an ascertained fact. Gauging the difficulties of the climb, he told me he considered the ascent from Zermatt a fraud utilized for the purpose of enriching local guides from the pockets of ambitious neophytes, but the descent to Breuil was "ganz anders."

In 1873, Christian Lauener, as well as Jaun, accompanied me in many first-class climbs. We made a new ascent of the Fletschhorn, from the east, and a first ascent of the Schallenhorn which we combined with the passage of the Moming. We further ascended Mont Blanc from the Miage Glacier (Mr. Kennedy's route), making no use of the rope until within a few minutes of the top.

In spite of the wretched weather of 1874, I was lucky enough to make my best expedition with Jaun, the Col des Grandes Jorasses. Its success was due to Jaun alone, for our porter was willing but dumbfounded. The dangers of the expedition have been much misunderstood, though they served to bring all Jaun's characteristic powers into exalted play. His indomitable pluck and perseverance, his unfaltering decision in sticking to his plan of attack, his prudence in leading us at one time a few yards above a couloir, so that we might be safe from the almost incessant cannonade of débris which was falling down it just below our feet, and then his skill in conducting us subsequently over the steepest and rottenest rocks I had ever encountered, were alike beyond all praise. Hardly moving a stone where all was movable, he yet gave timely warning if perchance a projectile had been launched on its career. His powers as a cragsman were displayed every half-hour, as, unroped, he scaled some point of vantage to see how the succeeding maze of rocks was to be faced or turned. His pace in getting from the Mallet Glacier to Chamonix, after a day of almost unparalleled exertion, was tremendous, and his unfailing resource, which had been used incessantly in a journey made up entirely of difficulties, never for a moment deserted him, bruised, benighted, and axeless, though we were; and lastly, his *bonhomie*, through all our trials, was never once ruffled, even when the porter indulged in prayer.

In 1875 bad weather prevented us doing much. We demonstrated, however, the perfect feasibility of the Finsteraarhorn from the Rothloch, and nothing but the chilly N.E. gale deprived us of an otherwise assured success when we were within a few minutes of the summit. Further we made, with Lord Wentworth, an attempt upon the Aiguille Verte from Argentière.

1876 was my last season of serious work in the Alps. Mr. J. Oakley Maund and Mons. Henri Cordier had joined me, with Andreas Maurer and Jacob Anderegg as guides. Our attack on the Aiguille Verte from Argentière was repeated, but on this occasion with perfect success. I, at the time, likened the climb to three Momings, interspersed with rock work on a par with the best bits of the Gabelhorn, and it was certainly incomparably the finest all-round climb of my experience. No guides could have behaved more splendidly than did our three men. But without Jaun we should not have succeeded, for to the highest qualities of a guide, he added the fresh experience of the previous year's attempt, and that knowledge formed an indispensable condition of our success. As it was, our work was so beset with difficulties that it was only just "pulled off." Immediately after this expedition we made the first ascents of the Courtes and the Droites. In the Engadine our failure to ascend the Piz Bernina by the arête dividing the Misauna Gletscher from that of the Morteratsch was due to Cordier, who had laid down our route for us, but the true way, ascending from the Misauna Gletscher to the summit direct, was noted by Jaun at the time, and afterwards successfully followed by Herr Güssfeldt. Similarly, we gave up Cordier's proposal for the Monte de Scersen. My suggested attack on the Rosegg from the Tschierva Gletscher was put into practicable shape by Jaun, and successfully carried through on the following day.

The same year I spent a fortnight in chamois-stalking with Jaun in the Val de Levigno and the Oberland. He was then very keen, and a good shot, and gave promise (a promise which has since been fulfilled) of being a Jäger of the highest class. His characteristics of courage, resource, good humour, and—a trait which is as specially welcome as it is seldom found amongst sportsmen—perfect unselfishness, were shown as usual, for they are part of Jaun's nature. None of the second generation of guides can show such a splendid record of new expeditions. When we take into consideration that it was 1868 when he made, as a young porter, his first new ascent, one is compelled to admit that among those who followed the pioneers of the golden age, his list is absolutely unique, if we judge of his expeditions from the standpoint of their difficulty and importance.

In 1868 he made the first ascent of the Grandes Jorasses. In 1872, he *crossed* both the Gabelhorn and the Rothhorn for the first time. The party started from Zermatt, making a col of the summit of the Gabelhorn to Zinal, and the following day returned to Zermatt over the Rothhorn. In 1873, he made, with the present writer, the first ascent of the Schallenhorn, and descended from the summit of the Aletschhorn to the Faulberg by an entirely new route down its northern face. In 1874, under the circumstances already narrated, he crossed the Col des Grandes Jorasses for the first time, and the following season, with Colonel Methuen and Colonel Montgomery, and his trusty comrade, Andreas Maurer, he made the second passage of the Dom Joch. In 1876 he made the first and only ascent of the Aiguille Verte from the Argentière Glacier, crossing over the summit of the mountain to the Montanvert. He has probably ascended this very difficult mountain under greater varieties of circumstances than any other living guide. During the same season he scaled Les Courtes and also Les Droites for the first time. In 1877 he made the first and only ascent of the Weisshorn from the Schallen Gletscher, and made a new route up the Gabelhorn. The following year he made the first ascent of Mont Maudit, a new route up the Bietschhorn, and the first and only passage over the summit of Mont Blanc *from* Chamonix to Courmayeur. This same year he also crossed the Col Dolent for the second time, the first passage having been made by Mr. Whymper thirteen years previously, under circumstances which up to this date had deterred any other party from attempting to repeat it.

During his career, Jaun has performed some very remarkable *tours de force*, and has spent much of his time with employers who were bent on making variations on peaks by new and what were often very difficult climbs. In 1877 he led a party up the north face of the Breithorn and down to the Riffelhaus in eight hours, including all halts. The same season he ascended the Gabelhorn, starting from and returning to Zermatt in thirteen hours, and on the occasion of the search party in connexion with the sad accident on the Lyskamm, he led two well-known amateurs from the top of the Lysjoch to the Riffelhaus in the extraordinary time of one hour and thirty minutes. The ascents of the Aiguille Verte from the Argentière Glacier and of Les Courtes and Les Droites were made in one week. In the first of these climbs the party left Argentière at 12 p.m. one Sunday night, and did not arrive at Chamonix till the following Tuesday at 11 a.m., and the length and difficulty of the other two ascents (one of which has not since been repeated) entitle this week's work to be considered, from a purely climbing point of view, as a *tour de force* unsurpassed in the history of the Alps. Jaun's splendid performance on the ice face of the Aiguille du Midi in 1878, during a terrific hurricane of wind and hail, and his subsequent descent to the Mer de Glace through the tremendous séracs of the Vallée Blanche, will long be remembered by those who accompanied him in the first ascent of that peak from the side of Chamonix.

Mr. C. D. Cunningham writes: "Like one other well-known guide, Jaun has always looked upon his *Führerbuch* as a most useless and unnecessary part of his kit." "Hans has an inveterate habit of leaving his book at home, of which we have only just succeeded in breaking him," wrote Mr. H. Seymour Hoare in 1882. The first entry is dated 1869, and is signed by Mr. T. S. Kennedy and another gentleman, who record with curt simplicity that "Jaun guided us up the Schreckhorn." Between the years 1869 and 1886 there are only some twenty entries in his book. These, however, with hardly a single exception, are signed by the best known amateurs in the Alps, and among them may be mentioned Mr. J. O. Maund, Mr. J. Walker Hartley, Mr. F. C. Hartley, Mr. Horace Walker, Colonel Methuen, Mr. W. E. Davidson, Herr Gruber, and Mr. H. Seymour Hoare. Every other guide can number among his clientèle some *Herr* whose going powers do not equal his enthusiasm for mountaineering, but there is not a single *Herr* whose name is intimately associated with that of Jaun whose powers are not of the first class, or who does not occupy a very distinguished place among other climbers. I remember on an off day that Hans was once lent, much against his will, to an American tourist who wished to cross the Mer de Glace. "Châpeau, sank franks, you savvy—now hurry up,"—were the terms in which the offer was made to him. And it was indeed in some ways an almost comical sight to see how carefully Jaun watched each step his new patron took, and to notice how anxiously he helped him up the huge soup-plate steps which the member of the Société, who acts as Cantonnier on that well-beaten track, was hewing out. It would be difficult to say whether Jaun or his charge looked the more uncomfortable, or which of them seemed most pleased when they arrived in safety on the other side of the Mauvais Pas. "That ' Foorurr,' as they call guides in Europe, was a real good man, he was; I shouldn't wonder if he had been up Mount Bloug. He hadn't no book or else I'd a given him a testimonial, but I fee'd him extra. I did." These very sincere words of commendation about Jaun's powers as a guide were overheard the same evening by some of his friends who were sitting drinking their coffee and smoking cigarettes in old Couttet's garden after *table d'hôte*."

In recent years Jaun has been chiefly employed by Mr. W. E. Davidson, whose name figures so largely in his list of new expeditions, and between whom and Hänserli exist the closest personal attachment and regard. "His reputation as a mountaineer," Mr. Davidson has written in Jaun's book, "is of course quite independent of any words of mine, for he is well known to all climbers as a guide with no superior in the Alps. To his modest and simple nature and his sterling worth, to his great courage, to his loyalty to his employers and devotion in all respects to their interests, no words of mine can possibly do justice."

Hans Jaun is one of the best known wood-carvers in the Oberland, and his productions, which are in every sense works of art, are much sought after. It is marvellous that any man who has received no regular artistic training should be able to produce an admirable and striking likeness in wood from a photograph. It is an axiom among many collectors that really good works of art always look well when they are arranged together, irrespective of their peculiar style or material. Jaun's work most undoubtedly stands this test, as any one must admit who has been in a certain cosy set of bachelor rooms in Jermyn Street, and seen there a statuette which Hänserli carved for the *Herr* whom of all others he probably holds first in his regard and affection. His treatment and rendering of chamois are most admirable, and no one has had better opportunities of studying their forms or is more familiar with their poses as they stand sentinel on the pinnacles of their native crags. From boyhood Jaun has been passionately fond of sport, and is now a first-class shot and a thorough sportsman. He has on several occasions acted as Shikari to Mr. J. Walker Hartley, and Mr. J. Oakley Maund, the two Englishmen whose names are most identified with chamois-shooting in the Alpine districts of Switzerland. 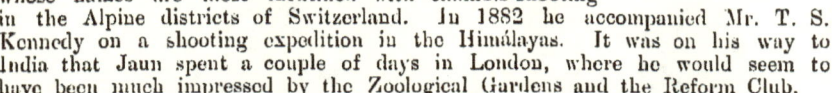 In 1882 he accompanied Mr. T. S. Kennedy on a shooting expedition in the Himálayas. It was on his way to India that Jaun spent a couple of days in London, where he would seem to have been much impressed by the Zoological Gardens and the Reform Club.

Among the living guides of the second generation Hans Jaun has no superior, and it would indeed be hard to select from the ranks of his contemporaries one who equals him. His knowledge of the various districts in the Alps is unrivalled. His list of new expeditions and rock *tentatives* of extraordinary difficulty speaks for itself. He has attained the greatest skill as a climber, and, with the exception of Melchior Anderegg, there is no guide who can equal his style, grace of movement, and perfect finish.

From his possessing these many good qualities in an exceptional degree he has, almost from the very first, been exclusively employed by amateurs in the front rank of climbers. Hence it is, that although every one who goes out yearly for a few weeks to the Alps is almost as familiar with the name of Jaun as with that of Melchior himself, and has heard of his many remarkable feats, there are comparatively few who have ever had the good fortune to see him on a mountain and to be able to judge of his capacity by comparing his style and powers with those of the guides they are familiar with. A strong bond of friendship has always existed between Hans and his old friends and patrons. His trustful, simple, and perfectly straightforward nature has led him to confide in them to the utmost, and speak of his life at Unterbach during the long monotonous winter months, broken only by some village festivity, or by an expedition after chamois with his friends the young Andereggs. While

it is indeed a rare testimony to the character of the man to hear with what affectionate regard those who have longest and best known him, and with whom his name will always be associated in his great climbing feats, speak of Hänserli.

T. M.

Ulrich Lauener.

ULRICH LAUENER.—"Ulch" as he is called in his native valley—the oldest of the living guides whose names are recorded in this work, was born at Lauterbrunnen in 1821. His career commenced before Melchior Anderegg or Christian Almer were known as guides. For some years Ulrich and his brother Christian may almost be said to have had the monopoly of guiding everywhere except in the Chamonix district. Ulrich even now recalls with some pride, how in his early days, when passing by the Zäsenberg, he used to hand over his sack to the shepherd, who for a consideration was always willing to carry it for him until they reached the glacier. This shepherd was none other than Christian Almer, who, in a very few years, became not only his rival, but more than his equal as a guide.

Ulrich is of the old school, one of the few remaining links between us and the early days of mountaineering. Melchior Anderegg has been called the 'King of Guides,' Ulrich is undoubtedly their *Doyen*. It is difficult to realize that he was in full practice as a guide, long before the first ascent of the Wetterhorn from Grindelwald in 1854, the date when systematic mountaineering may be said to have commenced. Mr. Justice Wills tells us in his fascinating book, how he went to Lauterbrunnen "to take counsel of Ulrich Lauener," as to the possibility of ascending the Wetterhorn. With Balmat, Simond, and the two *Gems-jäger*—of whom one was Christian Almer, 'the shepherd at the Zäsenberg'—Ulrich took part in that most memorable ascent. He it was who "pressed" to be allowed to take the *Flagge*, as that unwieldy iron machine, which cannot have weighed less than twenty or thirty pounds, was termed, and which one of the Chamonix guides of the party called with chilling cynicism a '*bêtise*,' to plant upon the summit. It was Ulrich who cut through the final ice-cornice, and led the party in triumph to the summit.

Turning over the pages of his *Führerbuch*, one notices how frequently he is referred to as a "pleasant companion," a character every one must endorse who ever smoked a pipe with the old guide, and heard him talk of his exploits in bygone days. And not a few of the rising generation, not only of guides but of amateurs, might do well to mark and inwardly digest many of his criticisms on the difference between past and present climbing. Those who knew Ulrich in his prime, speak of him as having been the '*beau idéal*' of a William Tell, dressed as was his wont in a dark green suit, with a *Wald-huhn* plume which he always wore in his hat; and they all vividly recall the splendid swagger of his gait. The portrait of him in Mr. Whymper's engraving of the 'Club-house at Zermatt,' quite bears out this description. Ulrich's tall figure, like a perfect giant, is seen towering in the background, with his ice-axe resting on his shoulder; and even those who have only known him in his later years, can well imagine from the old man's erect figure, and stately bearing, what he must have been at that period of his life. He seems in his early days to have been possessed of an overflowing geniality and a superfluity of good spirits, and his conversation was at all times racy and sententious. But dash and love of adventure are by no means the only qualities to be looked for in a guide with whom one starts on a new or dangerous climb.

One of the best known expeditions in which he took part was the passage of the Eiger-Joch, which he crossed for the first time with Mr. Leslie Stephen in 1859, and which that gentleman has described in 'The Playground of Europe.' "I had secured," he says, "the gigantic Ulrich Lauener, the most picturesque of guides. Tall, spare, blue-eyed, long-limbed and square-shouldered, with a jovial laugh and a not ungraceful swagger, he is the very model of a true mountaineer; and, except that his rule is apt to be rather autocratic, I would not wish for a pleasanter companion." Then he goes on to say that Ulrich had "certain views as to the superiority of the Teutonic over the Celtic races, which rather interfered with the harmony of the party at a later period. While cutting their way through a labyrinth of crevasses, the Chamonix guides warned us not to speak, for fear of bringing down some of the nicely poised ice-masses on our heads. On my translating this well-meant piece of advice to Lauener, he immediately selected the most dangerous-looking pinnacle in sight, and mounting to the top of it sent forth a series of screams, loud enough, I should have thought, to bring down the top of the Mönch." Ulrich was one of the Brother Smyth's party in the first ascent of the highest peak of Monte Rosa in 1855. He is, as I have said, a guide of the old school, and is one of the few remaining links between us and the early days of mountaineering. A man of strong will, he was always determined, even at the risk of offending an inexperienced employer, to see that all the proper precautions were taken for the safety of his party. He has a certain old-world courtesy of manner, and there is a great dignity about the way in which he expresses himself. The Rev. A. R. Abbott, with whom Ulrich has been at intervals between 1857 and 1872, writes in his *Führerbuch*: "He is still a most pleasant companion, a most reliable guide, and what I have ever found him, an honest man." No better testimony could be given to his skill, than the fact that during the forty odd years he has acted as guide, none of his *Herren* have ever met with any serious accident while under his care.

It is pleasant to read the following testimonial, written about one of the 'old guard' in the Alps, as Ulrich, who has nearly completed his fiftieth season of guiding, may well be styled. It is dated July, 1886: "I must express my astonishment and admiration at the way he bears his sixty-five years. I should not have believed his age, had he not told me before,—from the manner he came down the soft snow of the Petersgrat, and the surprising agility with which he descended the rather difficult *moraine* on the south side. Ulrich proved also a very pleasant, cheerful companion to me, as I was alone. I wonder how many years he will continue to be an efficient guide."

C. D. C.

Christian Lauener.

ULRICH'S junior by five years, CHRISTIAN LAUENER was born at Lauterbrunnen in 1826. The brothers commenced their career as guides at the same time, and have many characteristics in common. Especially in outward appearance and manner there is a strong family likeness between them. Both have the same emphatic mode of expressing themselves, the same stalwart figure, and dignified bearing. Both have what Mr. Justice Wills called "the true Lauener cut." In 'Vacation Tourists,' Professor Tyndall thus describes Christian's appearance: "In driving from Neuhaus to Interlaken a chaise met us and swiftly passed; within it I could discern the brown visage of my guide. We pulled up and shouted, the other vehicle stopped, Lauener leaped from it, and came bounding towards me with admirable energy, through the deep and splashing mud. 'Gott! wie der Kerl springt!' was the admiring exclamation of my coachman. Lauener is more than six feet high, but mainly a mass of bone, his legs are out of proportion longer than his trunk, and he wears a short-tail coat which augments the apparent discrepancy. Those massive levers were now used with extraordinary vigour to project his body through space; and it was gratifying to be thus assured that the man was in first-rate condition, and fully up to the hardest work."

No record of the two Laueners would be complete without some reference to their brother Johann, who was killed on the Jungfrau a good many years ago by a fall while chamois-hunting. He was a most remarkable man, and his great feats of strength and powers of endurance are still spoken of in Lauterbrunnen. Had he lived he would have been in the foremost rank of guides. Neither Christian nor Ulrich can be said to underrate his own powers, but each always speaks with unbounded admiration of Johann's skill as a climber, and they never tire of recalling the many instances of courage and daring, which have kept his name still in remembrance. The three brothers were passionately fond of sport, and, in 'A Chamois Hunt in the Oberland' (*Alpine Journal*, vol. iv.), an interesting account is given by the late Rev. W. H. Hawker of a bivouac with Ulrich and Christian. "The pipes being lighted, we were of course bound to talk the day's work over; and I now learnt how dangerous the rocks had been, Christian saying that on their return he was carrying the dead chamois, but that when they came to the worst part, even he, accustomed as he was to rocks, could not carry it over; and he added, with just pride, that he wished I could have seen how nobly Ulrich shouldered it, and walked as upright as a soldier across that fearful place. Ulrich disclaimed all merit, merely remarking somewhat naïvely that he had been more used to carrying chamois, and indeed I imagine that few, except his poor brother Johann, could ever beat him as a *chasseur*."

Ulrich and Christian were seldom together on the same rope. In their early days, even more than at the present time, good guides were scarce, and men who had such high reputations as leaders were always much in demand. With great courtesy, but with much firmness, Christian invariably conveyed to every one in his party the fact that he was in command of it. He would often ask ambitious tourists, who wished to 'do' some great peak, what they had already done in the way of mountaineering, and he would make inquiries not only as to their capabilities, but as to certain important details in their costume, in a way calculated to take away the breath of any of the English-speaking fraternity of mule-drivers who now inscribe "guide autorisé par le gouvernement" on the cards they thrust into the hands of Cook's tourists at the doors of mountain inns. It would be impossible to imagine the mishaps of past seasons, supposed to result from going up dangerous peaks in patent leather boots and cambric shirts, happening to any one under old Christian's charge. He never hesitated to express his opinions. Even the presence of a peer of the realm, who wished to have his violoncello carried to the summit of the Schreckhorn for his lordship's diversion, did not check Christian's sharp and somewhat caustic comments on the proceeding. On that occasion the party were sleeping out in the Kastenstein cave, and the owner of the cello insisted that his instrument should occupy a place at the camp-fire, to prevent the possibility of its suffering any ill-results from the keen glacier air.

In his best days Christian seems to have had great love and enthusiasm for his profession. For the employers whom he accompanied in the early days of his career, the old man still has a loyal regard. And when he speaks of the years he was in active service, one realizes how the engagements of those days, increased the mutual friendship and esteem which both guide and employer should always feel for each other. The name more frequently associated with Christian than any other is that of Mr. F. F. Tuckett, with whom he travelled for many seasons, and made several new expeditions, especially in the Tyrol, such as ascents of the Marmolata and Cima di Brenta by new routes, and (with Mr. E. R. Whitwell) first ascents of the Cimon della Pala, and Höhe Gaisl or Croda Rossa. The names of Professor Tyndall, the Rev. Dr. Hornby (the late Head Master and present Provost of Eton), Mr. T. W. Hinchliff, and Mr. John Ball, occur frequently in his book. Mr. Ball, in his list of well-known guides, refers to Christian as " A first-rate guide, good-tempered and obliging."

The principal new expeditions in the Alps in which he has taken part are :— The first passage of the tremendous Lauinen Thor with Professor Tyndall in 1860, the Weisse Frau in 1862 with Herr E. von Fellenberg, the Col du Grand Cornier in 1864 with Dr. Hornby's party, and the following year the ascent of the Silberhorn from the north. In 1866 he crossed for the first time the Ebnefluh Joch, Schmadri Joch, and Agassiz Joch; expeditions described by Dr. Hornby in the *Alpine Journal* (vol. iii.). In 1867 he reached the highest point of the Gletscherhorn. In 1873, with Mr. T. Middlemore, he made for the first time the ascent of the Schallhorn from the Moming Pass; and in 1874, with Mr. Whitwell, he ascended the Dent Blanche by an entirely new route, and made the first ascent of the Aiguille de Blaitière.

In his 'Glaciers of the Alps,' Professor Tyndall describes his celebrated ascent of Monte Rosa, which he accomplished alone, without guides. In the descent, near the bottom of the Kamm, he overtook an Englishman and his

guides who had been on the summit, and he relates the following incident, in which Christian displayed the greatest pluck and *sang-froid*. "It was an easy task for me," he says, "to fuse myself amongst them as if I had been an old acquaintance, and we joyfully slid, galloped, and rolled together down the residue of the mountain. The only exception was the young gentleman in Lauener's care. A day or two previously he had, I believe, injured himself in crossing the Gemmi, and long before he reached the summit of Monte Rosa his knee swelled, and he walked with great difficulty. But he persisted in ascending, and Lauener seeing his great courage, thought it a pity to leave him behind. I have stated that a portion of the Kamm was solid ice. On descending this Mr. F.'s footing gave way, and he slipped forward. Lauener was forced to accompany him, for the place was too steep and slippery to permit of their motion being checked. Both were on the point of going over the Lyskamm side of the mountain, where they would have indubitably been dashed to pieces. "There was no escape then," said Lauener, in describing the incident to me subsequently; "but I saw a possible rescue at the other side, so I sprang to the right, forcibly swinging my companion round; but in doing so, the bâton tripped me up; we both fell, and rolled rapidly over each other down the incline. I knew that some precipices were in advance of us, over which we should have gone, so, releasing myself from my companion, I threw myself in front of him, stopped myself with my axe, and thus placed a barrier before him."

The following *naïf* testimonial, written in 1878 by an Eton lad, shows a pleasant side of the old man's character. "Christian Lauener took me and my younger brother up the Eiger on September 12th. I am not in a position to criticize his skill as a guide, which is too well known to need further recommendation, but he took up in us two comparative novices without letting us feel uncomfortable or in difficulties. He is also a most pleasant companion."

While his brother Ulrich was still in harness, and Melchior, Christian Almer, and most of his contemporaries in their prime, Christian Lauener practically retired from the active life of a guide. He now keeps a small *Wirthshaus* in the outskirts of his native village.

C. D. C.

Christian Almer.

WHEN we reckon up the names of the explorers of the Alps, there is on the long roll one which specially attracts attention, for it occurs with astonishing frequency and in connection with the most widely separated districts. Need I say that I speak of CHRISTIAN ALMER, of Grindelwald, who has to his credit the longest and most splendid list of first ascents on record? Born on March 18th, 1826, his early life was passed as a cheesemaker on one of the Alps of his native valley, and as the shepherd at the Zäsenberg. In the course of the *Sonderbund* War of November, 1847, he took part in the advance on Luzern as a soldier in the 2nd Jäger Compagnie. It was, however, his passion for chamois-hunting which familiarized him with the upper regions of snow and ice, then scarcely known to any but hunters.

It is generally agreed that systematic mountaineering dates from the famous ascent of the Hasli Jungfrau, or outer peak of the Wetterhorn, made from Grindelwald on September 17th, 1854, by the present Mr. Justice Wills; and it lends a sort of dramatic completeness to Almer's unparalleled career as a guide to find that he shared in this memorable expedition. For he and his brother-in-law, Ulrich Kaufmann, were the two chamois-hunters who, as described in Mr. Wills's fascinating book, followed up the trail of his party, and overtook it on the *Sattel*. Balmat's anger with these "piratical adventurers" passed away when he found that they did not intend to steal a march on him, but wished only to take part in the ascent of the peak, the first made from their native valley. They were accordingly roped with the others, and are represented in the two illustrations (in Mr. Wills's book) of the party on their way from the *Sattel* to the summit. One of them had brought up a fir-tree, which was planted on the top next to Mr. Wills's iron standard—the bearer was Christian Almer. This was his first introduction to the Alpine world at large, for, though, as he has often told me, he had acted as guide before, it was only over passes, attempts on the higher peaks being at that time very rare. The Wetterhorn was Almer's first great feat, and it has always remained his favourite expedition, so that I have often jokingly remarked to him, that he was not happy unless he had been up the Wetterhorn at least once in the season. He repeated the ascent in 1855 with Mr. R. Chapman, and in 1856 went up the Jungfrau no less than three times, with Mr. R. Chapman, Mr. Eustace Anderson, and Dr. Sigmund Porges respectively, as I learn from his *Führerbuch*, from which also many of the following details are derived.

It was in 1857, however, that the first entries were made on the long roll of his first ascents—the conquest of the Mönch with Dr. S. Porges, a week after his ascent of the Klein Schreckhorn with Mr. E. Anderson. In 1858 he added to his list the Eiger, which he overcame in company with Mr. C. Barrington. He does not seem to have visited Zermatt and Chamonix until the season of 1860, and it was in the next summer that he first travelled with the Rev. H. B. George, his constant employer during many seasons. In 1862, with Mr. George and Mr. A. W. Moore, his new expeditions include the Jungfrau Joch, the Gross Viescherhorn (which it was proposed to call the Almerhorn), and the Sesia Joch, as well as the Mischabel Joch and Finsteraar Joch, with Mr. George. In 1863, with Mr. George and Mr. Macdonald, he made the perilous passage of the Col du Tour Noir, and later in that year he became the guide of the Rev. J. J. Hornby and the Rev. T. H. Philpott, with whom he was destined to make many brilliant expeditions in the Oberland district.

I am inclined on the whole to say that the summers of 1864 and 1865 witnessed his greatest Alpine triumphs, and that they mark the culminating point of his career. In 1864 alone, he and Mr. Moore passed from the Col de Voza to the Valley of Chamonix, over the summit of Mont Blanc, by way of the Aiguille du Goûter; while earlier in the same summer they had shared in that marvellous campaign of ten days in Dauphiné, when the spoils included the Col des Aiguilles d'Arves, the Brèche de la Meije, the Ecrins (monarch of the district), and the Col de la Pilatte. A little later he crossed the Moming Pass with Mr. Moore, and the Schallenjoch with Messrs. Hornby and Philpott.

In 1865 he was one of the leaders in that journey of Mr. Whymper's which is probably the most brilliant and successful ever carried out in the Alps. Within little over three weeks, these mighty hunters slew the Grand Cornier, the Grandes Jorasses (west peak), the Col Dolent, the Aiguille Verte, the Col de Talèfre, and Ruinette, besides making the third ascent of the Dent Blanche, and an attempt on the Matterhorn by the great gully in the eastern face. He parted from Mr. Whymper on July 7 (a week before the terrible accident on the

Matterhorn), to fulfil an engagement with Messrs. Hornby and Philpott, with whom he ascended the Lauterbrunnen Breithorn, and achieved that remarkable climb up the northern face of the Silberhorn, of which he still speaks with respect. Still later in the same season he guided Mr. George up the Jungfrau from the Wengern Alp—an ascent long thought to be absolutely impracticable—and accompanied him on the autumn journey which has been so vividly described in 'The Oberland and its Glaciers explored and illustrated with Ice-Axe and Camera,' and during which the first ascent of the Nesthorn was made.

Such is Almer's record of first ascents and passages for those two memorable seasons, the mere recollection of which is calculated to make later generations of climbers despair of coming anywhere near their Alpine forefathers.

In 1866, with Mr. Tuckett, he visited the Eastern Alps, 'bagging' the Cevedale, the Fornaccia, and the Saline; and we most of us know how, after that wonderful day which was fatal to two new peaks and three new passes, pride had a fall, and the whole party had a "night adventure in the Suldenthal," which has been graphically described by Mr. Tuckett in his paper in the *Alpine Journal* (vol. ii.). The same year Almer made, with Messrs. Hornby, Philpott, and Morshead, three new passes in the Oberland—the Ebneflub Joch, the Schmadri Joch, and the Agassiz Joch. In 1867, Almer's chief new expeditions were the crossing of the Jägerhorn from Macugnaga to the Riffel and the Lyskamm from Gressoney, both accomplished with Messrs. C. E. Mathews and Morshead.

It was in 1868 that by a lucky accident I first secured Almer's services and from that year onwards I have travelled with him during the whole or part of each summer. In fact, as time went on, I fear that I became more and more a monopolist of his unrivalled skill and knowledge; his chief new ascents with other employers being the Weisshorn from the Bies glacier, made in 1871 by Mr. Kitson (who had previously made several trips with him), and the Täschhorn from the Mischabeljoch, in 1876, with Mr. James Jackson.

Henceforward my narrative must be largely egotistical, for, from 1868 to 1875 inclusive, Almer was with my aunt and myself, and from 1876 to 1884 inclusive, with me alone.[1] We have wandered together through most districts in the Alps, and spent many happy days on many peaks and passes, old and new; but it is our explorations (begun in 1870) in the Alps south of Mont Blanc which have most largely added to Almer's list of first ascents and passages. I select some of the more important (adding the year in which they were made) to show what an extensive knowledge of these parts he gained, built on the foundation of his 1864 journey.

In the Maritime Alps, the Argentera (1879), the monarch of the group. In the Cottians, the Pointe Haute de Mary and the Aiguille

---

[1] It was soon after I became acquainted with Almer that, on July 11th, 1868, in order to cure me of a fit of bad temper caused by a failure on the Eiger owing to iced rocks, he of his own accord gave me his dog Tschingel. She had, indeed, already crossed (in 1865) the glacier pass from which she took her name, but it was only when she had to follow her new owners that she became a professional climber. Her list of glacier expeditions amounted to 55, including Mont Blanc, Monte Rosa, Finsteraarhorn, Jungfrau and Mönch (both from the Wengern Alp), Aletschhorn (twice), Grand Combin, and several first ascents and passages in Dauphiné. More than once we enjoyed considerable amusement because of the keen jealousy which this splendid list excited in the breasts of some of her two-footed human rivals. After my aunt's death on December 19th, 1876, Tschingel retired from active service, and herself died at the age of 14 years on June 16th, 1879.

de Chambeyron (1879), Pointe des Heuvières, the highest point of the Visolotto and Monte Viso from the N.E. (all in 1881). In Dauphiné, the Ailefroide and central peak of the Meije (1870), Grande Ruine, Pic des Agneaux and Râteau (1873), the Roche de la Muzelle (1875), the Aiguille des Arias (1876), the northern and highest pinnacle of the Pic d'Olan, Sirac, the Col des Avalanches, Crête de l'Encula and Crête de la Bérarde (all in 1877), Les Bans, the southern and the northern Aiguilles d'Arves (1878), the Pavé (1879), the Fifre, the Pointe du Sélé, and Pelvoux from the west (1881), Col de Gros Jean (1882). In the Tarentaise, the Mont Pourri from the north (1874), the Aiguille de Péclet, Tsantaleina from the north, the Aiguille de la Sassière by south-east ridge (all in 1878), the eastern Levanna from the east (1883). Besides these and many other minor first ascents, I may be allowed to mention two expeditions (both made for the second time), the most difficult we ever made together, and the success of which was wholly due to Almer's indomitable pluck and skill—the ascent of Mont Blanc from the Glacier de la Brenva (1870), and that of the highest point of the Meije (1878).

In addition to all these climbs made for the first time, he was the leader in a vast number of other ascents, made before, yet most commonly quite new to him. In 1876 he revisited the Eastern Alps with me, and explored the Pinzolo, Primiero, and Cortina Dolomites. He was rarely quite satisfied to ascend a peak by the usual route, very often devising some short cut or variation which saved time, though never at the expense of prudence. To him, too, is due the fashion of winter mountaineering, of which he was the chief pioneer, and which was destined to cost him so dear. In January, 1874, he led us up the Wetterhorn and the Jungfrau; in January, 1876, he was the leader in the first serious attempt made to ascend Mont Blanc in winter (a storm stopping the party on the Grand Plateau); and in January, 1879, he crowned his previous performances by the ascent of the Gross Schreckhorn.

Such a magnificent list—and if we were to count up all the peaks he has ascended and passes he has traversed, whether for the first time or not, it might be multiplied perhaps fifty-fold—is amply sufficient to prove his skill and his dash, and it is unnecessary to cite any other witnesses. Let me recall only the emphatic words used by Mr. Whymper when speaking of his campaign of 1865 : "His numerous employers concur in saying that there is not a truer heart or a surer foot to be found amongst the Alps."

But I should feel this account very imperfect unless I added a few words of grateful recollection of one who, by reason of the unfrequented districts which we so often explored together, was brought into far closer connection with me than is usual in the case of *Herr* and *Führer*, and who has been to me not merely a guide, but a faithful companion and a trusty friend. His skill in finding his way up an unknown peak, to the base of which we had been guided by the map, was something marvellous, and can scarcely be appreciated by any one who has not had the luck to see him at work. One keen glance at peak or pass was sufficient to discover not merely a way, but the best and safest way up. It is this skill too, which, through so many years of adventure, enables him to boast that in not a single instance has a serious mishap occurred to any member of his party—traveller, guide, or porter: once, and once only, before his last misfortune, had he met with injury himself, when a bit of ice fell on him during the descent of the Upper Grindelwald glacier, and broke several of his ribs. Always ready to try a difficult ascent, he invariably refused to run heedlessly into avoidable danger, and he was very emphatic in his disapproval of some recent climbing exploits. No one was

steadier on rocks, no one more untiring on a long ice slope than my old friend, no one more loyal to his employer and more willing to undergo inconvenience or exposure for his *Herr*. Rough and awkward in outward appearance, he was only at home in the mountains, which he loved for their own sake, for he was a true son of the Alps, in his strength as in his weaknesses.

We had parted late in 1884, hoping to travel together as usual in the summer of 1885, and I had fixed on the Cogne mountains as our hunting-ground, for that was perhaps the only considerable district in the Alps which he had never visited. But it was not to be. He tried the Jungfrau on January 7th, 1885, with a large party, and unluckily got very badly frost-bitten in both feet; one was cured, but the effects of the frost-bites in the case of the other were so terrible that it was necessary to amputate all the toes on it, and one of the first guides in the Alps became a cripple for life.[1] It was a sad fate for him, since, despite his years, his wonderful skill and strength showed no signs of failing, and he might well have counted on several more long campaigns amid the great hills. And I have lost the brave and faithful companion to whom I owe some of the happiest days I have ever spent, the recollection of which can only pass away with life. We can no longer continue our wanderings together, but the memory of my sturdy, simple-hearted, and devoted comrade will always remain with me, and as a guide he will ever be held in honour by all true lovers of the Alps, who remember how much we owe to his pluck, his enterprise, and his doggedness.

Almer's eldest son is Ulrich, of whom a detailed notice will be found in another part of this book. His second son, Christian (born 1859), has been with me in the mountains ever since 1876, at first under his father; while since the latter's enforced retirement, young Christian has been my chief, very frequently my sole guide. He is a most worthy inheritor of his famous name, and a most cheery and trusty comrade; while he possesses a most minute acquaintance with the South-Western Alps (from the Col de Tenda to the Little St. Bernard), such as no guide has ever yet enjoyed.

W. A. B. C.

Johann Baumann.

JOHANN BAUMANN—'Hans' as he is always called—was born at Grindelwald in 1830. Christian Almer's keen eye soon discovered that there was more than ordinary promise in the young guide. While Christian showed himself an apt tutor, Hans proved an equally ready scholar, and he has never failed to admit how much he owed to Almer's teaching, a subject to which he would often refer. The first expedition of any note in which he was engaged, was in 1862, when he acted as one of the porters in the first passage of the Jungfrau Joch, described by Mr. Leslie Stephen in his 'Playground of Europe.'

My first acquaintance with Baumann arose from a casual remark dropped at an Alpine Club meeting, when I happened to ask the Rev. H. B. George if he knew of a good guide who was at liberty for the coming season. He replied, "All the best guides are engaged, but you can't do better than take Hans Baumann. It is, I think, his first year as a guide, but he has done good work

---

[1] During the past two seasons old Christian has had engagements in the Oberland; last year he ascended the Jungfrau, and reached the final arête of the Schreckhorn, from where his party were compelled to return owing to a violent storm.—C.D.C.

as porter." This chance remark led to a friendship which has ended in my re-engaging him year after year for fifteen consecutive seasons. He has acted chiefly as guide to myself, often in company with Mr. A. W. Moore, and Mr. Horace Walker, and Jacob Anderegg. He made various excursions in Dauphiné with the Rev. C. Taylor, present Master of St. John's College, Cambridge, Mr. R. Pendlebury and Mr. F. Gardiner, and with the first two made the earliest serious attempt on the Aiguille du Dru. Mr. Dent, in his work 'Above the Snow Line,' says: "It should be noted that the line of attack chosen on this occasion—the first serious attempt on the peak—was devised by Hans Baumann, and it says much for his sagacity, that this very route proved years afterwards to be the right one." This expedition shows his special *forte*. Equally good on ice and rocks, he rarely failed on any occasion to select the best line of attack. This was a characteristic shown in the ascents of Mont Collon (1867) and the Gspaltenhorn (1869), which had been previously attempted without success. He again exhibited this power in the passage of the Dom Joch in 1869, in the ascent of the Dom from Saas in 1874, the ascent of the Mönch from the Eiger Joch in 1877, and the Eiger from the Eiger Joch in 1876. Writing shortly afterwards in the *Alpine Journal* (vol. viii.), when the incidents of the ascent were still fresh in my recollection, I thus described the chief difficulty we encountered after leaving the col, while making an unsuccessful attempt to accomplish the latter expedition. "If you will fancy yourselves passing along a house wall, here and there knocking out bricks for foothold, a little bothered by the necessity of getting round the windows, and suddenly brought to a stand by the corner of the house, it may give some idea of our position. Baumann cut an unusually good step, with a good grip for his right hand above it, and then leaning round the corner, with his axe in his left hand, cut another on the other side, but with all his skill found himself unable to pass from one to the other. At length, cutting a hole on the further side for his left hand, he literally took his axe between his teeth, grasped firmly with his hands one on one side of the corner, the other on the other, and fairly swung himself round till he could gain the necessary foothold." In 1868 he made the first passage of the Ochsenjoch, a pass closely allied to Mr. Leslie Stephen's Viescherjoch, but which Baumann always claims to be distinct. In 1871 he crossed the Tiefenmatten Joch, a brilliant discovery of Mr. A. W. Moore's. In 1873, with the Rev. C. Taylor and Mr. R. Pendlebury, he made the ascents of the Grande Aiguille, the Roche Faurio and the Sommet des Rouies, and the Brèche de la Charrière. In 1878 he accomplished a new route up the Wetterhorn from the Hühnergütz-gletscher, or the 'Kuhe-gletscher' as it is sometimes called in the district, a route on which he had been previously defeated by falling stones. All these added to his reputation, while the passage of Mont Blanc from Courmayeur in twenty-three and a half hours, and the ascent of the Grandes Jorasses in about twenty hours, showed powers of endurance seldom surpassed. In 1868 he ascended the Matterhorn from Zermatt, being the first Oberland guide to achieve this feat.

His long career as guide has never been marred by a fatal accident to any member of his party. On one occasion in the ascent of the Schreckhorn, while in the great couloir (in which in 1886 Herr Munz lost his life from an ice-avalanche), a shower of stones not only struck most of the party, but injured him so severely that it was with difficulty he gained the rocks before becoming insensible. On recovering he resumed work with his wonted pluck, only to be defeated by one of the worst gales it has ever been my bad luck to experience on a mountain. The most serious misadventure in which he was concerned, was on the Aiguille du Midi in 1869, when Jacob Anderegg had so narrow an escape of his life. How much the party owed to Baumann's coolness and skill it is difficult to say; while with two of their number wounded he led them successfully down, in spite of unusual difficulties caused by the frequent avalanches. A mishap on this course has been made the subject of one of the most graphic engravings of an Alpine accident ever published, which appeared in the *Alpine Journal* (vol. v.). The more serious accident which a little before so nearly cost Jacob his life, is not the subject of this sketch, but occurred some hundred feet nearer the summit. Writing at the time, I said: "Jacob was crossing a narrow gully, when suddenly, without any warning, as though he had trod on the keystone of the wall, the whole face some thirty or forty feet above him peeled off, and with a crash like thunder, hundreds of tons of rocks precipitated themselves on him. In an instant he was torn from his hold, and hurled down the precipice with them. Fortunately Walker was able to hold on, though the strain on him was something awful. As the uproar ceased and silence even more impressive succeeded, we looked in one another's faces in blank dismay. From our position it was impossible to see what had become of Jacob, and only the tight rope told us that his body at least, living or dead, was still fastened to us. In a voice singularly unlike his own, Walker at length cried out 'Jacob!' and our hearts sank within us as it passed without response. 'Jacob! ach Jacob!' Walker repeated; and I trust none of my readers may ever know the relief we felt when the reply came back, 'Ich lebe noch.' In Mr. Whymper's sketch Baumann is the first of the party, I am the next, followed by Mr. Horace Walker, Jacob Anderegg being the last on the rope. The chief point in which this graphic illustration lacks accuracy is, that Mr. Whymper has depicted a shower of stones, instead of a mingled avalanche of rocks and ice."

Like most quiet, reticent men, Hans Baumann requires to be known to be appreciated, but he then proves himself a right pleasant companion. Of his pluck we have already spoken. Benighted at high altitudes, I have been surprised to see how in all the discomfort which inevitably attends such bivouacs, he has come to the front, and in spite of the fatigue of which a lion's share always falls to the leading guide in a hard day's work, he has been ready to exert himself in every way for the comfort of his *Herren*, and by his genial good temper rapidly led all to follow his example and make the best of things. It is difficult to make those outside the magic circle understand the peculiar relationship that rapidly springs up between the *Herren* and their guides. Even when the latter has only accompanied you in one *grande course*, there will be warm greetings on both sides at every meeting for years, but when the guide is engaged not for a day only, nor even for a season, but for a succession of seasons, the mutual attachment becomes great indeed. Thus it proved with myself and Hans Baumann. My natural admiration of his great qualities as guide, was quickly followed by genuine esteem for his character as a man, and I soon found that I had obtained not only a first-rate guide, but an honest and trusted friend. G. E. F.

Peter Baumann.

PETER BAUMANN—'Old' Peter, as he is called to distinguish him from another guide of the same name—was born at Grindelwald in 1833. He is pre-eminently one of the old school, and began his career at a time when *Herren* and guides alike were content to learn the rudiments of their craft before attempting hazardous expeditions. Turning over the leaves of his *Führerbuch*, one recognizes many names well known in the Alps,—Mr. Leslie Stephen, Professor Tyndall, Mr. A. W. Moore, and others of the best known early Alpine pioneers. And it is impossible to meet Old Peter without instinctively becoming aware of the influence which long association with such men has had upon his bearing and character. There are few names familiar to readers of 'Peaks, Passes, and Glaciers,' or even of the more recent volumes of the *Alpine Journal*, which are not to be found in his book. And all have recorded not only the high estimation in which they hold Baumann as a guide, but the great respect and friendly feeling with which they regard him as a man. Somehow these certificates have a genuine ring of sincerity, which distinguish them from the conventional 'form of sound words' so often seen in guides' books.

Even in his early days Baumann never laid himself out for undertaking new or hazardous expeditions. Not that he was wanting in courage, for a braver, sturdier guide never faced danger on the mountains; but 'go' and love of adventure or excitement are not Peter's distinguishing characteristics. He has made few first ascents of any importance. Probably the best known first expeditions in which he has taken part are the Jungfrau-Joch and Viescher-Joch, which he crossed in 1862, with Mr. Leslie Stephen, and which that distinguished climber has graphically described in 'The Playground of Europe.' In 1873, he made a new route up the Schreckhorn from the Lauteraarsattel, an expedition which has not hitherto been repeated.

At an early period of his career, his powers as a guide were recognized, and it was not long before he had a considerable *clientèle*. He soon became known as possessing a thorough acquaintance with the great peaks of his own valley, and when guides came from other districts, they were only too glad to have Baumann as their leader on ground with which they were unacquainted. Like most thrifty well-to-do Switzers, Peter has invested his savings in land near his châlet. Finding ample employment at home, not only in acting as guide, but in looking after his possessions, he is naturally better acquainted with the Oberland than with any other district in the Alps.

He has ascended the Wetterhorn over a hundred times, and has been on the summit of the Schreckhorn nearly sixty times. Many an English and American tourist has gone home with a pleasant recollection of Swiss guides, and of what going in for mountaineering must be like, from some expedition conducted under the guidance of Old Peter. Though his name is chiefly associated with Grindelwald, he has greater geographical knowledge of the Alps than the majority of the guides in his native valley. He has been in Dauphiné, and a season seldom passes without his visiting Zermatt or Chamonix. Few guides know how to make the dreary evenings in a hut pass half so quickly as Old Peter. To say that he is a pleasant companion (to quote an expression so often found in his *Führerbuch*) conveys no idea of the thoughtful, well-informed, intelligent man he is. Of most powerful build, he at once impresses one as being a man of great

determination and force of character. Like many men of real strength, he has great gentleness of manner, and never forgets to consider those who have not the same powers of endurance as himself. He is well known in the valley of Grindelwald as being a first-rate shot, and in his early days had a great reputation as a wrestler. During his whole career as guide, no accident has ever happened to any one of his own party on a mountain; although he has been a witness of one of the most tragic and appalling scenes which ever took place in the Alps. In 1869, he was on the Schreckhorn arête with an Englishman, at the time of Mr. Elliott's accident, and saw, but was powerless to avert the fatal fall.

Few of us have opportunities of seeing guides display other qualities than those which are usually brought into play in the course of a long day's climb. But while these sketches were in preparation it was my lot, under trying circumstances, to see of what sterling, sturdy stuff Baumann was made,—to see him not only do what he felt to be his own duty, but by his example encourage others to do theirs. Writing to a friend at the time of the Schreckhorn accident (1886) in reference to the relief expedition, in which Baumann was one of the guides who took part, I said: "It was nearly nightfall before the guides who were carrying their mournful load reached the Schwarzegg hut. Our night's work proved not less difficult than we had imagined it would be. Rocks which in daylight were easy enough, became dangerous with no other light than that of a lantern. The task of lowering

down such a great weight was often a dangerous one, but nothing could have exceeded the care and reverence with which Peter and the guides, under his direction, handled their helpless burden." Only those who have taken part in such melancholy expeditions can fully appreciate the feeling of strength and confidence the presence of such a man as Baumann seems to inspire among his fellows.

Had Old Peter been born in Eskdale or Liddisdale, he would have had a seat on the School Board, and might even have aspired to become an elder of the Kirk. He is one of that class of men to whom Switzerland owes her prosperity. And it is impossible to turn over the illustrations of any work which deals with the early days of 'the little country' during her brave struggle to assert freedom, without seeing many types which remind one of Peter Baumann.

C. D. C.

Ulrich Almer.

MOUNTAINEERING qualities are not perhaps hereditary, but they are certainly contagious. "A worthy son of a worthy father," Ulrich does full justice to the name of Almer,—a veritable chip of the old block.

Eldest of Christian's sons, he was born at Grindelwald on May 8th, 1849. He went to school in his native village, and when at sixteen he had done with books, acted as tripod-bearer to the Rev. H. B. George's party during their interesting climbs in the Oberland in 1865, to which we are indebted for 'The Oberland and its Glaciers explored and illustrated with Ice-axe and Camera.' Ulrich had charge of the camera legs, and is mentioned by Mr. George as being "cat-like in his propensity for perching himself in uncanny places." He accompanied Mr. George and Mr. Mortimer in the first ascent of the Gross Nesthorn that same year, along with his father. In 1867 he made the second ascent of the western summit of the Grandes Jorasses with his father and Mr. George. He accompanied Mr. George and Mr. F. Morshead to the Tyrol in 1868. In 1869 he was with his father and the Rev. W. A. B. Coolidge in the Chamonix neighbourhood, and elsewhere.

The winter of 1869-70 he spent in England on the kind invitation of Mr. Hawthorne Kitson, an old patron of his father,—a visit of the greatest advantage to himself. In the morning he went on errands for the household, and in the afternoon saw something of engine-modelling in the Leeds foundry; whilst in the evening he had lessons in English, provided for him by Mr. Kitson.

By 1870 Ulrich had fairly won his spurs, after an apprenticeship such as few guides ever enjoyed. His Guide's Book dates from June of this year, when he again accompanied his father and Mr. Coolidge in Dauphiné, and included the first ascent of a point of the Meije (the Pic Central) slightly lower than the highest or western summit, a new route up the Pointe des Ecrins, and the first ascent of the Ailefroide, in his record of that season. In 1871 he was with his patron, Mr. Kitson, at Zermatt and elsewhere, making the first ascent of the Weisshorn from the Bies glacier; and later on in that season he was with his father and Mr. Coolidge on both sides of the Rhone. The year following he was once more in Dauphiné, and had now established himself as a mountaineer of no ordinary mettle. In 1873 he was with Mr. T. S. Kennedy in the first ascent of the peak of the Aiguille de Blaitière which towers over Chamonix, and made the first passage of the Col des Hirondelles with Mr. Leslie Stephen's and M. Loppé's party.

Eighteen hundred and seventy-five, his last year in Dauphiné, in which district he had made altogether many new ascents, is an important date in Ulrich's career. Since that time Ulrich and Christian have gone on entirely different tracks; and each season in the Alps, during the last decade, the son has year by year given increasing proof of his maturing excellence among leading guides. In the zenith of manhood, with sympathies in proportion to his liberal and varied education, Ulrich is cosmopolitan to the heart's core. Whether in his own native valley or at Zermatt, in the Saasthal or at Chamonix, he is on friendly terms with everybody. Many an evening has been spent by Chamonix guides in Ulrich's comfortable chalet on wet days at Grindelwald during the mountaineering season. Having travelled with many masters, he is faithful to them all. In him are combined the chief characteristics essential for a guide. With an unusually keen observation, and a capacity for grasping at once the powers of others; with a temperament never ruffled even under the most trying and provoking circumstances, his courage and bodily strength are alike remarkable. Calm in demeanour, he warms up on the mountain-side into the cheeriest and best-humoured guide imaginable. Always on the *qui-vive* to afford assistance, he never worries one with unnecessary or intrusive help. Friendly to a degree, he is never encroaching. With extraordinary dash, he is never foolhardy, and always knows when to turn back. His forte is on rocks, but he is first-rate on ice, and he is a perfect step-cutter; 'soup plates,' if need be, are the work of a moment. In the Ampezzo Dolomites, in the Zillerthal, in the Engadine, in the Alps of Glarus, as well as in the Pennines, the Eastern Graians, Dauphiné and the Oberland, his experience amongst the Alps is extensive. Of recent years his ascent of the Schreckhorn by the western arête (a route long coveted by Ulrich for his own), the Dent Blanche from Montet, and the Breithorn from the Schwarzthor occur to one the most readily as worthy of reference.

He knows what mountaineering means in winter as well as in summer. In 1874 he was with his father and Mr. Coolidge when they ascended the Wetterhorn and the Jungfrau in January, and was with the same party in the ascent of the Schreckhorn, in January, 1879. He ascended the Mönch along with another guide and a traveller on February 1st, 1887 (second winter ascent of that mountain); and on March 8th, 1887, he reached the summit of the Finsteraarhorn from the Agassiz Joch, alone with Herr Emil Boss, of Grindelwald, descending into the Rhone Valley by the Viescher Glacier. The following January (1888), he was leading guide in one of the most remarkable winter campaigns ever made in the High Alps. On the 5th of the month, he was on the summit of the Gross Lauteraarhorn; on the 6th, he made an ascent of one of the lower peaks on the Vieschergrat range, from the Schwarzegg hut (3360 mètres); and, on the 11th, he reached the top of the Gross Viescherhorn,—finishing up his rôle of *tours de force* with a passage over the Jungfrau to the Little Scheideck, from the Bergli hut. The mountain was crossed on the 16th, and the next night he and his party bivouacked in an ice cave above the ice fall on the Guggi glacier, on their way down to the Little Scheideck.

No guide has had a more chequered experience than Ulrich, although he is still comparatively young; and his splendid behaviour on three special occasions cannot go unnoticed here. In 1874, the year of Ulrich's marriage, in company with Mr. J. A. Garth Marshall and Johann Fischer, he left Courmayeur to ascend Mont Blanc by the Brouillard route. After bivouacking the first night in the open, about five hours from Courmayeur, they attained a considerable height next day (*Alpine Journal*, vol. vii. p. 111); but, on coming at

4 p.m. to a place which they could not circumvent, they turned back, as it was too late in the day to search for another means of passage. Having reached a point (by moonlight) whence they would have left the glacier in another five minutes—a large snow-bridge fell in, and all three were precipitated into a crevasse. Ulrich was stunned, and on regaining consciousness found himself midway between the corpses of his two companions. Escaping from this tomb of ice on to the level of the glacier, by means of a crack in the side of the crevasse, he walked down to Courmayeur, though considerably hurt, and later in the same day, headed a party to the scene of the accident for the recovery of the bodies, he himself riding a mule as far as the Fresnay châlets. After a third (very cold) night out, he went down once more to Courmayeur, and in a few days rode to Martigny. This catastrophe on Mont Blanc is remarkable as being the only one in which an accident with fatal results has happened to a party of which any one of the guides now living,

whose history is recorded in this book, was a member. It was an accident of a wholly exceptional character, and quite without precedent.

Six years later, a party of four were saved from certain annihilation solely through the extraordinary presence of mind, bodily strength, and activity of Ulrich. One of the rescued shall speak for himself and for all. "Ulrich Almer has been with us a few days. We have the most exceptional reasons for speaking in the highest praise of his abilities as a guide. He led us in a successful ascent of the Jungfrau, and on Saturday last, August 14th, was our first guide (together with Joseph Brantschen of St. Niklaus) in an unfinished ascent of the Ober Gabelhorn. We attacked the mountain from the Trift Alp, and had scaled the steep rocks and reached the eastern arête, along which at a distance of about twelve yards from the edge we were proceeding, when a huge mass of cornice fell, carrying with it the leading guide, Brantschen, and the two *voyageurs*. Almer, who alone remained on *terra firma*, showed extraordinary presence of mind and strength. Instantly on hearing the crack of the cornice, he leaped a yard backwards, plunged his axe into the snow, and planting himself as firmly as possible, was thus enabled to arrest the fall of the entire party down a precipice of some 2000 feet. Joseph Brantschen, who fell furthest down the precipice, dislocated his right shoulder, and this mischance involved a long, anxious, and to him most painful descent; and the return to Zermatt took us eight hours, the injured man being obliged to stop every two or three minutes from pain and exhaustion. It should be mentioned that the mass of cornice which fell measured (as far as we can judge) about forty yards long, by thirteen yards broad. There can be no doubt whatever that it is owing solely to Ulrich Almer's strength, presence of mind, and lightning-like rapidity of action, that the accident on the Gabelhorn did not terminate with the same fatal results as the Lyskamm catastrophe. Having had considerable experience of Almer's abilities,

I consider that he has no superior amongst the guides in Switzerland. (Signed) H. W. Majendie, A.C., August 18th, 1880, Zermatt." (Mr. R. L. Harrison, another of the party, countersigns Mr. Majendie's record.) The above speaks volumes for the value of the rope.

Once again, the indomitable pluck and endurance of this guide were exemplified in August, 1883, and this time under acute suffering, when during the descent of the Dent d'Hérens he was struck by an enormous stone (computed at 70 lbs. in weight by one of the party, at the time) shortly below the summit of the peak. It took the party, composed of Mr. C. E. Mathews, Mr. J. T. Wills, Melchior Anderegg, another (young) guide, and the wounded man nearly sixteen hours to reach the Stockje hut, the greater part of the night being spent on the Col de Valpelline. "But for his pluck we should have had to carry him all the way," writes Mr. Wills. As it was, Ulrich walked down to the Stockje with broken ribs.

With a career hitherto such as this, the portrait of Ulrich Almer deserves a page among "The Pioneers of the Alps." We may watch his future with interest and with confidence.

F. T. W.

Ulrich Kaufmann.

ULRICH KAUFMANN was born in Grindelwald in the year 1846, and like many of his kinsfolk became inured at an early age to the hardy life of a mountaineer. Chamois-hunting in winter, and assisting as porter in the tourist season, gradually trained him in the qualifications necessary for obtaining his guide's certificate. All those who employed him at the commencement of his career, found him to be a thoroughly reliable, steady, persevering man, and so retiring that his best qualities were apt to remain unobserved, till the emergency arose which brought them into action. The position he holds among guides is a somewhat remarkable one. All the laurels he has gained were won in his campaigns in the Himálayas and New Zealand. Although he has not made a single new expedition of any importance in the Alps, still no record of the leading Swiss guides would be at all complete without Kaufmann's name appearing in it. The names which occur most frequently in his *Führerbuch* are those of Messrs. C. and L. Pilkington, and amongst others Mr. J. Walker Hartley, Professor Roy, and Mr. Howard Barrett, express their high opinion of his qualities as a guide. Amongst the Grindelwaldners he was famous for his great strength. One day a number of them, assembled at the village forge, were testing their powers by trying to lift the anvil. Kaufmann came in and said he would not only lift it, but would carry it on his back through the village, and succeeded in doing so, to the admiration of all beholders.

In 1881 I determined to visit New Zealand, to see something of the glaciers of the Southern Alps, and if possible to ascend Mount Cook, the culminating peak of Australasia. As the mountaineering difficulties were likely to be serious, I determined to take with me a Swiss guide, and I wrote to Herr Emil Boss, of the Hôtel de l'Ours, Grindelwald, asking him to engage one of the Oberland men to accompany me. He at once recommended Ulrich Kaufmann, and what was still better, volunteered to join us himself. Herr Emil Boss, who is an officer in the Swiss Army, accustomed to foreign travel, and from youth upwards one of the keenest sportsmen in the Oberland, a man of splendid physique, proved my most valued companion, and amongst his many services may be mentioned this, that being a life-long friend of Kaufmann, he inspired him with courage to face the new and, to Kaufmann, altogether unrealized experiences of a tropical voyage and the many difficulties which necessarily lay in the way of a man who had never before been to the sea level, and who had to travel in British Colonies without knowing the English tongue. To say that Boss was the soul of our party, does not detract from Kaufmann's excellent qualities in his own particular department.

In New Zealand we had many days of wearisome work, carrying a tent and provisions over the loose boulders and through the dense scrub of the moraine of the Great Tasman Glacier. Kaufmann here did the heaviest work cheerfully, and when nearly worn out would simply hum a Swiss air and work

on. Boss said to me once or twice, during the hard work of that week, "I think Kaufmann is nearly done; he never sings to himself like that till he is played out."

The snow-line in New Zealand is so low, and the road over which we had to carry our sleeping gear and provisions so rough, that we had to pitch our highest camp 8000 feet below the summit of Mount Cook. After two fruitless attempts, we at last found the route to the summit of our peak. At 1.30 p.m. on the second day from our camp, the final slopes were reached, and here step-cutting commenced in earnest. Kaufmann hewed away at the hard ice for five hours without a pause. I should be afraid to say how many steps he cut in that time, for I did not attempt to count them. It was not till next morning, when we were leaving the narrow ledge, on which we had to stand out nine hours of a cold, stormy night, that he showed me the palms of his hands red with great blisters, and merely did so then as a kind of apology for not being able to wield his ice-axe as effectively as he could wish.

In February, 1883, Mr. W. W. Graham landed in Bombay, accompanied by Joseph Imboden, whom he had brought from St. Niklaus to assist him in ascents in the Himálayas. Serious hardships were encountered in a preliminary campaign in the Sikkim Himálaya, one result of which was that Imboden caught fever, and was compelled to return home. In this dilemma Mr. Graham wrote to Emil Boss for help, and to quote Mr. Graham's words, "In the pluckiest way, Boss himself came at a moment's notice, bringing Ulrich Kaufmann as guide, and a better pair of mountaineers I never wish to meet with." Mr. Graham read an account of his expedition before the Royal Geographical Society, which has been reprinted in the *Alpine Journal* (vol. xii.).

I saw Kaufmann once since his return; he looked somewhat worn, as if the hardships had made an impression on his stalwart frame. It is hard to criticize a living man, and mere meaningless adulation would simply be an insult. My experience of Kaufmann has left this impression on my mind. He is an humble-minded, unassuming man—so unassuming that it is difficult to get him to give any opinion as to the practicability or impracticability of any route which he has not traversed. Once, however, that a route is determined on, he will make it practicable in all its details, if it lies in human power to do so. Notwithstanding his travels, his life's experience has not been very wide; therefore, in an unexpected juncture his judgment might be at fault, but his fidelity never. I believe he would die or suffer any privation, rather than desert a man in a difficulty. Gentle and self-sacrificing in camp; daring, yet cautious on the mountain; endowed with unusual strength, Ulrich Kaufmann seems to me to come as near as possible to my ideal of what a good guide should be.

W. S. G.

Josef Imboden.

JOSEF IMBODEN was born at St. Niklaus in the year 1840. The story of the beginning of his life as guide is characteristic, and is best told in his own words: "I was never a porter," he said; "but when I was fifteen years old, and had saved twenty francs, I went and stayed at the Riffel, and asked gentlemen to take me as guide. They all asked me, 'Where is your book, young man?' I showed them my book, but there was nothing written in it. The twenty francs were nearly spent when I persuaded an Englishman to let me take him up the Cima di Jazzi. He was pleased, and the next day I took him up Monte Rosa alone. We then went to Chamonix together, and afterwards he wrote a great deal in my book: since then I have never wanted a gentleman to guide."

Though these first expeditions seem to show no lack of self-confidence, enterprise and love of adventure are not Imboden's distinguishing characteristics; and partly on this account, and partly because he was born ten years too late, Imboden has scarcely been concerned at all in the first ascents of the great Alpine peaks. For all that, he is not wanting in the qualities of a guide of the first rank. He possesses the instinctive faculty of seeing at a glance the best route up a mountain, and in stormy weather has frequently had opportunities of showing his very remarkable power of making a direct course across a snow-field without landmarks or a compass to assist him. He is a good rock climber, but probably his skill on ice is more marked; his judgment as to the state of the snow is excellent, and may be implicitly trusted. He has been a leading guide for many years, and no accident has ever happened to any member of a party under his charge. This fact alone is sufficient proof of his care and caution.

Many of his principal expeditions have been made in company with Mr. Percy W. Thomas, with whom he made in 1878 a new ascent of the Dom by the west arête and north-west face from the Kien Gletscher, and the same year carried out a long-cherished plan by ascending the Lyskamm by the wall of rocks on the south-east side of the mountain. The following year (1879), they made, on the suggestion of M. Loppé, a new route from the Glacier du Tour up the Aiguille du Chardonnet, which had remained unascended since Mr. Fowler's first ascent in 1865; and in 1880 made a determined attempt to climb the Eiger by the Mitteleggi arête; but this, like all attempts made by others from the same direction, was unsuccessful. In the same year, with Dr. Savage, he ascended the Gabelhorn from the Arben Gletscher by the south face, and added a seventh to the six routes up that peak then already known to be practicable. He accompanied Mr. Graham to the Himálayas in the spring of 1883, and there, to quote from Mr. Graham's paper read before the Geographical Society and printed in the *Alpine Journal*, "ascended a peak rather over 20,000 feet in height, and crossed the Guicho La, the pass between Pundim and the south-east arête of Kangchinjanga." Then an attack of jungle fever caused him to return home. Though his mountaineering experiences extend to every district in the Alps, Imboden has been very faithful to the peaks in whose shadow he was born. During the summer months he is now almost always to be found near Zermatt, and probably there is no one of the valley who has a more intimate knowledge than he has of the Zermatt range. Of the Weisshorn alone he has made about thirty ascents, a far larger number than any other guide can boast of.

Like one of old, Imboden is emphatically ἀνὴρ πολύτροπος, who
πολλῶν ἀνθρώπων ἴδεν ἄστεα καὶ νόον ἔγνω.

A guide in summer, he is always willing to go as a courier in the winter. In this capacity he has seen almost every country in Europe, including Hungary, Norway, and Sweden: he speaks German, French, and Italian well, and also some Norwegian. He spent part of two years in England, where he learned to speak excellent English. His varied experience, his strong sense of humour, and his love of telling stories, make him excellent company.

It is not, however, only as a guide pure and simple that Imboden stands well above the other guides at St. Niklaus and Zermatt. He has been President of the district Guides' Club for the past seven years: two years is the term of office, and he has therefore been three times re-elected. In the Zermatt valley there are few whose influence can be said to be greater than his. This may, perhaps, be in some degree ascribed to his wealth; for Imboden having begun with nothing, is now, for a guide, a rich man and a large landowner; his châlet is the smartest and best in the neighbourhood of St. Niklaus, and nobody in that district, where cows are the unit of wealth, has a larger herd. But his influence, whether increased or not by his wealth, is mainly due to himself, to his knowledge of men, and his force of character.

The esteem in which he is held by the other guides may be in some measure illustrated by the following incident. Some years ago, an ingenious and learned member of the Alpine Club took out to Chamonix, where he had arranged to join his guides, two imitation snakes,—one yellow, the other green. Chamonix was then a more popular mountaineering centre than it is now, and several of the best known guides of the Alps were collected at Couttet's with their *Herren*. Under some pretext or other all the guides were gathered into a group one afternoon, and the snakes suddenly produced from the grass. The effect was instantaneous. Men who were fearless on a mountain, were terrified at a coloured toy from the Baker Street Bazaar. The group dispersed: one guide did what he would never have dared to do under ordinary circumstances,—rushed into M. Couttet's sanctum, and endeavoured to hide himself under the bed; another retired to the observatory tower, and even the dinner-hour failed to tempt him to come down; a third rushed wildly through the village, and was only stopped by crashing through a paling which in his haste he had overlooked. The excitement produced by the snakes was so great that no other subject could be discussed among the guides then in Chamonix, and the next day one of their number came, representing the rest, to ask that the snakes should be conveyed to Zermatt; for they all agreed that *Imboden himself* could not stand up before them!

His authority over the other guides and his power of organization were especially conspicuous in the expeditions undertaken in search of the bodies of those who were killed in the accident on the Lyskamm in 1877, and on the Dent Blanche in 1882. On the latter occasion he led the search party during a violent snowstorm across the south-west face of the mountain, with a foot of snow on the rocks, and it was owing to his skill and correct knowledge of the locality that the bodies were found, though they were almost entirely hidden by the freshly fallen snow, at the bottom of the long couloir on the Dent Blanche which is so conspicuous from the Col d'Hérens. When the bodies had been recovered and drawn together, Imboden signed to the guides to kneel down in a circle round them; then he said a Litany while they chanted the responses. The lonely snow-field, the thickly falling snow, the black rocks of the Dent Blanche from time to time visible far above, and the chant of the kneeling guides heard through the gale, formed a solemn and impressive scene never to be forgotten. This expedition was both difficult and dangerous, and Imboden, though a very cautious man by nature, displayed courage and pluck of a very high order in leading it.

When the guides killed in this accident were a few days later buried at St. Niklaus, a stranger asked the name of the guide who so carefully ordered the funeral procession, and was so attentive to every detail. He was told that it was Josef Imboden.

G. S. B.

Aloys Pollinger.

THE subject of this notice was born at St. Niklaus in 1844. He made his first climbing expedition in the service of mountaineers in his twenty-first year. On that occasion, in 1864, he accompanied Mr. Puller over the Valpelline pass to Prarayen, returning by the Col de Vacornère to Breil. He soon began to attract notice, and for the last ten or fifteen years he has never lacked work.

ALOYS POLLINGER did not attain rank as a leading guide till after what may be called the great age of conquest was over. Nevertheless, his name cannot be omitted from the list of pioneers.

In 1877 he took part with Mr. J. W. Hartley, Mr. W. E. Davidson, and Mr. H. Seymour Hoare in the ascent of the Weisshorn by the S.E. face and the S. arête, an expedition which has not been repeated. He likewise shares the honour of having reached the summit of the Dent Blanche by no less than two new routes; first by the Zinal ridge or *Viereselgrat*, when Ulrich Almer was his fellow; afterwards by the Ferpècle arête, down which he led his party, the summit having been quitted at 4 p.m., and the night spent on the ridge. This latter route was soon afterwards taken in the reverse direction, and then again Pollinger led. He conquered the Breithorn from the Schwarzthor, an ascent little, if at all, less formidable than that of the Schreckhorn by the North-west arête or of the Eiger from the Bergli, in both of which Pollinger took part. Under Pollinger's guidance a lady, well known in the Alps, made one of the many new routes up the Dom which recent years have seen accomplished. Pollinger has a special gift of finding out new peaks and passes between St. Niklaus and the Turtmanthal, which no one ever succeeds in exactly identifying. He also invented an unpleasant way up Mont Collon by the S.S.E. buttress, and I daresay several more new routes and variations of which I have not heard.

He has ascended all the peaks of his own district again and again, the Matterhorn no less than forty-two times. Probably few guides know the Zermatt district as he does. He has, of course, been taken to other parts of the Alps, to Chamonix often enough, to the Graians, the Oberland, and Dauphiné more than once. He has never been in or near any accident.

Whilst taller and bigger than the average of the men in his valley, he walks with a peculiar swaying action of his own, and has a rather marked stoop. He usually wears a very big hat, from under the shadow of which a face of unusual friendliness looks forth upon his friends. His voice in speaking is exceptionally soft and rich, and his uniform gentleness and refinement have naturally made him a great favourite as a ladies' guide, but his courage, endurance, and pluck are no less remarkable.

Pollinger very readily adapts himself to circumstances, and often shows traces of a quiet humour. His genial simplicity is quite charming, and his

kindliness is irresistible. As a guide his powers seem to be of an all-round nature. He is an excellent rock-climber, but he is likewise good upon ice. Without having had the opportunities to which some less good guides owe the fortune of their fame, he has yet succeeded in making a solid reputation for himself, not only amongst climbers, but with his own comrades.

There are probably few Pennine guides with whom men from the Oberland or Chamonix would sooner travel than Pollinger. There is nothing theatrical in his manner on or off a mountain, but for quiet competence he is hardly likely to be surpassed.

W. M. C.

Peter Knubel.

PETER KNUBEL was born at St. Niklaus in 1838, and for many years has occupied a leading position among the not too numerous good guides of the Canton Valais. He was the first guide who ventured to ascend the Matterhorn from the Swiss side after the accident in 1865, when Lord Francis Douglas and Mr. Hadow were killed. In 1868, with the Rev. J. M. Elliott, who afterwards fell from the Schreckhorn, and J. M. Lochmatter, who perished on the Dent Blanche, he made the second ascent from Zermatt, a feat which naturally brought his name prominently before the climbing public. For many years Peter was considered to be the great authority on the Swiss side of the Matterhorn, in the same way that J. A. Carrel and J. J. Maquignaz had an unequalled knowledge of the Italian route. His name will always be associated with the early ascents of this mountain; he and his brothers practically erected the upper, or what is now called the "old" hut, a refuge familiar to many who may never even have seen it, from Mr. Whymper's beautiful engraving.

After acting for some years as porter he began his career as guide in the summer of 1863, at the age of thirty. In succeeding years he frequently accompanied Mr. Leighton Jordan, Mr. Robert Fowler, and Mr. Giles Puller, and in 1871 first became guide to the present writer, with whom he travelled for several years, and with him visited many districts of the Alps ranging from Grenoble to Innsbrück. He has also acted as guide in various parts of the Alps to Baron Albert de Rothschild.

In 1874 he accompanied Mr. F. C. Grove, Mr. A. W. Moore, Mr. Horace Walker, and myself to the Caucasus, and made the ascent of the highest point of Elbruz, the greatest mountain of the whole range. The point ascended by the Caucasian expedition of 1868, although practically the first ascent of Elbruz, is considered somewhat lower than the one ascended in 1874. Our journey has been graphically described by Mr. Grove in the 'Frosty Caucasus.' In 1869, with Mr. Robert Fowler, he made the first ascent of the Breithorn from the north, or from the Gorner Glacier; and in 1873 the first passage of the Rothhorn, now so favourite an expedition. During the same season he made several expeditions in Dauphiné, among which may be mentioned the first ascents of the Sommet des Rouies and the Roche Faurio, both important peaks in the district; also the second ascent of the central peak of the Meije. In the summer of 1876 he ascended most of the great peaks round Zermatt, and made the ascent of the Dent Blanche entirely by the great southern arête, a most difficult expedition which has not since been repeated.

In 1871, while descending the ridge of the Lyskamm, one of his party slipped, and, without a moment's hesitation, Knubel threw himself over the other side of the precipice and remained suspended by the rope till his companions had regained their foothold. This is one of the first instances of a gallant deed of this sort being performed on a mountain; a feat exactly similar to that which was performed in 1880 by Ulrich Almer, who saved the lives of his party on the Gabelhorn. It was indeed a strange and remarkable coincidence that five years later on this same mountain he should lose three brothers by a fall, caused by the ice-cornice giving way. In 1882, Johann Petrus, Knubel's brother-in-law, was killed on the Aiguille Blanche de Peuteret, and although none of Peter's *voyageurs* have ever encountered any accident while under his care, still, few guides have sadder memories to recall.

Peter Knubel may be described as a thoroughly "good all-round" guide, who possesses a better knowledge of ice-work than the majority of Valaisans. It is upon a difficult piece of rock work, such as the southern arête of the Dent Blanche, that he is seen at his best. Although enterprising and ambitious, he is at all times careful, and never omits any of the necessary safeguards to mountaineering, and in looking back upon the numerous expeditions made by him, rashness or want of discretion on his part never caused his employers to run the slightest risk. Knubel is a man of few words; quiet and reserved in manner. Probably in no *Führerbuch* do the words "cheerful companion" occur less frequently than in Peter's. But for all this he is none the less held in high esteem by his old friends, and by those who have had the opportunity of judging of his many sterling qualities. Like many men of his class, Knubel had an insatiable desire to possess land, and invested most of his savings in an alp near the Col du Torrent, which was practically rendered worthless by an earth-slip in the spring of 1877, and the estimation in which he was held by his friends could be seen by the handsome sum subscribed by them to assist him in his time of need.

F. G.

Alexander Burgener.

ALEXANDER BURGENER, living at Eisten, near Saas, Canton Valais, was born in 1846. When eighteen years of age he began chamois-hunting, and soon became known in the district as a successful sportsman. There seems to be a popular notion that every able-bodied male in a Swiss valley is a chamois-hunter. As a matter of fact, if this were the case and the sportsmen killed one apiece during the season, the whole race would become extinct in twelve months. Only specially qualified men do actually take up the sport, and Burgener won his spurs so early in life that he evidently had exceptional gifts as a mountaineer and as a hunter. A reputation is often more easily acquired than maintained, and hard work was needed to keep the position he soon gained of the boldest and most successful hunter of the valley. Not only was it necessary to excel in knowledge of this form of sport; it was essential also to out-climb rivals, and when Burgener first began the profession of guide, he was already an adept at rock climbing and snow work. From his elder brother, Franz, he learned some of the qualities necessary for guiding amateurs, and when the writer first made his acquaintance on the mountains, in 1868, Burgener had already softened down the rough and ready methods generally found in chamois-hunters who are nothing else. From 1868 to 1878, Burgener acted regularly as leading guide to the writer. A strong belief in his own powers, and the natural desire of a young man to earn a reputation among amateurs, led, in the early days of the alliance, to certain performances on the mountains on which the writer does not desire to dilate at present. It suffices to say that exploits such as an attempt on the Lyskamm in bad weather, made by an amateur and a guide alone, can hardly be considered orthodox, or even prudent. In those days we were not of an age very ready to take good advice. Wisdom however, in mountaineering as in other pursuits, comes late, and is chiefly characterized by a tendency to impart rather than to listen to sage counsel. Even now it is not hard to realize that Burgener had once a full share of the rashness of youth; but the quality lies dormant now for the most part, toned down by the tale of years, and rendered almost harmless by experience and developed powers. In the course of a tolerably long and varied experience in the Alps, the writer has never been benighted when with Burgener, though on one occasion the bivouac was not reached before 2.30 a.m. This happened on an expedition which Burgener still considers one of his greatest feats, namely, the first ascent of the Aiguille du Dru in 1878. How he worked on that occasion has been told already in the Alpine Journal. To this day the writer can recall distinctly Burgener's look when the summit was reached, and can see the tears of joy and pride that glistened in his eyes; ay, and can almost still feel the tremendous wring of the hand.

Alexander Burgener may be considered as one of the foremost men of the second generation of guides. Most of the great Swiss peaks had been vanquished before he began serious work. His principal new ascents in the Mont Blanc district, beside the Aiguille du Dru in 1878, were both peaks of the Aiguille de Charmoz in 1881, and some peaks near Saas. At this period the taste for discovering new routes up well-known peaks was fast developing, and the desire to do something new, when there was but little that was new to be done, led to a good deal of rather venturesome mountaineering. In this field Burgener became very prominent. Probably no guide has done more in the way of difficult variations of well-known expeditions. As instances may be mentioned, the ascent of the Rothhorn (Moming) from Zermatt (1872), the passage of the Col du Lion (1880), the rather sensational descent of the Mittelleggi arête in the Eiger (1885), and a climb up the Matterhorn from the Zmutt Glacier (1879). He also made the first ascent of the Aiguille Verte by way of the Charpoua Glacier, in 1881, but, as the Editor points out, this fine expedition was practically achieved by an English party a year earlier. Judging by the appearance of the rocks, the climb must have been a very difficult one.

Burgener has appeared as an author, and the *Oesterreichische Alpen-Zeitung* (vol. ii. No. 29) contains an article by him, entitled 'Der neue Aufstieg auf das Matterhorn.' Some of the paper is very well written.

In 1884, Burgener went with Monsieur de Déchy to the Caucasus, and made the first ascent of Adai Khokh. He also accompanied Dr. Güssfeldt to South America, but fell ill, and the expedition failed as far as mountaineering was concerned. In 1886 he made the first ascent of Tetnuld Tau (Central Caucasus), leading Mr. W. F. Donkin and the writer. Throughout the tour he displayed most valuable qualities. Like many men of slightly impulsive temper, he has much *sang-froid*, partly natural, partly cultivated. This attribute never failed during the rather trying conditions of Caucasian travel. On one occasion, when the native porters refused to carry a tent weighing rather over 20 lbs., he shouldered it in addition to an already heavy burden, and bore all in triumph to a bivouac high up.

Burgener has been twice to England, on one occasion remaining for some weeks, and he can speak English fairly well. He has good judgment really in estimating the climbing qualities of others, whether amateurs or professionals, but by no means underrates his own powers.

It is always difficult to estimate at their real value the merits of a guide who has led the same traveller for many years, for to the latter the man seems always immeasurably better than any other guide. Still, the writer has had some experience of other professionals in this department, and does not hesitate to place Alexander Burgener in the front rank, not only as a rock-climber, but as a guide on rock-mountains. He is a thorough ice-man also, but his best qualities are shown on difficult rocks. He has the keenest love for the mountains wherever they be, an attribute that all really good guides will invariably be found to possess. Possessed of great physical strength, of rather heavy build and loosely knit frame, he seems to force his way rather than climb up a difficult mountain. He has little of the neatness which is a characteristic of many of the Oberland guides; but he has extraordinary power. Once started on a difficult rock passage, it seems to the beholder an absolute certainty that he will conquer it, as he climbs on in a deliberate, continuous, dogged manner, that impresses as relentless and irresistible. If not neat and graceful, his method is at least effective. Probably he represents now more the 'school' of mountaineering, of which Michel Croz was one of the most brilliant examples in the days that are past; and this was a good school.

C. T. D.

François Dévouassoud.

It must always be a somewhat difficult and delicate task to put on paper a critical estimate of the character and capacity of living contemporaries. Yet this is what I believe the contributors to this volume are called upon to undertake. Undiscriminating panegyrics of the guides who have been our leaders and associates in the conquest of the Alps, would have no lasting interest for younger generations of mountaineers. We have to remember that these notices will appear in company, not with the conventional woodcuts of an illustrated newspaper, or the romantic portraits of an old-fashioned album, but with the realistic work of modern photographic art. We must endeavour to keep in sympathy with the artist. While not refusing the most favourable and characteristic aspect, we must make it our aim to depict with all possible sincerity the real man. For my own part I shall do my best to be just and faithful in this attempt, shall spare no pains to present a true likeness of one whom I have known intimately as a man and guide for more than twenty-three years. In so doing I may, I am aware, be thought by some readers to portray in several respects rather an ideal nature than an actual Savoyard yeoman. This risk I must be content to run; and I am the more content since I have assured myself that what is here written represents not merely my own individual feelings, but the unanimous opinion of those who have had the fullest opportunities of appreciating Dévouassoud's character. If, on the other hand, my guide or his comrades find that I have failed to do full justice to his skill and daring they will, I trust, take their revenge. How if it should turn out that our old companions have, as the years went by, been writing as well as receiving certificates? 'Le Club Alpin; études intimes, par quelques Guides' would be a taking title, and might serve to introduce a volume of curious interest, and, probably, considerable popularity with the public that has carried 'Tartarin sur les Alpes' through so many editions!

François Joseph Dévouassoud was born in September, 1831, at the hamlet of Les Barats, a few hundred yards west of the last houses of Chamonix. It lies on the path to Mont Blanc, and under the shadow of the great mountain, which for a few weeks at mid-winter hardly leaves it. François comes of one of the old families of the valley, members of which appear in documents of the fourteenth century, preserved among the records of Le Prieuré, as the Des Vuaczos. He is the eldest of three brothers, all of whom have served with credit as guides. For two years, between the ages of twelve and fourteen, he was sent to school at Sallanches, and again at the age of sixteen he went for about a year to the College at Bonneville, where at that time many youths of good family received instruction. He was among the best pupils, and showed a particular taste for geography. As in our own schools, Latin was taught at the expense of modern languages, and such facility as François has acquired in English and Italian has been gained in after-life. This superior education he afterwards put to use by keeping the winter school for the boys of Chamonix from 1850 to 1864.

Among the inhabitants of Chamonix, two distinct types seem to me to be recognizable. Of one—the townspeople or first families—Auguste Balmat, the companion of Mr. Justice Wills in his early ascents, and Michel Alphonse Couttet, who travelled frequently with my parents, and was my guide in my first glacier expeditions, were examples; tall, upright men, with little of the peasant in their bearing or address. The Dévouassouds, on the contrary, are a heavily-built race, and in François the family characteristics are fully developed. At first sight many might acquiesce in his own description of himself as "le gros paysan." But there are few who can be in his company for any length of time, without recognizing the applicability to him of the description given of his forerunner, De Saussure's guide, nicknamed on account of his bulk, "le grand Jorasse"—"dont l'âme sentimentale et délicate contrastait avec sa figure gigantesque et la simplicité de ses manières."

François' ordinary gait is the long, slow stride natural to the mountain folk before military service made all men march. His frame is massive, and he has a slight stoop of the shoulders which partly conceals his real height. His countenance is broad and smooth-shaven. Always full of sense and feeling, it has, when in repose, a pensive, somewhat melancholy cast. The lines of his mouth are indicative of a refined, educated nature. The tones of his voice are low and agreeable. One feels instinctively that he could hardly say a foolish, or an unkind thing. When he is interested, when he recognizes an old acquaintance, or fancies some one is sick or ailing, his eyes light up with sympathy, and his heart seems to shine through his features. His gentleness makes him a special favourite with children. Not only at Alpine inns, but in English nurseries and housekeepers' rooms, the arrival of "Mr. François" is hailed with respectful enthusiasm. Indeed, his good temper and unselfishness win him friends wherever he goes, with all ages and all classes.

Placed in different circumstances in life François Dévouassoud would probably have been a student and a traveller; primarily, I think, a student, for he is a great reader, and there is in his nature an undercurrent of love of repose, a disposition to leave well alone. On the other hand, he has what are not common among Alpine peasants, the curiosity of travel, a discriminating taste in scenery, and the love of new forms of adventure. Many brave guides will show dislike—to use no stronger word—of the unknown. I have been solemnly warned, near the Italian Lakes, by an Engadine guide, across whose brain dim visions of stilettos were presumably flitting, not to go out after dark. "Wir sind in Italien, Herr," he mysteriously muttered. Dévouassoud has proved himself imperturbable, whether asked to ride through the Hauran on an Arab steed, to walk between a double row of Suanetian daggers, or to ford swollen rivers in a Russian post-cart. He has been sent off alone, and without an interpreter, in charge of baggage on a two days' journey across Mingrelia. In a gale at sea he has appeared, quite undisturbed, to inform me that a tremendous crash was only lightning striking the foremast, and to recall Thackeray's delightful ballad by his ludicrous description of the misfortunes and terrors of his Turkish companions on the upper deck. He has borne equally well trials of a different description. He has taken tea with dignity with the Armenian Patriarch at Etchmiadzin, has handed coffee at Jerusalem to a Turkish Pasha, and has paid his respects to the Archbishop of Canterbury.

Dévouassoud has many qualifications as a fellow-traveller besides his gift of cheerfulness, and his equanimity in steep places—in the Horatian as much as in the literal sense of the words. He knows equally well when to efface himself, and when to come forward. His conversation is original and entertaining. He combines the varied interests, the power of observation, and more than the ordinary power of expression of an educated man with the simplicity and breadth of view of a peasant philosopher. His tact and courtesy are unfailing; no mere social acquirements, but the natural outcome of a singularly sympathetic and intelligent disposition. His letters are as good as his conversation. While on tours in the East and Spain, he wrote to English friends many admirable accounts of what he was seeing and doing. I remember in particular two—one giving his first impressions of Athens and the Piræus, the other describing the ceremonies of the Holy Week at Seville. He can be terse and picturesque, or humorous, in description. Thus when descending with me from the Lysjoch, one October afternoon, he explained the strange pyramid which rose opposite the closed door of the Riffelhaus as "le monument du Club Alpin Anglais." His eyes had been the first to recognize that it consisted of empty bottles! But his nature shows itself most, perhaps, in his singular tact in expressing feeling; in his way of going to the root of the matter, and saying the right thing in simple but sufficient words. With a strong sense of justice and no dull eye for character, he is the least controversial and most charitable man I have ever known. I do not mean only to say that he declines to take an interest in the Pass of Hannibal; or that he does not repeat stories against his former employers. If any matter of dispute, Alpine or other, is mentioned in his presence, his disposition invariably is to say the best possible for every one concerned. On the only occasion, as far as I know, when a personal attack was made—not by an Englishman—on himself, his comments were summed up in the words, "Poor man, I feel quite sorry that he should not have better informed himself."

A characteristic personal trait is his thoroughly British dislike of the formalities of good-byes. How often at railway stations, or on steamboat quays, from Charing Cross to Poti or Oran, has he gripped my hand, and walked off hurriedly without a glance over his shoulder. His sentiment at such moments runs too deep to show itself in surface bubbles of polite speech, such as are customary between foreigners or common acquaintances.

I ought, perhaps, to add that Dévouassoud has always shown not only the most complete disinterestedness in money-matters, but also a desire to spare as far as possible his employer's purse—sometimes, as I have learnt afterwards, at his own expense. Abstemious in all other respects, he is saved, in my eyes at least, from the imputation of having no vice by being a great smoker.

In the local affairs of his valley Dévouassoud has displayed a very discreet absence of ambition. He was entered on the Roll of Guides in 1849. For ten years he acted as treasurer to the Company, a post for which his—in youth—exquisitely neat hand must have been one of his qualifications. But in later life he has at one time stood out firmly, if quietly, against the obnoxious rules of the Company, at another refused all overtures to stand for the post of Guide-chef, preferring old cronies and a game of cards to the noisy discussions of the café and the bureau. At home he has led the ideal peasant's life. Though well-to-do in the world, he was long content to remain in the dark, low-roofed cottage inherited from his father, which he has only lately exchanged for a larger and more convenient dwelling. Here, when not engaged in travel, or visiting his friends in London, Oxford, or Cambridge, he may be found superintending the details of his farm and household; or surrounded by his well-filled bookshelves, his photographs and remembrances of foreign travel, and indulging himself in speculations on subjects beyond the grasp of nine-tenths of the tourists who hurry past his door on their way to Mont Blanc or the Glacier des Bossons. François has, perhaps, pressed his love of a quiet life rather far in avoiding matrimony; contenting himself with a sister as housekeeper, and concentrating his affections on her and a promising nephew.

As a guide Dévouassoud has lived up to the emphatic advice with which Mr. Whymper closes his memorable book:—" Climb if you will, but remember that courage and strength are naught without prudence, and that a momentary negligence may destroy the happiness of a lifetime. Do nothing in haste; look well to each step; and from the beginning think what may be the end." His ruling principle has been—"My first duty is to bring home my travellers safe and sound; my second is to carry out their wishes." This conception of a guide's duty has, as we all know, been sometimes disregarded, if not discredited, of late years. Men, if they have not avowed, have acted on the theory that a guide's business is to be ready to risk his life whenever his employers are ready to risk theirs, not to "reason why," but—if I may alter an 'and' to 'or' in the familiar quotation—"to do or die." Now, to Dévouassoud climbing on these terms would be impossible. His whole nature would insist on reasoning why. He is far too reflective and imaginative, too little subject to be carried away by the enthusiasm of the moment, to forget what he considers, rightly or wrongly, *his* responsibility, not to weigh the possible catastrophe against the probable victory. Sometimes he may have seemed to push caution to excess. He has certainly not been among the most brilliant leaders of forlorn hopes. He has, I am told, been thought to be deficient in dash by a generation, whose occupation and glory it has been to succeed in places where earlier mountaineers had either failed or turned aside. This is the defect of his qualities.

In matters of technical detail, even more than in great decisions, Dévouassoud is pre-eminently a safe guide. In my journey of 1864, when I was with two other young climbers, and we had often on glacier expeditions a porter who had never touched ice before, it was significant that the only risk of accident we ran was when a guide of Eastern Switzerland refused to employ the rope, and strode away with it over his shoulders across a crevassed névé! François makes a science of the use of the rope, and in difficult places is always on the look-out to see that it is taut and serviceable. No axe cuts more commodious steps in an ice-wall; no leader loss needs warning from those behind him to keep off a snow-cornice. He has a perfect appreciation of the conditions of snow and ice, and a keen eye for the tracks of falling missiles. He possesses in particular one faculty, which is based mainly on intelligence and varied experience, and is, therefore, often missing in men who are otherwise first-rate climbers. In selecting a route he regards not only what lies immediately in front, but the whole ascent; he does not, in order to avoid a difficulty near at hand, risk running into a worse one later on. Again, he is quick in adapting a line of ascent to the temporary local conditions of snow or ice. He has also a natural gift for topography; and he has acquired the facility of an educated man in the use of large-scale maps.

But it is only when things begin to go ill that Dévouassoud shows what he is capable of in the way of prompt and vigorous action. To see the full extent of his powers you must put him into a difficulty which has to be got out of. I remember no better instance than the way in which, rather than risk prolonged exposure to a blinding thunder-storm, he led Mr. Comyns Tucker and myself down the steepest gully of the Tödi, a gully never before trodden and only rendered passable by the perfect condition of the snow. The greater, in fact, the emergency, the stronger and more skilful he appears. Deferential even to a fault when all is fair, he will take the command and speak sternly enough when he feels safety is at stake. And what a tower of strength he is when he says quietly, "Allez comme vous voudrez, je vous tiens!" It is impossible to feel nervous; and the confidence he inspires has been justified by deeds.

According to their own testimony—you will hardly hear of it from François

—three members of the Alpine Club owe their lives to him. He succeeded in stopping himself and Mr. Coolidge when, through the rope being struck by a falling stone, they were both carried to the edge of a precipice on the Piz St. Michel. He saved Mr. J. H. Wainewright when he slipped and fell on the fatal slope of the Matterhorn. And, although first on the rope, he held up Mr. F. Pollock and Rubi after they had both fallen past him while descending the steep Swiss side of the Col d'Argentière.

François Dévouassoud's figure was never that of a gymnast. I can easily imagine rocks where a lighter man might have beaten him in sheer climbing; and if I have never seen him so beaten, my experience may in this sense be fairly held limited. But it is only just to call attention to some of his feats in the Eastern Alps. He made, with Mr. Comyns Tucker and Mr. H. Beachcroft, the first ascent of the Sass Maor of Primiero, described by Mr. Leslie Stephen as one of the most remarkable rock-towers of the Alps, and reckoned by M. Brulle, who has also had experience of the Meije and the Aiguille du Dru, "a delicate climb, calling for serious attention." He also first scaled—with Mr. Tucker and Mr. T. Carson—the eastern face of the Rosengarten Spitze, a long and excessively steep slope of smooth rock never since traversed, and considered by Mr. Tucker more dangerous, if less sensational, than the Sass Maor. That they should take longer to descend than to climb is a sure proof of the difficulty of rocks, and the character of these will perhaps be best indicated by the fact that they took three excellent cragsmen two and a half hours to climb—and five hours to descend.

Still, Dévouassoud's special gift undoubtedly lies in snow and ice-craft. If there are two ways, he instinctively selects the snowy one. In the mazes of an ice-fall—I have seen him in many—he is thoroughly at home; among the séracs he developes not only a marvellous power of hooking himself with his axe, which becomes a sort of claw, across crevasses, but also a sound judgment as to where such feats will be profitable—will serve to thread the maze, instead of leading deeper into its perplexities. It is where head and hand are both needed that he most shines.

It would be difficult to give any complete account of Dévouassoud's principal Alpine ascents. He was not brought much into contact with English mountaineers until he had almost reached middle life. This was, I think, due in part to his being a native of Chamonix, and subject to the rules of the Company of Guides. These rules—then far more narrow and rigidly enforced than at present—were, as all mountaineers know, admirably contrived not only to conceal merit, and discourage enterprise among the guides, but also to induce mountaineers to look elsewhere for their climbing companions. In those days it was only by virtue of a special providence that a young guide could hope to escape from the blighting influences of the old tariff and the *tour de rôle*. Chamonix had a fair start of the rest of the world as a school for glacier guides. It chose to realize the socialistic dream, to distribute employment and wages equally among the competent and the incompetent. Its decline and fall may be a warning to other Alpine centres, and even to more important communities.

Dévouassoud's first English employer, so far as I have been able to trace, was Mr. A. P. Whately, in 1852. But on this occasion he was only engaged for a few walks round Chamonix. In 1861 he visited the Zermatt district with the same gentleman, and made several glacier expeditions. My own acquaintance with him was made in September, 1863. I was then an Eton boy, with considerable knowledge of the Alps, and some little experience in mountaineering. I was to ascend Mont Blanc under the charge of old Michel Alphonse Couttet—old I thought him then, for he had already passed the limit of age at which Chamonix guides are struck off the roll, but he only died last March, at the ripe age of eighty-five. He chose François Dévouassoud as second guide. The expedition came off successfully, and I was delighted with my new companion.

In the following year Dévouassoud accompanied me and two college friends in a long cross-country ramble from Thonon on the Lake of Geneva to Trent in South Tyrol. We went over the high-level route, up Monte Rosa, the Rheinwaldhorn, Piz Sella, Piz Palü and the Königsspitze, and accomplished six new expeditions, including the first ascent of the Presanella, 11,688 feet, the highest summit of the Lombard Alps. In 1865, he and Peter Michel, a sturdy Oberlander, made a long journey with Mr. F. F. Tuckett, myself, and several companions through the Dolomites, the Tyrolese and Graubünden Alps. In its course we made twenty new expeditions, and on one occasion, among the Oetzthaler Ferner, crossed four glacier passes, and climbed three peaks—the Wildspitze, 12,390 feet, Weiss Kugel, 12,280 feet, and Langtauferer Spitze, 11,626 feet—in three consecutive days of seventeen, fifteen, and twenty hours respectively; a severe test of the endurance of guides, who, at a time when there were no huts and provisions in Tyrolese side-valleys, had also to act as porters. From these two journeys must be dated Dévouassoud's constant employment by English mountaineers. He came, therefore, into a good practice—to transfer to the Alps a legal expression—about the date of the fall of the Matterhorn, too late to have a share in the ascents of the more famous peaks of Switzerland. But within the next few seasons he had with Mr. Bishop, or Mr. Winterbotham, or myself, climbed several of the great peaks of the Oberland and Zermatt districts, found a new way to the upper ridge of the Bietschhorn, and made many ascents which at that date were not quite the commonplaces they have since become. Among his other principal English employers have been Mr. J. K. Wainewright, Mr. Melvill Beachcroft, Mr. W. Sidgwick, the Rev. H. B. George, Mr. H. E. Buxton, Mr. T. Carson, and the Revs. F. T. Wethered and W. A. B. Coolidge.

With me or Mr. Comyns Tucker, Dévouassoud has made in the Alps over fifty "new expeditions," and more old, above the snow-line. These, with a few exceptions, have been in the mountains east of the St. Gothard, that is, not in the loftiest portion of the Alpine chain. Thirty of them were between 13,000 and 11,000 feet, fifteen between 10,000 and 11,000 feet, and the remainder, mostly passes or rock-peaks in the Dolomites, under 10,000 feet. To the frequenters of Zermatt, or Grindelwald, the figures may seem insignificant. Yet on some of these climbs, the names of which might carry little or no meaning to the general reader, we met with difficulties or dangers which seemed to all of us as formidable as anything we had encountered on more lofty and familiar peaks.

In many of our expeditions Dévouassoud was the only guide engaged. In a few, such as Monte Viso and the first ascent of the Tinzenhorn—the 'little Matterhorn' of visitors to Davos—he was alone with one or other of us. I have a purpose in mentioning this detail. For I hold—as a rule, subject, no doubt, to certain exceptions—that ascents, however remarkable, made between two guides afford but a poor test of a traveller's mountaineering capacity. And on the same principle I consider that in estimating a guide's performances, the amount of support, moral and physical, that he had from comrades, or the extent to which he was thrown on his own resources, are important factors in the calculation.

Dévouassoud's ascents, new and old, extend from the Maritime Alps to the Pasterze Glacier; are co-extensive, therefore, with the Alpine snows. He has been up most, if not all, the highest peaks of the Ortelor, Adamello, and Val Masino groups, and many of those of the Bernina, Oberland, and Zermatt districts. His topographical knowledge of the Alpine chain as a whole is unequalled among guides. In this respect he holds a place among his comrades similar to that occupied by Mr. John Ball among English climbers. In his own country, however—though he has of course been up Mont Blanc over and over again—he has made but few noteworthy expeditions. The second passages of the difficult Col des Hirondelles and Col de Trélatête, and a new way up the Aiguille du Midi, are all that are recorded to his credit. His name occurs even less often than his brother Henri's in the table of first ascents. He has taken no part in the attacks on the last and most difficult Aiguilles. By a curious accident, the only maiden peak and pass—the Tour Ronde and its Col—I have myself climbed in the Mont Blanc chain were climbed with other guides. This considerable blank in his career I attribute partly to his being a member of the Chamonix Company, partly to his public reputation resting on his ice-craft, and principally to his frequent absences from home during the summer with employers, some of whom, like myself, do not belong to the most daring order of mountaineers.

It is, however, by no means my intention to suggest that François Dévouassoud's Alpine record equals, or even comes near, those of several of his contemporaries. To be appreciated fairly it must, of course, be read with a competent acquaintance with the Alps as a whole, and a reasonable allowance for the difficulties, now for the most part easily avoidable, which were encountered twenty years ago by the early Alpine explorers in their hasty raids upon unmapped, unhutted, and almost unknown peaks, passes, and glaciers. What I, with others of his old employers, believe is that, even when so read, his record gives but an inadequate idea of his powers. We are satisfied that, putting aside for the moment his Caucasian performances, we have in positions of very serious difficulty sufficiently tested his skill and judgment to be entitled to claim for him an honourable place among the Pioneers of the Alps.

But to the outer public, and to the Alpine men of a younger generation and more concentrated experiences, Dévouassoud is best known—and it is right that he should be best known—as the forerunner of a class, the members of which are still far from numerous—the guides who have been travellers and explorers as well as mountaineers. Partly by good fortune, but far more through his own qualities, he has enjoyed repeated opportunities of visiting distant lands. In 1868, he made with Mr. Comyns Tucker and myself the tour of the Levant; penetrating with us the tombs in the crags above Thebes, discovering the foundation of a temple on the top of El Kleib—the Hill of Bashan; wandering through the byways of the Armenian Highlands into Persia; and being beaten back by illness and the spring snows on Ararat. At Tiflis, Mr. A. W. Moore joined us, and we went on together to carry out my plan of breaking new ground for mountaineers in the central Caucasus. This adventure I should hardly have undertaken had I not felt assured that, besides two tried companions, I had at hand in Dévouassoud not only a first-rate mountain guide, but also the staunchest of comrades. It was mainly due to his skill and endurance that we succeeded at the first attempt in both climbing and crossing Kazbek (16,546 feet), ascending the south-eastern peak of Elbruz (18,431 feet), and forcing a pass through the séracs of the Karagam Glacier, the largest ice-stream yet measured in the Caucasian chain.

Nineteen years later—in 1887—François Dévouassoud returned with me to the Caucasus, bringing with him his brother Michel, and a young nephew, Joseph Désailloud. My travelling companion for the first half of my journey, was M. de Déchy, of Budapesth, an Alpine Clubman, who by his frequent visits to the Caucasus —including ascents of Elbruz and Adai Choch—and valuable photographs of its scenery, had earned for himself the charily-bestowed distinction of "Honorary Corresponding Fellow of the Royal Geographical Society." With M. de Déchy and myself, François and his comrades shared in two passages of the main chain by high glacier Cols, never before traversed by Europeans. With me he led in the first ascents of Tetnuld, a snow-pyramid a thousand feet higher than Mont Blanc, which looks down on the towered hamlets of Suanetia, and of a summit of about 15,000 feet on the northern side of the chain near Bezingi, which will perhaps be known hereafter as Uku. He also took part in many explorations and excursions on the southern slope of the mountains.

In less far-off regions, Dévouassoud has visited our own Lake Hills in winter; among Italian mountains he has climbed Dante's Pietra Pana, the marble heights of Carrara, and the Gran Sasso d'Italia, the highest crest of the Apennines in the Abruzzi; in Corsica, Monte Cinto, Monte Rotondo, and Monte d'Oro; in Algeria, the second peak of the Jebel Jurjura or Lesser Atlas. He has also made a long journey through Spain with a French gentleman, M. Astruc.

In 1885, Dévouassoud ascended the Finsteraarhorn and Jungfrau on two successive days. That his mountaineering and walking powers may last at least as long as their own is the wish of all his old employers. To some of them— to the writer at any rate—this sketch appears as but an inadequate tribute to one who, in many years of faithful service, has taught them to value him as a friend as highly as they have long esteemed him as a guide.

D. W. F.

François Couttet.

FRANÇOIS COUTTET, *dit* 'Baguette,' was born at Chamonix in 1828. The name 'Baguette' was given to his father, also a guide in the district, on account of his straight muscular limbs: it was afterwards adopted by his son to distinguish himself from two other guides of the same name. Young 'Baguette' was one of the porters through whose exertions the constitution of the Société des Guides was reorganized, and underwent considerable alterations in 1848; a period in the history of the Société which is referred to in the introductory chapter to this work. Two well-known names are pre-eminently associated with his career, those of Monsieur Loppé and Mr. A. Adams-Reilly. The latter he accompanied during the seasons he was engaged in making his survey of the chain of Mont Blanc; with the former he acted as guide for a considerable period. Monsieur Loppé always speaks of 'Baguette' as having the "vrai instinct des glaciers," to use his own most expressive phrase. A man who, by keen observation and intuitive perception, would always find a direction by which difficulties could as far as possible be avoided, he seems to have had the knack of readily perceiving, and always steering completely clear of obstacles which another guide would have overcome by force or by laborious step-cutting; greatly to the personal discomfort of all his *caravane*. One February I saw him display these qualities in a marked degree, while making an ascent of the Buet,

with some members of the French Alpine Club. Our party was fourteen in number; nine were Chamonix guides, including none other than that great personage for the time being, the Guide-Chef himself. A discussion took place as to our route. There were many counsellors, but very little wisdom brought to bear on the question. It was some years since Couttet had been on a mountain of any difficulty, as the Buet may fairly be termed at that time of year. But he seemed at once to grasp what our direction ought to be, and led us in triumph to the top, by a route which did not seem to have occurred to any one else of the party. His old employers always speak of him as having been a thoroughly "safe" guide, steady, always reliable and to be depended on. With one or two exceptions, he was taken more frequently out of his own valley than any of his contemporaries. As the *étiquettes* of his hôtel inform us, he has 'twenty-seven times made the ascent of Mont Blanc.' In 1858 he accompanied the first traveller, Mr. E. T. Coleman, who crossed the Col de Miage. The following year, with Mr. G. S. Lane Fox, he ascended the Aiguille du Midi. This peak is supposed to have been climbed by the Count de Bouillé's guides in 1856. The guides left M. le Count in a secure position some 200 feet from the summit, while they scrambled to the top. Tradition says that Jacques Balmat, the hero of Mont Blanc, had attempted this Aiguille, and pronounced it to be inaccessible. Mr. Lane Fox's expedition is one of considerable interest, as it resulted in the conquest of the first of the great Chamonix Aiguilles scaled by a traveller since the ascent of Mont Blanc in 1786. In the same year (1859), in company with Melchior Anderegg, he was the first to ascend Mont Blanc from Chamonix by Les Bosses. He accompanied Mr. Whymper in 1864 in an attempt on the Aiguille d'Argentière. The party reached a point some 250 feet from the summit, but were driven back by a violent gale. Describing this *tentative* in 'Scrambles amongst the Alps,' Mr. Whymper writes, "Ugh, how cold it was! How the wind blew! Couttet's hat was torn from its fastenings, and went on a tour in Switzerland." At the commencement of his career as guide, few men in the district had much taste for attempting new expeditions. There was more rivalry displayed in getting possession of the *Herren* who came to do the peaks, than in bagging the peaks themselves. Guiding was regarded at that time in Chamonix from a very prosaic point of view; the mere honour and glory of finding a new route up some difficult and probably dangerous peak, seemed worth little in comparison with the almost certainty of earning, say, the price of a cow on Mont Blanc or some other mountain which was sure to 'go.' Couttet was distinctly a good guide in a poor epoch.

In 1862, while Couttet was still acting as guide, he commenced to build a house for himself on a piece of ground he had purchased in Chamonix. Monsieur Loppé, who was there at the time, suggested that he should add an additional storey, where he and his family could pass a few weeks in summer, and escape from the noise and discomfort of hôtel life. The following season, M. Loppé occupied one *étage*, the other became a sort of bachelors' quarters for several members of the Alpine Club, with whom Couttet often went as guide. The idea then occurred to him of trying a more certain and profitable means of gaining his livelihood, and becoming *maître d'hôtel*. During the next few seasons his châlet became more and more popular, and in 1867 he found it necessary to lay the foundations of a larger house adjoining the old one. This is now the centre of the group of buildings which form his hôtel, and has the initials C. F., the date, and a couple of crossed ice-axes carved in one of the lintels. The following year Couttet said 'Good-bye' to guiding, and assumed all the dignities and importance of an hôtel-keeper. His little hostelry soon became known as being largely frequented by members of the Alpine Club. Season after season the same friends met there, and with the exception of the Monte Rosa at Zermatt, there is probably no hôtel in the Alps of which one has so often heard such pleasant reminiscences It was a comfortable, thoroughly home-like little place, in every sense of the word.

Any one who has stood in front of the 'Grand Hôtel Couttet,' the substantial pile into which the original little châlet has now grown, cannot regret

from Couttet's point of view that he ceased to be a guide, even when he was in the prime of his career. 'Baguette' always reminds me of one of a number of brothers, who with the rest commenced life in the army, but who very soon "cut the service and went into trade." Not long ago he came home with a couple of lakhs, to find his brothers reckoning up the years which must elapse before they could retire from active service on a modest pension. Personally I would much rather be one of the well-to-do countryfolk one sees driving through *barrières* in the early morning, than a hero in the Invalides; though the latter may wear a lot of medals, and even possess a sword and cocked hat. And when 'Baguette' takes a stroll in his garden after the day's work is done, I should imagine he had much more satisfaction in looking up at the well-built pile he has raised than at some break-neck peak, during the ascent of which for the first time by the S.S.E. arête, he had very nearly come to grief. Throughout his whole life Couttet has always shown the greatest diligence and energy in carrying out any work he has taken in hand. While still a guide he rented the Montanvert, and owned a share of the châlet at Planpraz. He was *entrepreneur* for the first *cabane* on the Grands Mulets. Step by step, by thrift and good management, he has made his way in the world. During the year which preceded the opening of his new hôtel, I spent a good deal of time at Chamonix, and could not help being struck with the fact of a man, who never had any technical training, being able to act as his own master-builder and contractor.

Old Couttet possesses many interesting souvenirs of his guiding days. He has one of M. Loppé's beautiful oil-paintings, representing a scene on the Séracs de Géant, at that spot where a whole party would probably have been killed but for his timely warning. The picture bears the artist's signature, above which is written: " À mon ancien guide et ami, F. Couttet 'Baguette,' souvenir affectueux." A framed copy of Mr. A. Adams-Reilly's survey of the chain of Mont Blanc, "presenté par l'auteur," hangs in the *fumoir*, a map which Couttet has used almost daily during the last twenty seasons, in helping old and young climbers to plan their expeditions. By its side hangs the *diplôme* which accompanied the *médaille d'honneur*, a "Récompense pour Belles Actions," which Couttet received in 1866, "pour porter secours aux frères Young, tombés d'un haut glacier dans les neiges, en faisant l'ascension du Mont Blanc." The diploma was given, it goes on to state, "de perpétuer dans sa famille et au milieu de ses concitoyens le souvenir de son honorable et courageuse conduite." There is an interesting account of this accident in M. Durier's 'Le Mont Blanc,' where a graphic description is given of "l'infatigable Baguette toujours attelé au cadavre." The fog was so dense that

Couttet was compelled to use a *cornet* as a sort of fog-horn, with which he signalled to those of the relief party who had deemed it more prudent to remain at the Grands Mulets. Couttet possesses a faded photograph of a group of about forty people on the Mer de Glace, many of whom are in full military uniform; a costume which, by the way, I have never seen worn on any glaciers except those in the vicinity of Chamonix. This group represents the Emperor Napoleon III., the Empress, and their suite, who visited Chamonix after the annexation of Savoy. Couttet was one of the guides attached to the Imperial party, and took part in a sort of mimic exhibition of the *modus operandi* of crossing a difficult glacier, which the guides arranged for the diversion and instruction of their distinguished *royageurs*. 'Baguette' was the leader, cut steps up a huge sérac, and when near the top was 'poussé par le dos' in the orthodox fashion, much to the edification of the Empress.

Personally I shall always have a warm regard for Old Couttet; ever since a certain day, now some fifteen years ago, when he started me on my first glacier expedition, and the same evening carried off my *bâton* to be marked 'Mauvais Pas' and 'Chapeau.' Many a long autumn and winter's evening has he wiled away with reminiscences of his guiding days, and the Albert-Smith-like ascents of Mont Blanc he has taken part in; the English captain who drank Château Lafite and ate fresh trout in the Grands Mulets; or the guide who carried numberless bottles of tisane in his pockets, and hung a thermometer on his back, in consequence of which "tout le monde l'appelait, Robinson! Robinson!" in occult allusion to the hero of Defoe. The doings of these celebrities possess a great freshness and novelty when related by Couttet, who by the way, is an excellent *raconteur*. His is one of those familiar faces we associate with certain districts in the Alps. And one always looks forward to his hearty welcome, the same now as in his less prosperous days. To his friends the proprietor of that 'Grand Hôtel de premier ordre' at Chamonix, will always be 'Baguette.'

C. D. C.

Michel Payot.

MICHEL CLEMENT PAYOT is a native of the village of Les Moussons, near Chamonix, and was born in 1840. His father was a farmer and local guide. Michel was apprenticed to a blacksmith and farrier, but at an early age manifested an inclination for the mountains. His first recorded mountain expedition was in 1858, when at the age of eighteen he volunteered as porter under Auguste Balmat, in Professor Tyndall's and Mr. Justice Wills's ascent of Mont Blanc, and gained a favourable notice in the Professor's narrative of that ascent ('Glaciers of the Alps,' p. 192). Subsequently he was employed by M. Gabriel Loppé, the well-known Alpine artist, with whom he travelled as porter and guide for several years. During this early period of his career he distinguished himself by a daring and skilful rescue of a fellow-porter, who had fallen into a deep crevasse while descending Mont Blanc. In another attempt at rescue under similar circumstances, which unfortunately was not successful, he was lowered to a great depth in an immense crevasse on the Petit Plateau, and for his gallant conduct on both these occasions a 'médaille d'honneur,' and a diploma of merit were awarded to him by the Ministry of the Interior of France.

In 1863 Payot became member of the Société des Guides, and in 1864 he was engaged by the late Mr. A. Adams-Reilly, who was then occupied in completing his map of the chain of Mont Blanc. In the early part of this season Mr. Whymper and the lamented Michel Croz joined forces with Mr. Reilly and Payot, and made the first ascents of the Mont Dolent, the Aiguille de Trélatête and the Aiguille d'Argentière: and also the first passage of the Col de Triolet. Later in the same year, with Mr. Reilly, Mr. John Birkbeck, junior, and Croz, Payot crossed the Dôme du Goûté from the Col de Miage, thus for the first time proving the feasibility of the ascent of Mont Blanc from the side of the Miage Glacier. In Mr. Reilly's paper on the expeditions just mentioned (*Alpine Journal*, vol. ii. p. 98) Payot is spoken of as "a novice educated by M. Loppé, but a novice who promises great things." Assuredly this promise has not remained unfulfilled. This season's work, in the company of such men, and under a leader like Michel Croz, had an immense effect on young Payot, and developed qualities which had hitherto been comparatively latent. I look on his association at this time with Croz as of especial importance; and although no formal or recognized relation of the kind existed between the two men, Croz may be regarded as teacher, and Payot as his favourite and an advanced pupil. From 1864 Michel Payot takes rank as a guide of the first class, and after Croz's death in 1865 may not inappropriately be considered as his Alpine successor among Chamonix guides.

Besides the expeditions already referred to, Michel Payot has made the first ascents of the following peaks: the Aiguille du Plan in 1871, the Aiguille de Rochefort over which he passed from Courmayeur to Chamonix in 1873, Mont Blanc by Broglia and Fresnay Glaciers in 1877, the Dôme de Rochefort, the highest point (3997 metres Mieulet's Map) between the Grandes Jorasses and the Aiguille de Rochefort in 1882. Also the Col between the Southern Miage and the Trélatête Glaciers, to which the rather absurd name of 'Col dit Infranchissable' has been given by M. Mieulet, other and more natural names having already been appropriated, and two new Cols between the Tour Ronde and the Aiguille du Géant.

In 1878 Payot accompanied me through a campaign in the Central Rocky mountains of the United States, which however was not productive of great results from a climber's point of view. But although disappointed in finding much mountain work for him, I found him in other respects a most useful companion, and full of resource in any contingency; a kind of 'Jack of all trades,' not qualified however by the ordinary proverbial ending of this designation. His knowledge of the treatment of horses and mules stood me in good service, as also did his remarkable dexterity in felling timber. Every man however has his weakness, and Michel's weakness showed itself in a mortal dread of Indians. There was an Indian war at that time in the Northern districts which we visited, and what he had heard as to their treatment of enemies who fell into their hands, produced in him a profound objection to even a remote possibility of his hair being left with them for ornamental purposes.

Although a good rock-climber, his strong point is ice-work, and he is at his best on a difficult glacier where the way has to be won through a complication of séracs and crevasses. On glaciers quite strange to him I have sometimes been amazed at his marvellous rapidity in taking in the situation and deciding on the best line of advance; sight and decision appear not infrequently to be almost simultaneous, and rarely have I found the decision to be unsound. An incident which occurred in the passage of the Col de Trélatête comes with especial vividness to my mind. This Col had been crossed twice previous to our passage, and the descent on the north side by the ice-fall to the main Trélatête Glacier, had in both cases been of extraordinary difficulty. After leaving the Col we walked down the snow-slopes in the middle of the glacier until we were just above the head of the ice-fall, where Michel halted. He gave a short comprehensive look downwards into the séracs, then turned his head towards the rocks on the left and said almost impatiently, " Pourquoi suivre un mauvais chemin, quand il y a une grande route à côté—dans une heure et demie nous sommes là bas," and immediately heading for the rocks he led us down them, and in ten minutes less than the time he mentioned we were racing down the smooth surface of the main glacier, having completely avoided all difficulties in the descent.

He is eminently a safe guide. His record is a clean one and unbroken by accident to any party of which he has been leader. Of his *Herr* he is singularly careful, and it is not out of place to relate an instance of which I was in more than one sense the *corpus vile*. Early one summer I arrived at Martigny straight from England, and proposed as a training walk with Payot alone, to walk up the Val d'Arpette, to find if possible a way over the Col at the head of this valley on to the snow plateau above the Glacier de Trient, and pass over the Col du Tour to Argentière. On arriving at the Col d'Arpette we found it impossible to cross direct on to the upper *névé* of the Trient glacier, and were obliged to descend to the north bank until we arrived at a point about half-way down the ice-fall. We then tried to ascend by the séracs near the bank where they appeared less broken than in the middle of the glacier, but were soon compelled to return and cross to the opposite bank. Here again we found advance impossible, so as a last chance we tried the very middle of the ice-fall, and after much hard work and no slight risk, being materially helped by some fallen séracs, we gained the upper glacier. All difficulty was now at an end, and gentle snow-slopes led up to the junction of the Trient and Orny glaciers, and thence to the Col du Tour. We halted for lunch, after which I suddenly became seriously ill, the result probably of unaccustomed exertion and want of training, and in an hour I was in a state of collapse. Several times did Michel endeavour to impress on me the urgent necessity for getting over the Col du Tour, and as I gave little attention to his entreaties, he lifted me on to my legs and tried to lead me along. His efforts were quite useless; my legs refused to work and I subsided on to the snow. It was half-past three o'clock, and the position was serious. Descent by the Glacier de Trient was not even to be thought of, and the distance to the Col was yet considerable. At last he cried out, "Il faut absolument que je vous porte;" and carry me he did. First, taking knapsacks, rope, and ice-axes to a distance of about 100 yards onwards, he laid them down and returned to me. Then he put me on his back and carried me about the same distance beyond the knapsacks, for which he returned after putting me in my turn on the glacier. These operations were repeated until we had passed the Col and descended a considerable distance on the Glacier du Tour, when I began to recover, and with many halts and descending very slowly, we arrived at last at the village of La Tour after nightfall.

Like many guides he is a keen hunter, and has besides a very fair knowledge of natural history, in which he takes a strong interest. His powers of observation, which are of no mean order, and his natural intelligence render him a pleasant companion, and his courteous manners and constant kindness are unfailing. As a lady's guide he has only one equal and no superior.

J. E.

Alphonse Payot.

ALPHONSE PAYOT, the youngest of the living guides whose names are recorded in this work, was born at Les Moussons, near Chamonix, in 1852. He is a younger brother of Michel Clement Payot, with whom he has been associated in many expeditions. Although he cannot be said to possess the knowledge and some of the more brilliant qualities of his brother, he is thoroughly skilful in his profession, is at the same time resolute and careful, and has a remarkable capacity for hard work. His extreme modesty, and his placid, and one might almost say too kindly nature, tend to do him some injustice, and with a stranger create a false estimate of his powers, which these qualities to some extent conceal; but such impression is only passing, and will vanish in presence of the first difficulty encountered.

His first expedition of importance was the passage (for the second time) of the 'Col dit Infranchissable' in 1871, when he was engaged by Mr. Arthur Milman as porter; and he continued at irregular intervals to act in the same capacity until 1876, when he passed into the rank of guide. The paucity of unclimbed peaks and new routes, and the comparatively recent commencement of his career, explain the absence in his case of an imposing list of first ascents or new passes.

My own experience of Alphonse dates from 1875, and the very first *course* which he made with me, the passage of the Col de l'Aiguille du Plan, showed

me that there was good stuff in the man, which a little experience would soon develop. A campaign in the Bernese Oberland the next year, fully confirmed the good impression I had received. He proved a very glutton for work, and appeared always to be rather sorry than otherwise when it was over. In 1877, he accompanied me in the first ascent of Mont Blanc by the Broglia and Fresnay Glacier route, on which occasion the greater portion of the work fell to him; and right well he did it. He had come in for his fair share of step-cutting before we arrived at the long arête leading up to the Mont Blanc de Courmayeur, and owing to the circumstance that he was leading when we were fairly committed to the ridge (which proved to be so narrow and steep that a change of order was imprudent if not impossible), he was compelled to remain in front and cut steps along its entire length until we reached the rocks near the summit. As the greater part of the ridge was hard ice, and large steps were necessary, the work was very severe, but he went through with it without a pause, and as cheerfully and philosophically as if step-cutting in hard ice were a permanent condition of existence.

A very noteworthy display of his skill in an emergency occurred during the descent, after an unsuccessful attempt on the Aiguille Verte by the Glacier de Charpoua in 1881. Our party, consisting of Mr. W. E. Davidson, Mr.

Frank C. Hartley and myself, with von Bergen, Lanier, and the two Payots, had arrived within a very short distance from the final arête. All difficulties had been overcome, and success was almost within our grasp (for at most another hour would have landed us on the summit), when bad weather, which for some hours had been threatening, broke on us, and we were compelled to retrace our steps. After descending the very long couloir above the Charpoua Glacier, we reached, just before nightfall, what we had found to be by far the worst place and greatest difficulty in the whole ascent, viz. the rocks which connect the couloir with the glacier just above the bergschrund. These rocks, which were interspersed with patches of ice, were bad enough in broad daylight, but now the fading light had considerably enhanced their difficulty, and haste was necessary, for our position was rather critical. Alphonse here came to the front, and how he led the party on to the glacier, remains still a mystery to me. In the morning the passage of the bergschrund and the rocks had cost us nearly an hour and a half's good work; he now led us down the rocks

and over the schrund in little more than half an hour, and certainly not less than half of the distance was covered in the dark, or by the fitful light of an uncertain moon.

He is an indefatigable chamois-hunter, and an excellent shot. Many pleasant recollections have I of evenings passed in camp or bivouac after the day's sport was over, when by the fire we talked over the chances of the day or discussed the plans for the morrow. His imperturbable good humour was proof alike against bad sport and bad weather. There is, indeed, much of the Mark Tapley temperament in him, and when benighted far from our sleeping quarters, or when our bivouac was exceptionally uncomfortable, his good-natured taciturnity would relax into modified jollity "under creditable circumstances."

He knows the Pennine and Bernese Alps well, and has travelled much in the Graian Alps and the Tarentaise, of which he has a good knowledge. Although rather a thoroughly good all-round man than pre-eminent in one special department, I would say if compelled to give a preference that he excels in rock climbing, and his steadiness and certainty as rear-guard in the descent of difficult rocks are not easily forgotten.

J. E.

Edouard Cupelin.

EDOUARD CUPELIN, "Canut" as he is called by his friends, was born in the valley of Chamonix in 1840. In Savoy "un Canut" seems to be the generic pseudonym for a tall powerful man, who walks with a long stride. The name has probably been derived from some distorted version of the well-known tale, told of the monarch who seems to have been placed at a disadvantage by the *haute diplomatie* of some member of his household, who told him he could stem a rising tide by merely putting his toes against the waves. Even François Dévouassoud's etymological researches may never settle this knotty question satisfactorily; but at all events we may safely admit that it is only with regard to his great strength of limb, that the name is at all applicable to the Canute of Chamonix. If my recollection of 'Little Arthur's History' is at all accurate, the incident concludes by King Canute sharply rebuking those nobles who were standing around his royal person. And any one who has ever met that most good-natured of all Chamonix guides, could hardly imagine that any amount of provocation would make Cupelin rebuke even the most incompetent among the newly joined of the Société des Guides, far less a "noble."

In his early days Cupelin was *soutien de famille*, and consequently escaped the years of military service which in so many cases have marred the career of Chamonix guides, just at the moment when their capabilities were beginning to be known and recognized by amateurs. He is related to François Couttet, whom he often used to accompany as porter, and from whom he learned the rudiments of his craft. To see "Baguette" and "Canut" together on the same rope must always have reminded one of the "Two Fishermen" of Japan, who are so constantly carved as Netsukes, and whose abnormally long and short proportions are looked upon by the Japanese as a symbol of self-help. "Baguette" often speaks of Cupelin as "un de mes élèves," and amongst all the numerous guides and amateurs of whose mountaineering education that veteran claims to have laid the foundation, Cupelin may undoubtedly be considered his most distinguished pupil.

The first entry in his *livret* is dated 1861, and is signed by Monsieur Bisson, the well-known photographer to Napoleon III., the forerunner of those who have since enabled us to adorn our walls and fill our bookshelves with really artistic photographic views of the great peaks, and scenes in the Alps we love so well. With Monsieur Bisson, Cupelin made his first ascent of Mont Blanc and went up the Buet; it was on the latter occasion that the celebrated panoramic view was taken from the summit, the copies of which have in recent years become so extremely rare and valuable owing to the original negative having been accidentally broken. On the

margin of most of the impressions is engraved, "L'ascension dirigée par Auguste Balmat." Two years later, Cupelin was employed as porter by Monsieur Miculet, during a portion of the time he was engaged in making the surveys for his celebrated map. In 1864 Cupelin commenced to travel with Mr. D. J. Abercrombie, the first Englishman who gave him engagements of any length, and in the same year he made his first new expedition. With the brothers Wills, Mr. A. Millman, and Mr. F. Taylor, he reached the summit of the Col des Grandes Jorasses from Chamonix; they returned, however, by the same route and did not attempt to cross the Col. "The expedition occupied no less than twenty-one hours," the then Mr. Alfred Wills wrote at the time in Cupelin's guide's book, "and involved difficulties of ice and snow of no common order. Cupelin was called 'porter,' but he acted in every respect as one of our guides, and we have great pleasure in bearing our testimony to his capacity as a mountaineer, and to his good temper and general good conduct in every respect. We think him in every way qualified to be a guide, and one of a high order." Monsieur Miculet wrote,—"Je n'ai eu qu'à me louer de son énergie et de son intelligence, je le recommande à tous les voyageurs qui désirent entreprendre des courses longues et périlleuses."

Many of the entries in Cupelin's *livret* have been made at long and irregular intervals; and, unlike the great majority of guides, it never seems to have occurred to him that the certificates in his book form in reality a record of his climbing achievements. Among the best-known names which one finds may be mentioned those of Mr. C. E. Mathews, M. Paul Perret, Mr. W. Leighton Jordan, and Mr. Henry Pasteur, who says,—"I consider him one of the best, strongest, and pleasantest guides I have ever met. I have travelled with him in the Alps for many years." The next certificate in the book is from Mr. C. E. Mathews, who says,—"I think Mr. Pasteur's commendation on the other side is well deserved." The name most frequently found in Cupelin's *livret* is that of Dr. Marcet, with whom he visited the Canary Islands and made the ascent of Teneriffe.

Few Chamonix guides have had more constant employment than Cupelin; but, notwithstanding this, his record of first expeditions is an insignificant one. In 1864 he reached from the Chamonix side the summit of the Col des Grandes Jorasses; in 1873 he made the first ascent of the Schwartzhorn, in 1882 he scaled Mont Mallet by a new route, and in 1883 made the first passage of the Col du Tacul.

In guiding, more than in almost any other profession, a career is moulded and a reputation gained through the individuals who may chance to form the *clientèle* of the guide. He rarely has the chance of independently showing what his powers really are, or of giving proof of his capacity as a guide except while he is fulfilling an engagement. A guide may number among his patrons some *Herr* who is bent on doing *courses* which are absolutely new; others may spend the greater part of each season with some individual who is more of the student than the athlete, in studying the topography of the lower valleys, thus it is that the guide's name is always more or less bound up with that of his employer, whose peculiar fads and idiosyncrasies he helps in carrying out and pursuing.

Cupelin's powers as a guide are perhaps displayed to best advantage on difficult rocks. Taking into consideration the fact that he is a man of such powerful build, all his movements are wonderfully graceful. With the exception of Alexander Burgener, I doubt if there is any one of the guides in the first rank who impresses one so much with his gigantic strength.

Cupelin, however, has none of that clumsiness of movement which is so conspicuous in Burgener's "form." One of the most genial of Imboden's many admirers recounts, how, when Josef had completed the final arrangements for making an ascent of the Rothhorn with some ambitious "tripper" (who found that he had still a couple of days to spare before his return ticket would become overdue), he said half apologetically to the bystanders, "It does not matter, he may slip as much as he likes, I can hold him up." This was exactly the reflection which occurred to me about Cupelin regarding myself while going up the sheer precipice of the Géant, and on one of the "nastiest" places on the higher Dru, when one looked up and saw him standing on a tiny foothold above, apparently as firmly placed as if he himself was a part of the mountain. The fact of Cupelin being on the rope would inspire the most timid novice with confidence. With the exception of two or perhaps three guides he has climbed a greater number of the peaks in his own district, than any of the four hundred members of the Société des Guides can boast of. He is one of those Chamonix guides whose names can be counted on the fingers of one hand who has a practical acquaintance with the great peaks of the Oberland or in the Zermatt district. He has been in Dauphiné and in the Tyrol. He has made the ascent of Mont Blanc fifty-seven times, an exceptional number when we take into account the large portion of each season which has been spent by him out of his own valley. Like all guides of any merit he has suffered much from the stringent and despotic rules of the Société des Guides. When I made Cupelin's acquaintance some years ago, it chanced to be the commencement of the season, when there were hardly any tourists in Chamonix. I well remember his being compelled to refuse three separate engagements to go up Mont Blanc, owing to the slow rate at which the names on the roster of guides were moving, and his consequent inability to take his *tour du rôle*.

No Chamonix guide can show a larger record of winter ascents than Edouard Cupelin. In the winter of 1882 he took part with the present writer in a number of winter expeditions, some of which are referred to in the chapter on 'Mountaineering in Winter.' He subsequently accompanied a well-known lady mountaineer in the excursions she made between November, 1882, and March, 1883, among which may be mentioned the first winter ascent of the Aiguille du Midi, the Col des Grands Montets, the Col de Chardonnet, the Fenêtre de Saleinaz, the Col d'Argentière, and the first actual passage of the Col du Tacul. These, as well as many other *courses* he made with the same lady, have been graphically described by her in the 'High Alps in Winter,' and 'High Life.' The latter work is dedicated to Cupelin, and his portrait is given as a frontispiece.

It is indeed a bitter irony of fate that, while none of the many *voyageurs* whom Cupelin has so skilfully and carefully guided has ever met with the slightest mishap while under his care, he himself should have been the victim of an accident. He is the only one of the living guides whose names are recorded in this work, who has been compelled to go on the "retired list," so far, at least, as his being able to attempt the more difficult and dangerous peaks. While making the ascent of the Aiguille Verte on the 12th of August, 1884, a stone was dislodged which struck the rope, with the result that Cupelin was thrown "out of his steps," fell a considerable number of feet, and severely injured his right knee. Those who know Cupelin can well imagine that when the great boulder fell, which sent him flying into space, his first thought would be for the safety of his *voyageur* and not for his own. And, with characteristic generosity, he always maintains that the accident could not possibly have been avoided, and stoutly protests that not an atom of blame can be attached to any

of the party; a rare test of the perfect fairness of a man who has been disabled for life, and who has consequently lost the whole of his professional income. He has now taken a lease of the Pierre Pointue and the *cabane* at the Grands Mulets, and although he has only played the part of "mine host" for a single season, he has already given most ample and practical proof that in his new calling he will have as great success, and be as popular among his patrons as he used to be when a guide.

Cupelin has an abundant store of good spirits, which no amount of hardship or unpleasant surroundings can ruffle. In the chapter in 'High Life' in which a passage of the Stelvio in winter is described, many pleasant traits in his character are alluded to. "For an hour or so," the authoress writes, "I pushed steadily forward, ploughing through powdery snow, which often reached to my waist. On looking back, I noticed that at every step Cupelin sank nearly twice as deeply into the snow as we had done, and that he appeared to be in an unaccountable state of intense heat and fatigue. As soon as he got quite close to us, the mystery was suddenly solved, for on his back fastened with shawls, and her face as white as the snow itself, was my maid, in a state of complete unconsciousness." They were compelled to seek shelter in a roadmender's house, which was of course unoccupied at that season of the year. "A blow or two from his (Cupelin's) powerful axe sent in the door with a crash." On entering they found no furniture of any sort, not even a "bundle of hay or straw; the place was as bare as it possibly could be. The operation of making ourselves comfortable was carried out in this wise. First of all Cupelin brought up the door which he had broken in. It was placed across the two portmanteaus, thus forming a table. A candle, which Cupelin triumphantly produced from the depths of one of his pockets, was lit and made to stand upright on the table. The night was bitterly cold. I had the rope as my pillow, and a thin shawl as my sole wrap, and, when he had settled us, Cupelin took some stones which he had put in the fire to heat, and placed them against our feet. He himself would not lie down, but sat over the crackling wood, carefully gathering the little bits together from time to time, and thus economizing our limited stock of fuel."

In many ways he has more the "cut" and temperament of the Oberländer than of the Chamoniard. He possesses, however, in a marked degree all that courtesy of manner which is so strong a characteristic even of those Chamonix guides who are by no means near the top of their profession. He often reminds one irresistibly of a big, good-natured schoolboy who is out for a holiday; no one of a party ever seems to enjoy the ascent half so much as he does, no matter how hard the work may have been, of which he always contrives to do the greater share. In appearance he is undoubtedly the *beau idéal* of a guide.

C. D. C.

J. J. Maquignaz.

Of the four great nations whose boundaries march with Switzerland, perhaps none has more thoroughly explored its own frontiers and mountains than Italy. As well in the Southern Graians as in the Ortler and Adamello districts, Italian climbers have ascended nearly every peak which has a claim to notice. The love for their own country, and the delight in all that is beautiful, which are the especial birthrights of every Italian, coupled with that sturdy *physique* so peculiarly characteristic of the races of Northern Italy, have made it only natural that they should scale the great stone and ice ramparts of their native land. In this work of exploration and conquest, there is one man who, *par excellence*, has taken a foremost part. JEAN JOSEPH MAQUIGNAZ was born, as his friend and rival Jean Antoine Carrel, at Val Tournanche in 1829. This tiny village has probably produced more good all-round guides than any other of its size throughout the whole of the Alps. In one respect Maquignaz holds a unique position among guides. No one else of any distinction in the craft has ever identified himself so completely with his own nationality, or has shown such loyal pride in the laurels he has helped his countrymen to win. "He had received many offers for the Géant," Signor Alessandro Sella writes, "but did not accept them because he would only have the Italian flag on the summit." All Maquignaz's best achievements and new expeditions have been on his own mountains, and many a climber at Zermatt, who may possibly never have seen him, is familiar with his name as being the great authority on the southern side of the range. As the list of his first ascents shows, Maquignaz has in recent years been chiefly employed by the various members of the Sella family, but among the other well-known Italians he has travelled with, may be mentioned the names of Signor Baretti, Professor of Geology at Turin, Signor Felix Giordano, the well-known engineer, and the Cavaliere Alessandro Martelli.

Comparatively few Englishmen have been with him; the name best known among them being that of Professor Tyndall, with whom he crossed the Matterhorn for the first time; an expedition to which we shall presently have occasion to refer. In recording it at the time in Maquignaz's *livret*, Professor Tyndall wrote of him, "that he was calm in danger, strong where strength is required." And out of the hundreds of certificates which have been written of guides, it would indeed be hard to find such a truthful and accurate delineation of character more happily expressed.

Maquignaz's name will always be associated with the early history of the Matterhorn, the mountain on which he first became known as a bold and fearless rock-climber. It was in 1867, after that peak had twice been ascended from the Italian side by J. A. Carrel, that a party of Val Tournanche guides set out in order to try and discover for themselves the route by which they also might be able to conduct travellers to the summit. They were eight in number; Maquignaz and his brother and five other Val Tournanche guides, including J. B. Carrel, whose daughter accompanied the party. The two Maquignaz succeeded in reaching the summit, and this very laudable expedition was rewarded by their discovery of a much easier route than that taken by J. A. Carrel in his two previous ascents. The brothers had not long to wait before they commenced to reap the fruit of their energy and enterprise; and in a few weeks they again made the ascent with Mr. W. Leighton Jordan.

The following season (1868), Maquignaz crossed the Matterhorn from Breuil to Zermatt with Professor Tyndall, and five days later he returned by exactly the reverse route from Zermatt to Breuil with M. F. Thioly and M. J. Hoiler of Geneva. In one of the most spirited chapters in 'Hours of Exercise in the Alps,' Professor Tyndall describes his own expedition. "My desire," he says, "was to finish for ever my contest with the Matterhorn by making a pass over its summit from Breuil to Zermatt." Speaking of Maquignaz, he goes on to say, "He was the leader of our little party, and a brave, cool, and competent leader he proved himself to be. He was silent save when he answered to his brother's anxious and oft-repeated questions, 'Es-tu bien placé, Joseph?'" Along with being perfectly cool and brave, he seemed to be perfectly truthful. He did not pretend to be 'bien placé' when he was not, nor avow a power of holding which he knew he did not possess." Then he goes on to say, "Joseph, if I may use the term, is a man of high boiling-point, his constitutional *sang-froid* resisting the ebullition of fear."

It was in 1882 that Maquignaz made the first ascent of the Aiguille du Géant, with Signor Alessandro Sella and three other members of that well-known family. His name was thus brought once more prominently before the climbing public. Whatever individual opinions may be held as to how far it is legitimate or not to use 'artificial means' in a new ascent; all must unite in admiration of the indomitable pluck, perseverance and courage which Maquignaz and his companions displayed during the successive attempts which paved the way for their ultimate ascent. On more than one occasion, Maquignaz's son and nephew (the other guides of the party) stood one above the other on his shoulders, he supporting their weight till the highest of the three could fix a rope, or drive a stanchion into a fissure in the rock. And any one who has seen a somewhat similar *tour de force* in the 'ring' of a circus, can understand the nerve required for the performance of such a feat upon a tiny bracket of rock, on the side of the smooth sloping precipices of the Géant. During their *tentatives*, Maquignaz took with him a fir-pole three mètres and a half in length, which was used as a ladder, and was left by him on the lower of the twin summits of the peak. The higher summit, which under ordinary circumstances is perfectly easy of access in some ten minutes from the lower, was not attained until somewhat later in the year by a subsequent party. This *bâton* has been the means of determining the exact difference in height between the two summits. In 1883 it was planted on the lower peak, and by crouching down upon the higher of the two, and using a half-empty bottle as a level, the top of the fir-pole seemed to be exactly the same height as the point from which we were making the observation. A good idea of the rocks of the Géant may be formed from one of Mr. Donkin's enlarged photographs, in which a well-known member of the Alpine Club and his two guides are seen standing on the top of the higher peak. For the last two years this photograph has been exhibited in Spooner's window in the Strand, and many a British workman going home from his day's labours, has been heard to express in more or less forcible Saxon to his mates, the extreme perplexity which he evidently felt as to the means by which the party had arrived at their elevated position; and this feeling any one who has ever examined the peak itself from the Col du Géant with a glass, will certainly have shared. Maquignaz possesses an interesting *souvenir* of the ascent. Pasted in his *livret* is a telegram from his old patron, Quintino Sella, the distinguished statesman, who, as father of three of the chief actors in the ascent, and President of the Italian Alpine Club, congratulates Maquignaz in the hour of his triumph. "Come Padre, come Presidente Club Alpino Italiano, plaudo vivamente vostro coraggio, vostra prudenza ascenzione Dente Gigante, senza disgrazie sarà vanto vostro onore guide Alpine Italiano."

Maquignaz's name also will always be especially associated with mountaineering in winter. Few guides can show a better record of work done at that season of the year. Among his principal ascents are—The Matterhorn from Breuil, on the 17th March, 1882, with Signor Vittorio Sella. On the 30th January, 1884, with the same gentleman, he ascended the Dufour-spitze; and the following year, on the 2nd March, 1885, made the ascent of the Grand Paradis from Valsavaranche. On the 22nd of March, 1885, with the Signori Vittorio Corradino, and Alfonso Sella, starting from the Col d'Olen, he reached the summit of the Lyskamm by the S.W. arête. This expedition occupied twenty-two hours. On the 18th January, 1886, he crossed the Lys Joch to Zermatt, making *en route* the ascent of the Signal Kuppe with the Signori Corradino and Gaudenzio Sella. In January, 1888, with the four Signori Sella and Emile Rey, he crossed the summit of Mont Blanc from the *cabane* of the Aiguilles-Grises to Chamonix, a feat which may be considered as one of the most remarkable *tours de force* ever made in the high Alps in winter. I am indebted to Cavaliere Alessandro Martelli, the well-known member of the Italian Alpine Club, for a list of Maquignaz's new expeditions, from which I have selected the most important. In 1867 a variation of J. A. Carrel's route on the Italian side of the Matterhorn, which has since been generally adopted. In 1874 the Becca de l'Invergnan or Grande Rousse de Valgrisanche, and the Col de la Grande Rousse de Valgrisanche, with Cav. Martelli, the Abbé Gorret and Signor Leopoldo Barale. With Signor Lüigi Vaccarone in 1878, he ascended the Tour du Grand St.

Pierre from the south. And in 1882, he made the first ascent of the Aiguille du Géant, with Signori Alessandro, Gaudenzio, Alfonso and Corradino Sella.

Maquignaz is as popular among his friends, as he is justly esteemed and respected by his employers. Many Italian guides seem to have the doggedness and courage of the Oberländer with the refinement and courtesy of the best class of Chamoniards. And with these are blended all the frankness, cheerful temperament and enthusiasm of their own race. All these characteristics Maquignaz possesses in a very marked degree, and he may be taken as a typical representative of the best school of Italian guides.

C. D. C.

J.-A. Carrel.

Every man who has reached the top of the tree in his profession—from an Archbishop or a Lord Chancellor downward—is prone to recall some incident

in his early career from which he dates the first upward step on the ladder which led to supreme distinction. This may chance to be some brilliant stroke of genius he has unexpectedly displayed, but it is far more frequently an occasion when the opportunity has arisen of giving proof of hard work or long research, honestly and ungrudgingly undertaken, without any thought at the time of immediate reward and of profiting by the labours which a less conscientious man would have been tempted either to scamp altogether or to perform in a slovenly manner. In no other profession do we more frequently meet with instances of this than in that of a guide, and no better case in point could be cited than that of JEAN-ANTOINE CARREL, whose name was first brought to the notice of climbers by the frequent attacks he made on the Matterhorn.

In Carrel's early days the inhabitants of the valleys within sight of that weird mass of rock still firmly believed the uncanny legends about the spirits who were said to harbour on its precipitous slopes. The "Mountain Gloom" hung over Zermatt as heavily in 1865 as it had done a century before. The Cervin must hold as prominent a place in Carrel's recollection of his childhood and early days, as it has since taken in his career as a guide. When Jean-Antoine was a bad boy, as the greatest statesmen and divines, and even the most eminent guides, are admitted sometimes to have been, the censors of juvenile morality in Tournanche doubtless employed some expression equivalent to "Matterhorn Bogey will fetch you" with which to terrify the young evil-doer. On half-holidays, when playing with his friend Jean Joseph Maquignaz (who, by the way, was born in 1829—the same year as himself), and the other village lads, they were doubtless wont to make mimic ascents of the Cervin on the rocks which rise among the tiny patches of cultivation in the valley. And little did the neighbours dream at the time, as they looked up for a moment from their hoe or their sickle, that one of these noisy, laughing urchins was destined to play such a distinguished part in the history of that great peak. The Matterhorn is to Val Tournanche what Mont Blanc is to Chamonix, and the former peak seems to have exercised as powerful a fascination for Jean-Antoine Carrel, as the latter had for Jacques Balmat.

Referring to the ordinary routine of a guide at the time of the commencement of Carrel's career, Signor A. Martelli writes, "The profession of guide at Val Tournanche had then no other scope than to conduct travellers over the Théodule and make ascents of the Breithorn." It is easy to understand how a man of such fearless and adventurous nature as Carrel longed for more ambitious and worthier outlets for his energies than excursions such as these could furnish, and so during the years 1858 and 1859 we find him taking part in several of the first attempts ever made to gain the summit of the Cervin. Those who were chiefly associated with him in these *tentatives* were Jean Jacques Carrel, Victor Carrel, the Abbé Gorret, and Gabriel Maquignaz. The subject of the present sketch is one of the very few distinguished guides, and their names may be counted on the fingers of one hand, who have systematically made attempts on unascended peaks either by themselves or accompanied only by their neighbours, and have done so, not for the mere sake of bagging the prize-money, but rather in order to gain for themselves the laurels of victory. This is a very remarkable trait in Carrel's character.

In the account of his "first scramble on the Matterhorn," in Mr. Whymper's well-known work, to which I am greatly indebted for many of the details in this sketch, that distinguished climber relates his first meeting with Carrel in 1861. "Up to this time," he writes, "my experience with guides had not been fortunate, and I was inclined, improperly, to rate them at a low value. They represented to me pointers out of paths, and large consumers of meat and drink, but little more; and, with the recollection of Mont Pelvoux, I should have greatly preferred the company of a couple of my countrymen to any number of guides." Then he goes on to say, "When walking up towards Breil we inquired for another man of all the knowing ones, and they with one voice proclaimed Jean-Antoine Carrel, of the village of Val Tournanche, the cock of his valley. We sought, of course, for Carrel, and found him a well-made, resolute-looking fellow, with a certain defiant air which was rather taking. Yes, he would go. Twenty francs a day, whatever was the result, was his price. I assented. But I must take his comrade. 'Why so?' Oh, it was absolutely impossible to get along without another man. I demurred, the negotiations broke off, and we went up to Breil." In the same chapter Mr. Whymper relates how, when he was passing the night in the highest cow-shed in the valley, previous to his first attempt on the great peak, he saw, stealing up the hill-side, the forms of Jean-Antoine Carrel and the comrade. 'Oh, ho!' I said, 'you have repented?' 'Not at all; you deceive yourself.' 'Why, then, have you come here?' 'Because we ourselves are going on the mountain to-morrow.' 'Oh, then it is *not* necessary to have more than three?' 'Not for us.' I admired their pluck, and had a strong inclination to engage the pair, but finally decided against it. The comrade turned out to be J. J. Carrel, who had been with Mr. Hawkins, and was nearly related to the other man. Both were bold mountaineers, but Jean-Antoine was incomparably the better man of the two, and he is the finest rock-climber I have ever seen. He was the only man who persistently refused to accept defeat, and who continued to believe, in spite of all discouragements, that the great mountain was not inaccessible, and that it could be ascended from the side of his native valley."

The following season (1862) Carrel received an engagement from Mr. Whymper and Mr. Reginald Macdonald. "We thought ourselves fortunate," writes the former, "for Carrel clearly considered the mountain a kind of preserve and regarded our late attempt as an act of poaching." The various attacks Mr. Whymper made on the Cervin between the years 1861 and 1865 are most graphically described in his popular volume, and together form one of the most fascinating narratives of mountain conquest. Before his final and successful assault, and when the hopes of victory had become almost assured, Mr. Whymper once more wished to engage Jean-Antoine; but in spite of this tempting offer, Carrel was naturally bound to fulfil an engagement he had made with the Signori Sella and Giordano, who intended to make an attempt from the Italian side. Thus it was that Carrel did not stand by Mr. Whymper's side on the summit on the eventful morning of the 14th of July. The pages in which Mr. Whymper describes his arrival on the summit are, perhaps, the most thrilling and exciting in the whole of his work. All the way from Zermatt, Lord Francis Douglas, the Rev. C. Hudson, and the rest of the party had constantly raised many false alarms of "men on the summit." They knew that Carrel's party were at that very time making their way up the cliffs on the other side. "The higher we rose the more intense became the excitement," wrote Mr. Whymper. Even when they reached the ridge which formed the summit they did not know but that the Italians might have been at its further extremity. "I hastened to the southern end, scanning the snow right and left eagerly. Hurrah! again; it was untrodden. 'Where were the men?' I peered over the cliff, half doubting, half expectant. I saw them immediately—mere dots on the ridge, at an immense distance below. Up went my arms and my hat. 'Croz, we must make those fellows hear us;' we yelled until we were hoarse. The Italians seemed to regard us, we could not be certain. 'Croz, we must make them hear us, they shall hear us!' I seized a block of rock and hurled it down, and called upon my companion, in the name of friendship, to do the same. We drove our sticks in, and prized away the crags, and soon a torrent of stones poured down the cliffs. There was no doubt about it this time, the Italians turned and fled." It was indeed a "most merciful dispensation," as we say north of the Tweed, that the Italians had the good sense to keep out of the way of the cannonade which Mr. Whymper and his friends kept up, else a catastrophe might have taken place on the southern side, even of a more appalling nature than the one which occurred a few hours later on the Zermatt face of the mountain. The unfortunate Italians doubtless occupied an equally unenviable position to that in which Mr. Whymper depicts himself in that beautiful engraving of "A Cannonade on the Matterhorn," which faces page 127 in 'Scrambles amongst the Alps.' Writing afterwards of the hour of his triumph, and referring to those who had so nearly taken the prize from his grasp, Mr. Whymper says:—"Still, I would that the leader of that party could have stood with us at that moment, for our victorious shouts conveyed to him the disappointment of the ambition of a lifetime. He was the man of all those who attempted the ascent of the Matterhorn, who most deserved to be the first upon its summit. He was the first to doubt its inaccessibility, and he was the only man who persisted in believing that its ascent would be accomplished." It had been the "aim of his life to make the ascent from the side of Italy for the honour of his native valley." It would be impossible for guides of any nationality to exhibit a greater amount of patriotism in their work of conquest among the great peaks which form their frontier, than those of Italy; and any regrets which Carrel experienced from not being the leader of those who first scaled the peak must have been more than counterbalanced when a couple of days later in company with the Abbé Gorret, he and J. Baptiste Bic gained the summit by the Italian side, and planted upon it the flag of the country they both loved so well. The conflict for the Matterhorn was as hard as it had been long; it occupied some seven seasons. The interest in the drama was kept up to its close; and, as we have seen, the last heat in the final struggle became almost a "neck and neck" race.

Carrel's name will always be inseparably associated with that of Mr. Whymper. Along with his son Louis he accompanied that distinguished climber in an expedition among the great Andes of Ecuador; they left Southampton in November, 1879, and returned to London in August of the following year. Their greatest achievements were the ascents of Chimborazo (20,517 feet), and of Cotopaxi (19,550 feet). Mr. Whymper's diary is given in the tenth volume of the *Alpine Journal*, and from its perusal we can form a good idea of the amount of hard work which the party had to undertake, and the privations they endured. The following extracts may be taken as a fair sample of the sixty odd pages of diary in the *Alpine Journal*, and give some conception of the almost insurmountable obstacles and difficulties this brave trio of explorers encountered at nearly every step.

From the First to the Second Camp on Chimborazo.

Dec. 27.—Shortly after arrival all the party except Perring had frightful headaches, and felt much exhausted (although all had ridden up the entire distance from Guaranda), and retired to bed early, feeling incapable of making the least exertion. The height of the second camp was 16,600 feet. Minimum temperature in night was again 21° Fahr.

Dec. 28.—Three inches of snow around the tent in the morning. All except Perring completely incapable, and lying panting in the tent. Found that much of the tinned meat had gone bad, and had it thrown away down the mountain side.

Dec. 29.—The Carrels were somewhat better and were eager to be off exploring. Sent them away at 7.50 a.m. to continue the ascent of the ridge on which the camp was placed, instructing them not to try to go to any great height, and to look out for another and higher camping-place. They returned at 6.30 p.m. quite exhausted, having made a push towards the summit and reached a height of nearly 19,000 feet.

Dec. 30.—At the second camp. Both Carrels *hors de combat*, lying down in the tent most of the day. Eyes of both badly inflamed, especially J.-A. Carrel's. Louis becoming better towards midday, sent him with Perring to fetch up the second tent from the first camp. They returned just at nightfall, having found it as much as they could manage to carry.

Out of the two hundred and twelve days which the party passed in the interior of the country, there were only four at which they found themselves under 6000 feet above the level of the sea. Thirty-six nights were passed at elevations over 14,000 feet. The continued bad weather which the party seems to have encountered must have thrown a gloom in more senses than one over the expedition. Writing of their second ascent of Chimborazo, Mr. Whymper says, "Our last ascent in Ecuador, like the first one, and all intermediate ones, rendered no view from the summit." On his return to England, Mr. Whymper gave an account of his travels at an Extraordinary General Meeting of the Alpine Club, which was honoured by the presence of H.R.H. the Prince of Wales, and a "distinguished and select company." Mr. Whymper on that occasion succeeded "in attracting the attention of Royalty itself" to his platform, a distinction which I believe only one other Alpine lecturer can lay claim to.

The Cavaliere Alessandro Martelli has kindly furnished me with a list of the new expeditions made by Jean-Antoine Carrel, from which the following are selected. As early as 1857 he made the first ascent of the Tête du Lion in company with the Abbé Gorret. In 1863 he scaled for the first time the Pic du Grand Tournalin from Val Tournanche, and made the first passage of the Breuiljoch from Breuil to Zermatt. As we have already stated, he made the first ascent of the Matterhorn from the Italian side in 1865. In 1872 he made the first ascent of Mont Blanc from the Italian side, by way of the Aiguilles Grises, with Mr. T. S. Kennedy. During 1875 he made the first passage of the Col Budden, and scaled for the first time the Punta Sella with Signor Guisoppe Corona. Mr. R. H. Budden has kindly pointed to me that J.-A. Carrel has made routes up the following great peaks from the Italian side: Matterhorn, Mont Blanc, Monte Rosa, and the Dent d'Hérens. His expedition to South America with Mr. Whymper, during which Chimborazo and Cotopaxi were ascended, may be considered the most remarkable one yet undertaken by Alpine guides in distant regions. No mountaineers have ever returned from any quarter of the globe with such a long list of splendid achievements, and probably none have ever experienced so many hardships, or carried on their work under more unfortunate conditions, so far at least as weather and surroundings were concerned.

Each guide whose life is given in this work has, like the *Herren* who employ him, some marked trait of character, some peculiarity in his "form," which even those whom he had only accompanied on a single glacier expedition cannot fail to have remarked, and which they afterwards always associate with him. A. may be noted for his clumsy if otherwise effective method, B. for his great strength, and in the irreproachable blandness of C.'s manners we may still recognize the influence which the years he spent in a Jesuit Seminary have exercised upon his bearing. No guide in the Alps conveys the idea of being possessed of such dogged determination as Jean-Antoine Carrel. There is something about the set of his mouth which almost reminds one of a bull-dog. Not the *bouledogue* in the caricatures of the Englishman in Paris, but the trusty companion whom we all must have met at some time or other, who is never averse to our advances, save when it appears to him we try to assume his master's place or encroach upon his rights. Any one who has ever been with Carrel on a mountain must have been impressed with his enormous strength. Some seasons ago while we were crossing the Col d'Herens, an unsuspected snow-bridge gave way, and I suddenly found myself in the most ignominious of all positions which it is possible for a climber to occupy —suspended in mid-air in a huge crevasse, with the rope gradually tightening round my chest in a way which was highly suggestive of the fact that if it was much tighter breathing would become difficult. And never shall I forget the gruff though cheery tones of Carrel's voice when he called out from above, "Ne craignez rien." It made one almost wish to pause for a moment to look down at the wonderful forms of pale blue and green ice in the huge cavern below me, before endeavouring with the assistance of the guides "to land." It is, however, as a cragsman rather than as an ice-man that Carrel is seen at his best. He may be said to climb in the most "powerful form," and those who have watched him on a difficult piece of rock will not easily forget the masterly and determined way in which he swarms up places which one would have considered to be perfectly impossible. For many years he and J. J. Maquignaz were justly considered to be the two great authorities on the Italian side of the Matterhorn.

Carrel has a fund of dry humour, and his conversation is always racy and very much to the point. In his younger days he must have been the "Lauener" of the Italian guides. There is that "splendid swagger" about his gait and manner which was such a marked characteristic of the three brothers of Lauterbrunnen. Indeed, there is probably more of the Oberlander about Carrel than any of the other well-known Italian guides. With his great strength and determination of character, are combined many of those qualities which have won for such a large number of guides of his race the warm esteem in which they are held, not only among their own countrymen, but by climbers of every nationality.

Carrel is called the "Bersagliere," from his having served in that most distinguished corps. He was "out" in two campaigns and fought at Solferino. No guide was ever more jealous for the honour of his country, and of all the many brave sons of Italy who have scaled her great mountain boundaries, no name is worthier to be held in remembrance than that of Jean-Antoine Carrel.

C. D. C.

Emile Rey.

EMILE REY was born at Courmayeur in 1846. Not till he was thirty years of age did he receive his first offer of a long engagement; but during 1876 and the two following years he was retained for the greater part of each season by Lord Wentworth. It was, however, with Mr. J. Baumann and Mr. J. O. Maund that his name began to be known as one of the boldest and most skilful rock-climbers in the Alps. With them he made a series of most difficult *tentatives*, among which may be mentioned those on the Aiguille du Plan from the Plan des Aiguilles, and the Eiger from the Mitteleggi arête. Referring to this latter attempt, Mr. Baumann wrote in Emile's *livret* in 1881: "Rey alone and unroped succeeded in turning a very difficult overhanging rock, and proceeded along the arête to a point which has never before been reached." This feat it is impossible for any one fully to appreciate, who has not stood on some part of that stupendous ridge of rock and ice. That Rey should have surpassed his two companions on this occasion, must not for one moment be regarded as a reflection on their skill and courage. He was the junior, and had not established the position he now holds as a guide. His keen Italian temperament was brought into contrast with the more easy-going natures of the Oberländer.

Rey's career did not begin till what has been called the "great age of conquest" in the Alps was over. But, taking into consideration the period at which he got into practice as a guide, his list of new expeditions is a highly creditable one. In 1877, while with Lord Wentworth, he ascended for the first time the Aiguille (Noire) de Peuteret, and Les Jumeaux de Valtournanche. In 1879 he took part in the first ascent of the Aiguille de Talèfre with Mr. G. FitzGerald, Mr. F. J. Cullinan, and Mr. J. Baumann. While with me in 1882, we made a first ascent of the Calotte de Rochefort, the chief summit of Les Periades, and went up the Aiguille de Talèfre, for the first time from the Italian side. In 1883 we made together the first ascent of the Lower Peak of the Aiguille du Midi. With Mr. H. S. King, C.I.E., and A. Supersax he made, in 1885, the first ascent of the Aiguille Blanche de Peuteret, thus scaling the last unascended peak in the great chain of Mont Blanc. With Herr Gruber, with whom Rey has done considerable work, he had on a previous occasion reached, from the Glacier de Brouillard, the Col which connects the Aiguille Blanche with the *massif* of Mont Blanc. The second ascents of the higher and lower peaks of the Aiguille du Dru were also made by Rey. The latter, with Mr. J. Walker Hartley, who (with Mr. C. T. Dent) made the first ascent of the Higher Peak, was accomplished without the aid of the iron stanchions employed in its first ascent, and was in the opinion of both these most experienced climbers, the hardest ascent that they have ever made. In four consecutive days Rey made the third, fourth, and fifth ascents of the Higher Peak of the Dru. One of these was the first occasion on which the peak was climbed direct from the Montanvert, without sleeping out. Referring to this feat, Mr. C. T. Dent writes: "Mr. W. E. Davidson, in a recent ascent of the mountain, was able to find his way without invoking the assistance of either ladder or fixed ropes. In a marvellously short space of time, too, did he get up and down the peak on which we had spent hours without number." In January, 1888, with the four Signori Sella and the three Maquignaz, he crossed the summit of Mont Blanc from the *cabane* of the Aiguilles Grises to Chamonix (being the third winter ascent of Mont Blanc, and the first from the Italian side), a feat which may fairly be

described as one of the most remarkable *tours de force* ever made in the high Alps in winter. Emile spent some weeks with me in England in the winter of 1884; while in Scotland we went up Ben Nevis, an ascent which he refers to more frequently than to some of his greater feats in the Alps. It is described in vol. xii. of the *Alpine Journal*.

Unlike his contemporaries at Meiringen, Jaun, Maurer, and von Bergen, Rey never had the advantage of serving an apprenticeship, as it were, with an older or more experienced guide. Nor was it from love of sport, while chamois-hunting, that Rey learned the rudiments of his craft, as so many guides have done. His reputation as one of the first rock-climbers in the Alps, and the position he holds among other guides, are the result of his own aptitude and ability, the great enthusiasm he has for his profession, and the energy and earnestness with which he pursues it. Any one who has seen Rey, Melchior, and Jaun together on a mountain, must recognize, at once, that influence which Melchior's guiding has exercised upon the younger men in his own district. Their wonderful grace of movement in scaling difficult rocks, or in step-cutting, has never yet been attained by any other 'school' of guides. Be this as it may, Rey has at least all their energy and dash, and displays to the fullest extent the same calm and unflinching courage under all circumstances, and resource in the presence of sudden danger. No greater compliment could be paid him as a guide, than to class his name with those of Hans Jaun and Andreas Maurer, men with whom he was associated on the Eiger (as elsewhere) in one of the most splendid *tentatives* on difficult rocks ever recorded. Rey always expressed the greatest admiration for the guiding powers of these men; and this was one of the reasons which led him to spend a winter in Meiringen in order to learn German, so that he might be better able to work with the Oberländer with whom he saw it would be his fate, if he were to be a leading guide, to be constantly brought into contact.

By trade, Rey is a *menuisier*, and any one who has slept in the *cabanes* of the Grand Paradis, Col du Géant, Grandes Jorasses, or Aiguilles Grises, must testify to their admirable construction, and in so doing to the thoroughness of his work. Possessed of a good business, in prosperous circumstances, and belonging to a class in life somewhat superior to the majority of guides, he has had every inducement to lead a 'stay-at-home' existence. None of Rey's *Herren* has ever yet met with an accident while with him on a mountain. He was leader of the search-party which brought the remains of Professor F. M. Balfour and his guide Petrus, killed in 1882, in an attempt on the Aiguille Blanche de Peuterct, back to Courmayeur. In the autumn of 1886 he was again engaged in a similar task, in bringing down to Grindelwald the body of Herr Munz, who was killed by an ice-avalanche on the Schreckhorn; Rey, with another party, being on the mountain at the same time, some ten minutes in advance of Herr Munz and his guides. On such occasions the onlooker, no matter how well he may have imagined himself to be acquainted with all the members of the party, may yet recognize, for the first time, qualities in those who are taking an active share in the sad day's work, which he never before associated with their character. And any one who, like myself, saw the guides engaged in their melancholy task, must always recollect the great force of character and power of organization Emile Rey displayed. Always taking the lead, but never once seeming to take command of his fellow-guides, he was on both those mournful days the moving spirit of the whole party.

Emile has always expressed decided views about the labourer being worthy of his hire; and he acts up to the opinions which many men hold regarding their own professions, although they are often loth to admit them when considering the claims of those who have risen to the top of the tree in humbler callings, but whose knowledge and experience they may, nevertheless, have availed themselves of. Rey never underrates his own power as a guide, and does not attempt to conceal that he is proud of the reputation he has won. He always draws a most distinct line between those of the higher and those of the lower grades in his craft. One morning, at the Montanvert, we were watching the arrival of the 'polyglots,' as an ingenious person once christened that crowd composed of nearly every nationality, who may daily be seen making their toilsome pilgrimage from Chamonix. Among them was an Englishman, who had first provided himself with green spectacles, a veil, and socks to go over his patent leather shoes, and who only wanted a guide to complete his preparations. Going up to Rey, and pointing first to the Mer de Glace, and then to the Chapeau, he inquired "Combiang?" "Voilà, Monsieur," replied Rey,

taking off his hat, and indicating with his left hand a group of rather poor specimens of the distinguished Société des Guides, "Voilà les guides pour la Mer de Glace; moi, je suis pour 'la Grande Montagne.'"

Throughout his whole connection with me as guide, during engagements each year lasting over a longer time than most members of the Alpine Club care to stay in the Alps, no act of his ever has tended to lessen in the slightest degree the great regard I have for him, or to mar the good fellowship which exists between us. On arriving in a hut at the end of a long day, no one can be more unmindful of his own wants or comforts. No guide ever entered more readily into whatever course his Herr suggested, whether it was an afternoon's scramble on the glacier, or the ascent of one of the great peaks. It would indeed be difficult to find a bolder cragsman, or a man more determined to gain his summit, no matter what difficulties may be in the way. But I have always found him ready to draw the line when foolhardiness was about to take the place of courage. Rey is always in condition; he never smokes, and is temperate in every sense of the word. In looking back upon the two occasions when it seemed that our climbing days must come to an end, I recall how the thought of what appeared for the moment to be inevitable, faded in the presence of the strong arm, the cool head, and indomitable pluck of my guide. His great courtesy and natural refinement of feeling, together with the naïve simplicity with which he often expresses himself, have gained for him many friends outside the climbing world. Whilst staying with me in England, he received numberless proofs of his great popularity amongst all those with whom he was thrown into contact. From my Presbyterian housekeeper, who at first naturally looked upon him with suspicion, because as a foreigner he was dimly associated in her mind with the 'Scarrlett Leddy,' to the Editor of the *Nineteenth Century*, with whom he spent an intellectual afternoon at Madame Tussaud's, every one had a good word for him.

Emile will always take the foremost place in the recollections which begin to gather round those years we have spent together amongst the mountains. In looking back upon past seasons in the Alps, I can never forget how much he has contributed to the success and pleasure of my mountaineering life.

C. D. C.

"IN MEMORIAM."

Auguste Balmat.

Most movements show in the course of their history some particular period in which the foremost place is occupied by a conspicuous figure who belongs neither to the new order of things nor to the old. It is not always easy to assign to such men the exact place which they should hold in the story of their art, but their relations both to its past and future are peculiar and striking, and their influence on its development is often considerable.

The subject of this memoir occupies among the Pioneers of the Alps the position which I have endeavoured to indicate in the foregoing sentences. He belongs neither to the class of his great-uncle Jacques Balmat, nor has he founded a school like Melchior Anderegg, yet he has a portion of the spirit of both; he does not possess their unique renown, but he holds a position of his own which is not contested by any rival, and if he has rendered services to his art, less conspicuous than those of either of them, they have been nevertheless hardly less useful. To the younger generation Auguste Balmat is but "nominis umbra;" one must read the records of the Alps to understand his history. A pleasant thing it is to turn over the leaves of these early writers, for early they seem, though they only wrote thirty years ago. To the late Professor Forbes and to Mr. Justice Wills the world owes a debt for their Alpine "Fasti" hardly less than that which it owes them for their contributions to the Science of Geology or to the elucidation of the law. They are refreshing to the mind, and there is a novelty and cheerfulness about their descriptions which is as charming as it is in the present day rare. Balmat was the constant companion of both these early chroniclers and makers of Alpine story, and to their faithful record of his career we owe most of our knowledge of the work which he did and the services he rendered to mountaineering.

Balmat was a native of Chamonix, to which place the feats of his great-uncle on the glaciers of Mont Blanc have given the prerogative claim to be held the metropolis of mountaineering, although his successors (with many brilliant exceptions) have ever sought to make that claim of none effect through their traditions. The original Balmat disappeared from the scene of his triumphs in a mysterious manner, though there is little doubt, from the very interesting investigations of Mr. Justice Wills (in 'Eagle's Nest,' p. 37), that he fell down a crevasse while searching for gold. In the valley, however, a gleam of red fire seems to have flickered over the end of his career, and adds a certain tinge of romance to the family record. Auguste Balmat, who was born in 1808, had no doubt acquired the few and simple maxims of his craft as they were known in his early days, with the intelligence and perseverance which distinguished his later efforts, and he must have been in some way conspicuous among his fellow-guides, for we find him chosen by the Curé to accompany Professor Forbes on the 24th June, 1842. This we learn was an irregular proceeding, he was chosen "out of his turn." Thus early in his history is Balmat in conflict with the strict order of things, and as his range of vision widened so do we find his antagonism to the rules of the Société des Guides growing in intensity. Between the man of Science and his guide a true and abiding friendship soon sprang up, the former valuing the fidelity and courage of Balmat, and the latter soon beginning to enter with interest into the scientific labours of his employer. He absolutely refused remuneration not only for the long hours spent with the investigator on the ice, but also for his laborious visits to their posts of observation during the winter. In after years, when ill-health had long prevented Forbes from revisiting his beloved Alps, he writes of Balmat with the warmth and affection of old and long-tried attachment. "I long to welcome him to my native town," he writes in 1858, and the same year he says, when speaking of the absence of Balmat's name from the first records of the Alpine Club, "he would still be invaluable to any man with ever so slight a tincture of Science." "I really thirst to see him again," he writes the next year; and on Balmat's death, in 1862, he writes to Dr. Symonds, "You have seen, no doubt, that our poor friend Auguste Balmat is dead. It was to me almost like a family bereavement, and has removed one of the lifelong hopes to which I clung of revisiting Chamonix in his company, with his sympathy and help." There must have been something more than fidelity and capacity to thread his way among crevasses, in the man of whom Forbes could thus speak.

But the feats of Balmat as a climber are chiefly to be found in the accounts given us of their adventures together above the snow-line by the writer of 'Wanderings among the High Alps' and 'The Eagle's Nest.' From perusing these works it is quite evident that Balmat was by no means on the level of the ordinary products of his native valley and its peculiar guide organization; he is ever ready to try something new, but never lets the love of adventure overpower the dictates of caution. He was eminently endowed with the suavity and courtesy of demeanour which still distinguish the guides of Chamonix as a school, while he possessed the thirst for continued exploration with which at the present day they are not as a body tormented. To him the mountains had lost the uncanny aspect which they bore to the climbers of the first period, but they had not assumed the garb of familiarity which in these days robs them of some of their charm. In his view their difficulties were to be met, and conquered, but there were many rules handed down by his predecessors which were to be duly observed if disaster or discomfort were to be avoided. The way over the Col du Géant was not so well known then as it is now, and the performances of Balmat along those crevasses (even now at times sufficiently formidable) elicited from the other guide the enthusiastic remark that he was "un véritable diable pour la glace." From Wills's account of their passage of the Adler Pass, it is evident he was not so much at home on rocks, though it appears he could find a way with great ease over a glacier he had not seen before; this being due to the fact, as is somewhere pointed out, that he worked by observation, not by rule of thumb, knowing well the nature of the ice, never having recourse to heaps of stones and such signs as are set up by man to point where a passage could be most safely found. He took a constant pleasure in the surrounding objects of his "course." Wills tells us that when they were on their way up to the Allalein Glacier, "Balmat as usual went grubbing about everywhere for stones, flowers, or anything else he could pick up, nothing escaped his quick eye. His knowledge is so considerable on many scientific subjects, especially in all that relates to the structure and action of glaciers, that one can seldom be long in his society without learning something." It is this intense interest in his surroundings and in the concomitants of the climb, as much as in the climb itself, which seems to connect him with the earlier school of guides, even as his love of enterprise connects him with the new.

Balmat's name cannot be linked with any number of great "first ascents." Even though he made one of the party which scaled the Wetterhorn for the first time from Grindelwald, he was not the leader in that adventure, the opening scene of the Alpine drama which seems now to have reached its fifth act. Ulrich Lauener was the avowed leader, but Balmat's counsel and experience entitled him to no small part of the credit for this performance. We have only to look at the roll of mountaineering exploits before and after the ascent of the Wetterhorn to grasp the significance of the feat. First ascents before that date (at least of peaks of any magnitude) are few and far between, but since that date conquests have succeeded one another with startling rapidity, until now the hardy climber who would scale fresh mountain-tops must seek his victims on the borders of India or among the volcanoes of Peru. As Goethe said of the skirmish of Valmy, "it has inaugurated a new epoch." Like that cannonade, which without rising to the dignity of a pitched battle yet sufficed to keep at bay the troops of Brunswick, the ascent of the Wetterhorn, though not equalling in adventures and hairbreadth escapes many similar succeeding struggles, is yet notable as the beginning of a new order and the herald of feats which, perhaps, before it was accomplished were hardly dreamed of. Balmat's conduct during the ascent is noteworthy as indicating the almost reverent spirit in which he approached an enterprise of any magnitude among the mountains. He reproved Lauener for noisy expressions of delight on the way up, regarding his shouts and his flagstaff as both more or less a challenge to Providence, though he would permit no audible appeal to Higher Powers during the descent as likely to shake the nerves. I only mention these two apparently trivial incidents as indicating the frame of mind in which Balmat regarded nature; though ready enough "Desipere in loco," he seems to have regarded mountaineering as De Tocqueville tells us we should regard life, "as a solemn business which it is our duty to carry through and terminate with honour." Both previously and subsequently to the Wetterhorn ascent, Balmat made many interesting expeditions. In the neighbourhood of Chamonix and Zermatt he made many exploring expeditions over the glaciers, and may claim the honour of having been the first Chamonix guide to introduce a lady to the mysteries of the upper ice-world of that locality. It is amusing to read the account of the preparations for this expedition which was so novel in conception and so entirely foreign to the notions of the "guide chef" in 1854, that it was only by imparting their designs "in awful secrecy" to a select few that the conspirators succeeded in evading the imposition of many unnecessary guides and troops of importunate spectators. It is satisfactory to know that the scheme was a complete success. These conflicts with the guide system of his native place were frequent in Balmat's career, and he generally came off victorious; the most notable of them deserves special mention as it is connected with an act of devotion on his part in the interests of Science which alone would serve to place him high among his fellows. In 1858 he accompanied Mr. Wills and Professor Tyndall in the month of September to the summit of Mont Blanc, in order to embed there some self-registering thermometers. The travellers were enveloped near the top in a dense mass of cloud, accompanied with snow and wind. The cold was awful, and the party had to remain some time at the top in order to bury the thermometers. Balmat actually dug the holes with his hands (the proper instrument having been left behind), and his companions only know of his devotion when they emerged, half-frozen, from their improvised shelter and found his hands so frozen that it took an hour's assiduity to restore anything like life to them. Any one who has suffered the pangs of returning circulation in a slight degree can appreciate the fortitude with which Balmat endured sufferings voluntarily incurred for the sake of his friends and for Science. But a more amusing adventure awaited the guides on their return to the valley. They had ventured to make the ascent without the regulation number of guides, they had despised the authority of traditions and of the Société des Guides. Balmat was haled before the Juge de Paix at St. Gervais; but the Government Intendant took his part, and a great blow was inflicted on the party of obstruction.

During the trial the following remark was made, which deserves to be inscribed in letters of gold in some conspicuous spot in Chamonix. "Il serait mieux que les glaciers descendraient un peu plus bas et écraseraient quelques de ces gens si ignorants, si rétrogrades, afin que les autres pourraient marcher un peu mieux sans eux." (This incident is told at greater length in the Introduction to this work.)

One is glad to learn that although Balmat refused any pecuniary remuneration for his gallant conduct on Mont Blanc, he received from the illustrious Savants gathered together at a meeting of the British Association shortly afterwards rounds of enthusiastic applause when Professor Tyndall recounted the incident of the burying of the thermometer in the midst of the raging snowstorm. In the same year Balmat ascended Monte Rosa with Mr. Wills, and this seems to have been one of the last of his great climbs, though we must not forget to mention that he spent the night on Mont Blanc with Professor Tyndall's party in 1859, a feat never since attempted. A new generation of climbers had arisen, and soon created a new class of guides. Professor Forbes mentions in a letter of that year, with strong feeling, that Balmat "is too good to sink into a mere ladies' guide." That this was no doubt true, his performances in the summer of that year sufficiently prove, but his active career was practically at the end. He had ushered in the new order, but did not actively participate in its triumphs, though he must have sympathized with them. True to his rôle of opposition to antiquated prejudice, he rendered Mr. Wills yeoman's service in his struggle with the high and dry Church party in Sixt when endeavouring to induce them to sell him a parcel of land for the building of a house, whence the Curé pictured the descent of heresy in its most malignant forms on his defenceless flock. The party of reform triumphed and the house was built, so well known to many travellers since as "The Eagle's Nest." It was here that Balmat died in October, 1862, watched and tended to the last by his companion "in many difficulties and some dangers." His death was caused by grief at pecuniary embarrassment, brought about by his own reckless kindness to his friends and neighbours. During the whole of his career he had always shown the most perfect disinterestedness regarding money-matters. A broken heart was a sad end for one who had ever shown kindliness to all men, devotion to science, and reverence for nature. Since his time there have been many guides more adventurous and skilful, but few who have understood as well the real dignity of their calling, and none whose career it can be more pleasant to record both by reason of its unique position in Alpine story and of the noble qualities of the hero.

W. B. D.

Auguste Simond.

AUGUSTE SIMOND was a native of the valley of Chamonix. He was born in 1816, and died in 1870, at the comparatively early age of fifty-four. He lived in a picturesque cottage near Argentière, on the right bank of the Arve, close to the water's edge, approached by a foot-bridge over the river from the path to the Col de Balme. He was a friend of the well-known Auguste Balmat.

The first record of his mountain work is in connection with the ascent of the Wetterhorn, from Grindelwald, made in the autumn of 1854, by Mr. Alfred, now Mr. Justice Wills, described in the 'Wanderings in the High Alps,' pp. 267—315, and so frequently alluded to in these pages.

In the year 1856 Simond was recommended by Auguste Balmat to my brother and myself, and acted as our guide in the expeditions among the mountains of Bagnes described in the fourth chapter of the first series of 'Peaks, Passes, and Glaciers.' From the Val de Bagnes we went by way of the Col d'Érin to Zermatt, and finally, in company with a very large party, made one of the early ascents of Monte Rosa. In 1857, Simond again accompanied me as guide. He was engaged in the first ascent of the Finsteraarhorn by English travellers, described in Chapter XI. of the volume above-mentioned, and a few days later in the first ascent by a traveller of the Grand Combin, in which, however, owing to the loss of time caused by wading through fresh snow, we succeeded only in reaching the summit of the northern and slightly lower of the two culminating pinnacles. This was the last excursion I made with Simond. He had suffered considerably from the labour of making footholes in the snow, and in following seasons recommended me to younger men. I saw him again at Chamonix in 1866, when he seemed in feeble health.

Auguste Simond practised his vocation at a time which formed an epoch in the history of mountaineering. He had been bred under the influence of the strict Chamonix traditions, when the average climber limited his ambition to a visit to the Jardin, and the more daring regarded the passage of the Col du Géant or the ascent of Mont Blanc as the crowning effort of a life. He belonged to a school of which Auguste Balmat may be cited as a typical representative. They were men familiar with all the well-trodden routes of their own district, as a rule, good leaders on ice and snow, prudent and persevering, and invariably courteous and loyal to their employers. But they suffered from the benumbing effect of the Chamonix rules, which by putting every man on the same level, denied to superior capacity its just pecuniary reward. It is not surprising that some of these men, when suddenly called upon to traverse the Alps from Monte Viso to the Gross Glockner and to engage continually in new expeditions, should occasionally fail in technical skill or be deficient in dash and enterprise.

In Simond's time the now familiar *piolet* was all but unknown. He travelled with an ordinary alpenstock and a common hatchet. On one excursion from the Riffel the latter was forgotten, and his party returned helpless from the foot of the Adler, when within a short distance of the summit of the Strahlhorn. In 1856, after a long study of the Grand Combin, he pronounced it "inaccessible," but in the following year his dogged tenacity in pounding steps in the soft snow, with which the mountain was covered, alone enabled the party to reach the summit. Although he cannot be said to have been in the front rank of his profession, his many good qualities endeared him to his employers, by whom he will always be gratefully remembered.

W. M.

Christian Michel.

IF Chamonix was the cradle of mountain guides, the Bernese Oberland has been to them as a fostering-mother. A district which has produced the Lauener, the Michels, the Almers, the Baumanns, the Kaufmanns, the Andereggs, the Jauns, and the Maurers, can give an account of itself equal to that of any Alpine centre—in regard to guides.

Christian, who was born in 1817, was the elder of the two brothers Michel, known in their day as reliable among their own mountains; and Christian, certainly, had experience further afield. Amongst his principal expeditions, the first ascent of the Gross Schreckhorn, in 1861, when along with his brother Peter and Christian Kaufmann, he guided Mr. Leslie Stephen, stands out perhaps as the foremost and the most noticeable. Readers of 'Peaks, Passes, and Glaciers' will not have forgotten the graphic epigram of Mr. Stephen, when he likens their "flattened out" quartett—at a certain *mauvais pas* on the rocks—to "beasts of ill repute nailed to a barn." Christian was leading at the moment.

In 1862, he travelled with Mr. F. W. Jacomb over the Strahleck to the Grimsel Hospice; thence over the Gauli Joch up the Ewig Schneehorn, and so *viâ* the Urner Alp and Weitsattel to Rosenlaui. This ascent of the Ewig Schneehorn was the first by an Englishman. In the same year he formed one of the party of guides who pioneered Mr. Leslie Stephen, the late Mr. A. W. Moore, and others in the first passage of the Jungfrau Joch, an expedition made memorable on account of the plucky endurance of Peter Rubi, who carried a ponderous ladder all day on his back, to enable the party to scale the crevasses of the Guggi glacier. A maiden passage of the Viescher Joch was also effected by Christian, in 1862, along with Mr. Leslie Stephen's party—thus opening out a route direct from the Grindelwald Eismeer to the Viescher glacier (the Agassiz Joch was not crossed until five years later).

In 1863 Christian and Peter accompanied Herr Baedeker and Herr von Fellenberg in their ascent of the Silberhorn, by a roundabout route viâ the Guggi glacier and the head of the Giessen glacier, from the Wengern Alp, having passed the previous night under the Schneehorn; he was Mr. Jacomb's principal guide in the first passage of the saddle between the Bergli Stock and the Rosenhorn, now known as the Bergli Joch; and, with Peter, he crossed the Jungfrau Joch as guide to Mr. Jacomb and Mr. Reunison by a route different from that which had been taken by Mr. Leslie Stephen's party the previous year, as they skirted the actual base of the Jungfrau itself much more closely than on the occasion of the first passage of the Joch. He was with Mr. Jacomb and Mr. Chater, the same year, in a new mountain route from the Eggischhorn to Zermatt,—first, by the Binnen and Lang Thals south of the Rhone valley over the Ritter Joch to Cormi; thence by the Kaltenwasser Joch, between Monte Leone and the Wasenhorn, to Simpeln; and afterwards by the Flotsch Joch, between the Laquinhorn and the Rossbodenhorn, to Saas im Grund. Rockwork and ice couloirs swept with stones combined to render this expedition very hazardous and difficult.

In 1864 he went with Mr. F. F. Tuckett to the Eastern Alps. The enterprise of this year was great. Commencing in the Bernese Oberland, and amongst other expeditions in that district making with Mr. Tuckett the first passage of the Beichgrat,—they went over the Joch pass into the valley of Engelberg, and left the Oberland behind by the Grassen Joch, the first time in all likelihood that it had been used. On their way to the Engadine they started from the Plazbi chålets, which lie towards the head of the Val Tuors in the Albula district, for the highest summit of the Piz Kesch, which they reached, and thence descended to Madulein by the Eschia Pass—both new expeditions. During the next few days in the Grisons, Mr. Tuckett and his friends, Mr. E. N. Buxton and Mr. H. E. Buxton, accompanied by their guides Christian Michel, Franz Biener, and Peter Jenni, crossed the Fuorcla Sella to the Fellaria Alp, and made thence in a single expedition, next day, the maiden passage of the Fuorcla Crast' Agüzza, the first ascent of the Piz Zupo by travellers, the first passage of the Fuorcla Zupo which lies between the Piz Zupo and the Bella Vista,—and so back on to the upper névé of the Fellaria Glacier and the watershed of the Palü Glacier, recrossing the frontier once again into the Grisons by a pass which Mr. Tuckett has named after the Pizzo di Verona, at the southern base of which it lies. They slept at Le Prese. The actual distance covered that day was not excessive, but the achievement of three new passes and an almost virgin summit on the same day is worthy of mention. The party, excepting Peter Jenni, thence moved on to the Ortler district, where they accomplished the following:—Monte Confinale, first ascent by travellers,—the first passage of the Madatsch Joch, and the discovery of the true character and rank as well as the first ascent of Monte Cristallo, thus unravelling the mystery in which this group had long been shrouded. The second ascent of the Königsspitze and the first passage of the Königs Joch rapidly succeeded, and a new route up the Ortler, the summit of which had not been reached at all for thirty years previously. The above are specimens selected from a longer total of expeditions, to which Christian was a partner in that eventful year. It may be doubted whether at any epoch of Alpine history, a greater number of events has often been scored by any one of Christian's successors in a single campaign than those which are credited to him in 1864, especially when the varied field over which they extend is taken into account. Mr. Tuckett rewards his guide by writing these words in his Führerbuch: "He is first-rate on ice and rock, and appears able to bear almost any amount of fatigue, and when associated with other guides is always ready to do more than his own share of the work."

Christian was more than forty years of age when he ascended the Schreckhorn with Mr. Leslie Stephen, so that it cannot be any great matter for surprise to find that the expeditions entered in his Führerbuch, which by the way commences with Mr. Stephen's notice of the Schreckhorn climb, are not very numerous in any year, except in 1864. After leaving Mr. Tuckett that season, he joined Mr. P. H. Lawrence, and was with him, chiefly in the Bernina group and other parts of the Grisons and in the neighbourhood of the Disgrazia, from August 12th to October 7th. In 1866 he made the first ascent of the Wellhorn with Herr von Fellenberg, and with him climbed the Mönch from the

Little Scheideck for the first time; and he revisited the Bernina district with Dr. Hermann Weber in the same season. In 1867 he ascended the Eiger with Professor Tyndall, who writes that he cannot too strongly recommend him,— "He is a first-rate guide both on rocks and ice. I have never travelled with a more careful man." His records cease at the end of the season of 1875, and the last testimonial given to his worth bears out the experiences of former employers. After that date his health no longer allowed of active work, until he died on June 20th, 1880. He was a man of few words, solid, and steady, superior as a guide to his brother Peter. "What seemed to excite him more than anything else," says Mr. Jacomb, "was, when I boiled a top or pass with the hypsometrical apparatus. He would lie down in the snow, with his eye level with the thermometer, watching eagerly for the rise as the boiling-point was reached, and exclaiming, 'Es kommt! Es kommt!'" Physically very strong, his legs perhaps were better than his head. He was slow on foot, and seems to have been drowsy in the morning before a start. Referring to their bivouacs together, Mr. Jacomb says of a certain *gîte*, "I had been for some hours wet through, so I immediately divested myself of my habiliments, which were hung to drip, whilst I put on the scant supply my knapsack contained, and squeezed myself into the apology for a couch in the corner of the unusually small and ill-provided châlet. Swallowing the contents of a bowl of hot milk, I was endeavouring to snatch half an hour's sleep before my enemies, the fleas, awoke and discovered the rich prize drifted to them by the storm, when Michel crept in by my side, and squeezed me still tighter against the wall, saying, by way of apology, 'Ich wollt en wenig schlafe.' And sleep he did, as he always does, and not only a little, but undisturbed through the livelong night, in a most aggravating way to luckless self."

Since the days of his Schreckhorn ascent, he has left his name upon Alpine annals more on account of a few brilliant episodes, than of any very severe amount of continuous work.

F. T. W.

Peter Bohren.

No one who has ever seen him on a mountain can forget the quaint, wiry, little figure of Peter Bohren. He was known as 'Peterli,' having been so called by his mother, because he was such a little boy. Peterli was not more than five feet in his stature. His career is of interest chronologically, as marking the point of departure from old-fashioned to newer-fashioned days among the Alps. When Peterli was in his prime, mountaineering was rapidly emerging from a period, during which it had been regarded with absolute disrepute and suspicion, into the status of recognized Pastime and Sport, on its own intrinsic merits.

Peter Bohren brought into notice no less a guide than Christian Almer. The former was the mentor of the latter in guidecraft. This remarkable guide was the first to show that diminutive stature is in no way preventative to strength and agility on the mountains. The little man was activity and courage personified. With a thorough knowledge of the lie of snow and of snow-bridges, he was first-rate on ice, and if possible still better on rocks. With plenty of dash, although never imprudent, he was reliable on all occasions of difficulty. Sparkling with vivacity, with an eagle eye, good-humoured and helpful, this 'Gletscher-Wolf,' as he was called, had an iron will and determination of his own. The vigour with which he would cut up an ice slope in his little woollen night-cap, the patience with which he would plod through an opposing snow-field, were alike characteristic of this fine guide. He was thorough in all he did. I shall not easily forget his—"Herr, you are master in the valley; I am master here," when a member of our party had feebly ventured to question the *mot d'ordre* of Bohren, on quitting the knife-edge summit of the Wetterhorn. In camp, Peterli was a clever and genial companion. The *cuisine* of many a mountain *gîte* has been indebted to his skill, and he was an excellent hand with the *casserole*. His knowledge of French was most useful to himself and to others. He was an economical guide, never running up the prices in making arrangements for a party, but always anxious to save his employers as much trouble and expense as possible. The scope of his experience, although perhaps more limited than that of some of his juniors, was a large one. The Oberland east of the Gemmi was naturally the country he knew best of all. His knowledge of the Grindelwald, Eggischhorn, Bel Alp, and Grimsel districts was complete. Next to his own country, Zermatt was best known to him, whilst his experiences in the chain and neighbourhood of Mont Blanc were considerable. He did not make any expeditions of importance or of any special interest until that memorable year in Alpine annals, 1854, in which he was one of Mr. Justice Wills's guides, on September 17th, to the summit of the Wetterhorn (the first ascent of that mountain from Grindelwald). The fir-tree which Christian Almer planted on the mountain's top that day was a 'landmark' in the history of mountaineering. It dates an important epoch in the Alps.

Among Peterli's more prominent ascents, the following may be mentioned. In 1857, he and Christian Almer reached the summit of the Klein Schreckhorn with Mr. Eustace Anderson, bivouacking the previous night under rocks near the Gleckstein; and in 1858 he was with Christian once more in the first ascent of the Eiger, with Mr. Charles Barrington. In June, 1859, Peterli (this time with Victor Tairraz of Chamonix and J. Bennen of Laax) was, to adopt Mr. F. F. Tuckett's words written in Bohren's book, "quick, intelligent, obliging, as plucky as can be desired,"—when the Aletschhorn was conquered by the party described in 'Peaks, Passes, and Glaciers' (Second Series, vol. ii. pp. 33, etc.).

The September of 1859, too, is noticeable in this guide's history, as in that month he crossed the Col de Miage, with Lord Monk Bretton (then Mr. J. G. Dodson, M.P. for East Sussex) and others, in a single day from Courmayeur to Chamonix; while just previous to the passage of this Col in the Mont Blanc range, he had formed one of the party with F. Couttet ('Baguette') and Mr. G. S. Lane-Fox in the ascent of the Aiguille du Midi, from Mont Fréty,—which was then almost virgin, having been once ascended previously by the Count de Bouillé's guides, while the Count himself sat down upon a friendly rock below the summit—sending his flag to be affixed to a pole on the top by proxy. This ascent by Mr. Lane-Fox's party is the more remarkable from the fact that this eastern outlier of Mont Blanc was the first Aiguille, west of the Mer de Glace, climbed by a *voyageur* since Jacques Balmat's and Dr. Paccard's joint ascent of Mont Blanc itself in 1786. The year 1862 found Bohren again on the south side of the Rhone, but this time in the Saas and Zermatt valleys, when he accompanied the Rev. Coutts Trotter, the Rev. H. B. George, and others over the Mischabel-Joch, first passage, and ascended the Lyskamm for the first time after the Rev. J. F. Hardy and his party had set foot on its summit in 1861. Mr. Coutts Trotter thus writes in Bohren's book, in 1862: "He is almost as much at home on a pass he has never seen as in his own country." In 1868 he appears among his own mountains, as making the first ascents of the Ebenfluh and the Dreieckhorn with Mr. T. L. Murray Browne. And probably these were the last of his new peaks.

In December, 1871, he accompanied the late Mr. A. W. Moore and Mr. Horace Walker in their winter campaign from Grindelwald—the first ever ventured on. After hunting and shooting for some days on the Mettenberg slopes and elsewhere around the valley, their party, consisting of Mr. Moore, Mr. Walker, Peter Bohren, Melchior Anderegg, and Christian Almer, started (December 23rd) at 3 p.m. from the village for the Finsteraar-Joch, which they reached in the middle of the night, or rather at 1.15 a.m. on the 24th. Descending to the foot of the Finsteraar-Firn, they rounded the Strahleckhörner rocks, and recrossed by the Strahleck pass to Grindelwald, which they reached in twenty-two hours from the time of starting. He was also one of Herr Bischoff's guides in the first winter ascent of the Mönch in January, 1874.

It seems almost more than an ordinary coincidence that he should have died, literally in harness, upon those very grass slopes on which he had bivouacked with Mr. Justice Wills in 1854, in their ascent of the Wetterhorn; and again with Mr. Eustace Anderson and Christian Almer, in their ascent of the Klein Schreckhorn in 1857.  The peaks of the great Wetterhörner and Schreckhörner, on whose rocks he had hunted and whose summits were so peculiarly his own, had just risen to his eyes when he died on the slopes with a knapsack on his back. He was sixty years of age, having been born in 1822. He lies buried under the shadow of his mountains, in the churchyard of Grindelwald. His long-tried and faithful friend Peter Baumann wrote thus of Peter Bohren's death in 1882: "Tuesday (July 4th) was a fine day. That afternoon Peter Bohren and I started with a traveller for the Gleckstein hut, to ascend the Wetterhorn next day. About a quarter of an hour's walk below the hut, old Peter remained behind, being very tired, and told us to go on, while he would follow later. Arriving at the hut, I saw him coming on, but suddenly he sat down and seemed to fall. I called to him, but it was too late; he was dead—his face was already cold. It was a sad sight. I carried him to the hut. That was a long night for me. Early in the morning we started downwards, and five guides went up to bring him down." *Finis coronat opus.*

F. T. W.

Franz Andermatten.

FRANZ JOSEF ANDERMATTEN was born about the year 1823, at the hamlet of Almagel within Saas. He first emerges upon the field of Alpine history as *Knecht* of Johann Josef Imseng, the well-known Curé, first of Randa, afterwards of Saas. Who shall relate on how many unrecorded hunting, scrambling, and other expeditions Franz accompanied his master?

The Curé was a strong, cordial, brave man, hospitable and enterprising, a daring chamois-hunter, and a pastor beloved by his folk. When apparently about sixty years of age, he could still scramble and tramp the twenty-four hours round without over-fatigue. The early literature of Alpine adventure frequently mentions his name, and always in kindly tone. More than most he deserves to be remembered as an Alpine Pioneer, a veritable enthusiast of the hills—" Oh! nous serons gais là-haut," he used to say.

Franz was just such another as his master, warm-hearted, brave, unselfish, without a trace of meanness, ready for any adventure, humorous, excited when he heard a marmot, wild if he saw a chamois. In his youth he was probably a little hare-brained; he was certainly very strong. In Franz the Curé found a companion so much the more sympathetic as the undertaking in hand was the more venturesome. Imseng was one of the few natives of this part of the Alps who felt an interest in exploring the regions of everlasting snow. He and the Curé of Zermatt together discovered the Adler pass in the year 1848 or earlier. Franz at an early age imbibed from the Curé this interest in exploration for its own sake. The love of adventure remained strong in him to the last, and he always preferred a new expedition to an old one. Possibly it was also from Imseng that he inherited a conscious delight in the smaller beauties as well as the sublimer grandeur of the Alps, which distinguished him so sharply from the general run of guides.

In 1847 Herr Melchior Ulrich came to Saas on what was practically a journey of discovery. He repeated his visit to this and the neighbouring valleys more than once, and thereafter wrote his still interesting account of the ' Seitenthäler des Wallis und der Monterosa' (Zurich, 1850, 8vo). This pamphlet, or rather the papers upon which it was founded, contributed to the Zurich Naturforschungen Gesellschaft, contains the first published account of expeditions in which Franz Andermatten took part. He possibly made the first passage of the Allalin pass, carrying provisions for Ulrich and the Curé on the 13th August, 1847—an exciting and memorable expedition for its day. He certainly accompanied the same zealous pair when, in the following year, they made the first passage of the Ried Pass and the first ascent of the Ulrichshorn, but he was still only a porter, Stephen Binner and M. zum Taugwald being the guides. Perhaps it was in the same capacity that he went with Ulrich, Studer, and Imseng in 1849 over the newly discovered Adler pass.

In 1850 Franz appears as an explorer on his own account. He and a companion had to find their way from Simplon home. They elected not to go the long round involved by the usual route up the Zwischbergen valley, but to find a more direct passage. This they accomplished by traversing the top of the Thälihorn, thence crossing the snow-field to the Zwischbergen pass, and descending upon Almagel. I have been told that Franz accompanied the present Mr. Justice Wills over the Adler in 1853. If so, he must have been the " strong man of Saas" described in the interesting account of that expedition. The said strong man lingers in the judge's memory as "a silent, short, thick-set man," but silent I cannot believe Franz ever to have been. At all events, Andermatten was not without employment during these years. If not yet famous as a guide, at a time when the only " famous" guides out of Chamonix were the brothers Lauener, he was at any rate known as the best local man, and is so recorded with sufficient emphasis in the 1854 edition of Murray's guide-book.

The first series of ' Peaks, Passes, and Glaciers' contains the record of two expeditions in which Franz was the leading guide. He is described as " landlord of the Monte Rosa hôtel at Saas." It was generally known that Imseng was the real landlord of one of the Saas hotels, but (as humorously described in Wills's ' Wanderings') he used always to speak as though he were merely a kindly mediator between an unseen host and the visitor. Perhaps he played off Franz as host on Mr. Ames. Franz it was, at any rate, who led that gentleman and three other Englishmen to the top of the virgin Laquinhorn, on the 25th of August, 1856, Curé Imseng being likewise of the party. A few days later Mr. Ames and Franz made the first ascent of the Allalinhorn, reaching it from the Allalin pass. "Andermatten's pet object," says Mr. Ames, "was now attained. He cheered and jodelled enthusiastically, exclaiming at intervals 'Der Herr Pfarrer sucht uns gewiss mit dem Spiegel,' and seeing a quantity of loose rocks lying on one side of the peak where there was no snow, he called on us to assist him in building a *Steinmann*. The present writer once had the delight of spending a cloudless hour or two with Franz by the side of this same pile of stones. Franz was in his best form, full of spirits, the wealth of which, with him, usually culminated on an Alpine summit. His great joke was to imitate the mountain-top behaviour of the various nationalities. "What does the German do, Franz?" and Franz would strike an heroic attitude, wave his hat to the biggest mountain near, and cry, "Das ist jetzt famös!" "And what does the Englishman do?" "Looks round once, and then falls to on the victuals."

The ascent of the Nadelhorn in 1858 is the next conquest in which I can find it recorded that Franz Andermatten had a share. The record is indeed not an easy one to discover, for it appeared in the *Walliser Wochenblatt* (October 2) of that year. The party consisted entirely of Swiss, and of course included the Curé, though he remained behind some distance below the top. The mountain was in an exceptionally icy condition, and no less than 1470 steps had to be cut along the arête, where usually few are required. Franz carried a huge wooden cross, which was triumphantly erected on the summit, and remained visible there for many years.

In 1860 Franz took Mr. Leslie Stephen to the top of the Allalinhorn from the Fee pass, over which, at a later date, he led me on the occasion of its first passage. That very pass was the object of Mr. Stephen's expedition; but when they reached the col, Franz insisted on their going over the peak to the Allalin pass, and so to Zermatt. He was reasoned with, but it was of no avail, he insisted, and, says Mr. Stephen, "I felt the rope tighten round my waist, and Franz was off like a steam-engine, with his small train of travellers and guides panting behind him. One long slope of snow (fortunately in good order) lay between us and the summit, and straight up that slope we were dragged at our best pace, without halt or hesitation. At half-past two we were sitting at the top, round the little cairn which Franz had previously erected, loosing the ropes, and allowing our internal arrangements to return to their natural state." This was the third year in which Franz and Mr. Stephen had travelled together; they may therefore have made other expeditions worth mention, but of which no account has reached me.

Andermatten's preposterously big ice-axe (it was as big as any two average weapons of the kind) hewed the way to the summit of the Biesjoch for two French gentlemen in 1862. The bare record of the expedition is alone preserved. In the following year he and Curé Imseng piloted Mr. Watson and his party to the virgin summit of the Balfrinhorn, as is more fully described in the first volume of the *Alpine Journal*.

On the occasion of the Matterhorn accident, in the memorable year 1865, Franz came out very well. The other guides, obedient to the orders of the Zermatt curé, refused to start with a forlorn-hope expedition on the Sunday. Franz's curé was fortunately the other side of the Mischabelhörner, but, Curé or no curé, he would have gone, as in fact he went. There was a fund of humanity in him that could not be bound in by any conventionalities when it was warmly aroused.

He had none of the local or class jealousies common amongst guides

He was as ready to climb with a Zermatt or St. Niklaus colleague as with one from his own village. He liked to see foreign guides in his own district. When climbing without guides began, Franz was almost the only guide to express pleasure at the movement. He has been known to urge his own employers to make important expeditions without professional assistance, and once at any rate he offered to accompany a party of amateurs on the lower part of an ascent, in order to carry their packs, and set them on the right road.

From 1865 to his death, in 1883, Franz lived the life of an active and popular guide. Others in his place would have grown rich; he declined to do so. He firmly refused to raise his prices, saying that he had always been accustomed to receive such and such payment. He never counted the money paid to him, and seldom knew, even at his own small tariff, how much was his due. He kept no record of the number of days he had been with an employer, nor of how many peaks and passes had been done in them. Thus his friends were able to cheat him a little in his own favour, but he found it out if they offered him much more than his price, and firmly declined to accept it. Not that Franz was one of those "happy-go-lucky" people who live upon debts and make others pay for their lordly carelessness. He was always anxious to earn what he thought fair pay, and would go as porter rather than be unemployed. He has been met, quite late in life, when his reputation as a guide was secure, carrying a burden of very nearly an English hundredweight for a few francs over the Monte Moro pass. He was always a splendid weight-carrier, and many are the stories told about him in that capacity; how, when his back and shoulders were piled with knapsacks, he would say that he had room for another in front, and the like.

He drank but little, and seldom ate on a mountain. He hardly ever wore dark spectacles, even on the most glaring snow-field. With all his poverty he had within him the lightest heart ever carried by a guide. He was always happy, always thoughtful for others, always polite. There was a charming natural refinement about him, rare in men of any country or station. He married at least three times, and had about eighteen children, some of whom he educated to be guides. Pleasant it was to watch the process of education going on, and to hear the little asides in which Franz instructed his boy in manners and conduct as well as in the mountain craft.

He was never in any accident on the mountains, and he died peacefully in his bed. In August, 1883, he caught a cold on some mountain expedition, crossing, I believe, from Saas to Zermatt. Inflammation of the lungs rapidly set in. His wife and an English lady whom he had often led upon the mountains, hurried round to Zermatt in time to find him alive and perfectly conscious and happy as usual. In a few hours he died, and the world was the poorer by one bright soul. He was buried at Saas, and all the valley mourned for a lost friend.

W. M. C.

J. J. Bennen.

JOHANN JOSEPH BENNEN, of Laax, in the Upper Rhone Valley, was born in the year 1824. Coming first into prominent notice in 1858, his life was brought to an untimely and tragic close in 1864. During that short period, however, many great peaks unconquered, and passes untraversed, still challenged the enterprise of guides and travellers; and the career of Bennen, a guide who accomplished work of considerable interest, has fortunately been described with graphic and sympathetic pen by eminent English mountaineers who were closely associated with him.

One of his employers, Mr. Vaughan Hawkins, wrote of him in his lifetime: "Johann Joseph Bennen, of Laax, is a man so remarkable that I cannot resist the desire to say a few words about his character. Born within the limits of the German tongue, and living amidst the mountains and glaciers of the Oberland, he belongs by race and character to a class of men of whom the Laueners, Melchior Anderegg, Bortis, Christian Almer, Peter Bohren, are also examples,—a type of Mountain race, having many simple, heroic qualities. Bennen, as he surpasses in those qualities which fit a man for a leader in hazardous expeditions, combining boldness and prudence with an ease and power peculiar to himself, so he has a faculty of conceiving and planning his achievements, a way of concentrating his mind upon an idea with clearness and decision, which I never observed in any man of the kind. Tyndall said to him, 'Sie sind der Garibaldi der Führer, Bennen!' to which he answered in his simple way, 'Nicht wahr?'—an amusing touch of simple vanity, a dash of pardonable bounce, being one of his not least amiable characteristics. Thoroughly sincere, devoted to his friends, without a trace of underhand self-seeking in his relations to his employers, there is an independence about him, a superiority to most of his class, which makes him, I always fancy, rather an isolated man, though no one can make more friends wherever he goes, or be more pleasant and thoroughly cheerful under all circumstances. Unmarried, he works quietly most of the year at his trade of a carpenter, unless when he is out alone or with his friend Bortis (a splendid mountaineer) in the chase after chamois, of which he is passionately fond. Pious he is, and observant of religious duties. A perfect Nature's gentleman, he is to me the most delightful of companions." Professor Tyndall, referring to their first meeting in 1858, at the Eggischhorn, where Bennen had for some time acted as a guide attached to the hôtel, spoke of him as "a remarkable-looking man, between thirty and forty years old, of middle stature, but very strongly built. His countenance was frank and firm, while a light of good-nature at times twinkled in his eye. The proprietor had spoken to me many times of his strength and courage, winding up his praises by the assurance that if I were killed in Bennen's company there would be two lives lost, for that the guide would assuredly sacrifice himself in the effort to save his Herr."

It was during the ascent of the Finsteraarhorn, their first expedition together, the work being severe, that Bennen turned and said to the Professor, "Ich fühle mich jetzt ganz wie der Tyroler einmal," and went on to relate the story of the conversation between a priest and an honest Tyrolese, who complained to his Father-Confessor that religion and an extreme passion for the fair sex struggled within him, and neither could expel the other. "Mein Sohn!" said the priest, "Frauen zu lieben und in Himmel zu kommen, das geht nicht." "Herr Pfarrer," sagte der Tyroler, "*es muss gehen*." "Und so sag' ich jetzt," cried Bennen. The same persistent spirit, manifested on the Weisshorn's jagged arête and the cliffs of the old Weissthor, accomplished expeditions more arduous than the ascent of the "Dark Eagle Peak," although that, undertaken, as on the occasion in question, by two persons only, each well burdened, is suited only to strong climbers. Guide and traveller, however, shared the work loyally, and a heavy boiling-water apparatus which, borne in the interests of science on the Professor's back, swung round annoyingly in climbing, was not suffered to add to the burden of the guide.

The expeditious with which Bennen's name is especially associated,—all, as it happened, made in the company of English mountaineers,—are early attempts upon the Matterhorn, the first ascents of the Aletschhorn and Weisshorn, the first recorded passages of the old Weissthor (by two routes), the Zwillingejoch, the Col de la Reuse d'Arolla, the Col du Mont Tondu, and the first ascent of Mont Blanc made completely by the St. Gervais route—that is to say, by the Aiguille and Dôme du Gouté, and Bosses du Dromadaire, without trenching at any point upon the ordinary way from Chamonix.

The first attempt upon the stately Aletschhorn, second in height of the Bernese Alps, was made in 1859, by Mr. F. F. Tuckett. Provided with able guides (Victor Tairraz and Peter Bohren), he secured in addition the services of "the trusty Bennen," and the first ascent was successfully accomplished. The second ascent, made in the same year by Messrs. Dunville and Bruce, was also made under Bennen's guidance. He was not, however, destined to work only in his own district.

The tale of the memorable series of attempts upon the mighty Matterhorn has been told by Mr. Whymper—attempts continued with a varying degree of encouragement, now on one side, now on another, until in 1865 the mountain was ascended both from the Swiss and the Italian sides. Before the year 1859 some few attacks only had been made, from the side of Italy, led chiefly by Jean Antoine Carrel, of the Val Tournanche. Guides, as a body, shrank from conflict with a peak to them so weird, so awe-inspiring. Were not its savage crags the trysting-place of evil spirits? The terrible tragedy which attended its conquest—the revenge of a vanquished monster—perhaps served at the time to confirm unreasoning timidity. Nowadays the tendency, which has proved fatal, is to underrate the foe.

Bennen, almost alone among Swiss guides, did not yield to the feeling prevalent at one time in regard to the mountain, and gallantly attacking it on two occasions (in 1860 with Mr. Vaughan Hawkins, and in 1862 with Mr. Hawkins and Professor Tyndall), he succeeded in reaching each time a point beyond any previously attained. These attempts were made from the Italian side, apparently considered at the time as the more hopeful. We are told that in ascending the mountain on which he met his death, the Matterhorn showed its black head over one of the arêtes of the Haut de Cry, and Bennen was asked whether he thought it would ever be ascended. His answer was a decided "Yes." Poor fellow! He, who would have been no unworthy conqueror, was never again to assail its stupendous crags.

The season of 1861 was an active one for Bennen. Crossing the Lysjoch to Gressonay with Mr. Tuckett and Messrs. C. H. and W. J. Fox, and 'cheery, steady' Peter Perren, the party returned to the Riffel from Macugnaga by one of the difficult and hazardous passages of the Old Weissthor, across the ridge between Monte Rosa and the Cima de Jazzi. Starting again from Macugnaga some weeks later with Professor Tyndall and a porter, he led once more up to and across the same ridge by a route differing from, though lying near to that followed by Mr. Tuckett's party. After exposure to two stone avalanches, fortunately without injury, the party had next to descend an ice slope. "Andermatten (the porter) slipped here, shot down the slope, and knocked Bennen off his legs, but before the rope had jerked me off mine, Bennen had stopped his flight. The porter's hat was shaken from his head and lost." How, straining slowly upward amid the maze of crags, the party were forced to scale smooth, vertical cliffs, "the ugliest place beneath over which a human body could well be suspended," how "Andermatten, with his long unkempt hair and face white with excitement, hung midway between heaven and earth, supported by the rope alone," Professor Tyndall has graphically related. The expedition is one which seems to involve something more than difficulty.

In the same year Mr. Tuckett's party, before mentioned, made the first passage of the Col de la Reuse d'Arolla, from Prerayen to Chermontane in the Val de Bagnes. They also made, from the Lysjoch, the first attempt upon the Lyskamm, which, however, was frustrated by the state of the snow and a violent wind—the pleasure of first conquest some weeks later being reserved for the party led by Mr. Hardy. Bennen, with Mr. Tuckett, thereafter made a new pass of use and interest, now known as the Col du Mont Tondu, between the Col de la Seigne and Contamines, and repeated the ascent of the Grand Paradis, first achieved by others in the previous year.

Until 1861 the ascent of Mont Blanc by the St. Gervais route, that is to say, from the Pavillon de Bellevue and Aiguille du Goûté, had been made only by trenching each time more or less upon the ordinary way from Chamonix. Each portion of the route from the Aiguille du Goûté to the summit, without descent to the Grand Plateau, had been traversed at one time or another; but in that year Messrs. Leslie Stephen and Tuckett, with Melchior Anderegg, Bennen, and P. Perren, put the keystone to the route, passing for the first time direct from the Aiguille to the Dôme du Goûté, and thence to the Bosses du Dromadaire and summit.

At the commencement of the climbing season of 1861 one niche certainly in mountaineering history had yet to be filled. The Weisshorn, second in height of the Swiss Alps proper—peak of most graceful outline, most attractive grandeur—was still unascended. Professor Tyndall, after a preliminary reconnaissance of the mountain by Bennen and an Oberland guide named Wenger, started with them from Randa on the 18th August, 1861, and bivouacking above the village, mounted next day to the long, high, narrow, broken ridge, which leads towards the summit from the east. Difficulties soon appeared. At one point, "the arête narrowed to a mere wall, which, however, as rock, would present no serious difficulty. But upon the wall of rock is placed a second wall of snow, which dwindles to a knife-edge at the top. It is white and pure, of very fine grain, and a little moist. How to pass this snow catenary I knew not. . . . Bennen's practical sagacity, however, was greater than mine. He tried the snow by squeezing it with his foot, and to my astonishment commenced to cross. Even after the pressure of his feet the space he had to stand on did not exceed a handbreadth. I followed him, exactly like a boy walking along a horizontal pole, with toes turned outwards. Right and left the precipices were appalling. . . . We reached the opposite rock, and a smile rippled over Bennen's countenance as he turned towards me. 'Had the snow,' he said, 'been less perfect, I should not have thought of attempting it, but I knew after I set my foot upon the ridge that we might pass without fear.' Bennen's instinctive act is justified by theory. . . . My guide, unaided by any theory, did a thing from which I, though backed by all the theories in the world, should have shrunk in dismay."

The climb proved long and hard. Hour after hour slipped away. At one juncture "Bennen laid his face upon his axe for a moment, a kind of sickly despair was in his eye as he turned to me, remarking, 'Lieber Herr, die Spitze ist noch sehr weit oben.' But a gulp of wine mightily refreshed him, and looking at the mountain with a firmer eye, he exclaimed, 'Herr! wir mussen ihn haben;' and his voice, as he spoke, rang like steel within my heart. I thought of Englishmen in battle, of the qualities which had made them famous —it was mainly the quality of not knowing when to yield." At length, working steadily upwards, "a knife-edge of pure white snow ran up to a little point. We passed along the edge, reached that point, and instantly swept with our eyes the whole range of the horizon. The crown of the Weisshorn was underneath our feet." The descent proved also long and difficult. Professor Tyndall has related how the track of a chamois, whose line of movement on the cliffs had been carefully noted by Bennen during his reconnaissance, proved of assistance at a juncture of threatening difficulty in the descent.

"Between the first-class Alpine guide and any man worthy to work with him a warm regard and respect will certainly grow up." And between Bennen and his employers this was so. Professor Tyndall said of him in later days, "All my knowledge of Bennen as a man and a guide serves simply to confirm my opinion of his excellence. He is a man of approved courage, strength, and caution. He is also tender and kind." Present on the scenes of two accidents which might easily have proved fatal, he appears to have exhibited a commendable self-forgetfulness and kindly solicitude. The story of the accident in 1861 to Mr. Birkbeck, who fell more than 1700 feet of vertical height from the Col de Mingo, down an ice slope of appalling steepness, is narrated in 'Peaks, Passes, and Glaciers' (2nd Series, vol. i.), and the strong effect upon the guides of the harrowing circumstances in which the party were placed is there alluded to. "The German Guides gave vent to frequent bursts of tears from time to time during the day." The other incident referred to, the entombment of a porter in a crevasse of the Aletsch Glacier, and his providential rescue, is thrillingly narrated in 'Hours of Exercise in the Alps.' About one hour had elapsed since the man had disappeared in the crevasse, when Professor Tyndall's party fortunately arrived on the spot; and although nothing was to be seen of him, the sound of a low moan gave hope to the rescuers. No rope proper was at hand—that of the party lay in the crevasse, coiled round the porter's body —but one was contrived of coats, waistcoats, and braces, with which the Professor and Bennen were with difficulty lowered singly into the awful chasm. Then, with all care, they began to clear away the snow and ice. A layer two or three feet thick was thus removed, and finally from the frozen mass issued a single human hand. Bennen worked with the energy of madness. The ice-fragments round the man had regelated—he had literally to be hewn out of the ice. Raised, insensible, after an hour's work, to the surface of the glacier, he was borne with difficulty to the Faulberg Cave; and tended carefully through an anxious night, he made a satisfactory recovery.

In 1863, Professor Tyndall and Bennen crossed the Oberaarjoch, their last journey together. Later, Mr. Stephen Winkworth, with Bennen and J. B. Croz of Chamonix, made the first passage of the Zwillingejoch, an expedition of some difficulty; and shortly afterwards the same party, with Mrs. Winkworth, made an attempt upon the Zinal Rothhorn from Zermatt, abandoned through want of time when a considerable height had been attained. Monte Rosa surmounted, the same party next accomplished ascents of the Aletschhorn and Jungfrau, ascents notable as the first made of these two peaks by a lady. Minor excursions ended Bennen's work for the season of 1863, fated to be his last.

Mr. P. C. Gosset and M. Boissonnet, accompanied by Bennen and three local guides or porters of Ardon, in the Valais, started on the 28th February, 1864, to ascend the Haut de Cry, a mountain of 9698 feet. Having reached a considerable height, the party proceeded to mount a snow-field, lying steeply before them somewhat in the form of a large, high couloir. "Bennen did not seem to like the look of the snow very much, and told us he was afraid of starting an avalanche; but the local guides assured us that our position was perfectly safe. We asked whether it would not be better to return, and cross the couloir higher up; but the Ardon men objected, mistaking the proposed precaution for fear, and the two leading men, Bevard and Nance, continued their work. Bennen had not moved—he was evidently undecided—but seeing some hard snow again he advanced. He had made but a few steps when we heard a deep, cutting sound. The snow-field split in two just above us. The cleft was at first quite narrow, not more than an inch broad. An awful silence ensued; it lasted but a few seconds, and then it was broken by Bennen's voice, "Wir sind alle verloren!" His words were slow and solemn, and those who knew him felt what they really meant when spoken by such a man as Bennen. They were his last words. Borne downwards in the avalanche, crushed and buried in the hissing snow, two of the party—M. Boissonnet and Bennen,—emerged no more alive. The others narrowly escaped.

Thus, yielding in a fatal moment to the opinion of others less capable (though presumably better acquainted with the mountain), misled for an instant as to the true state of the snow, although conversant with its condition in winter as in summer, there perished miserably one of the best and bravest guides the Valais has ever seen. His body, recovered three days later from under eight feet of snow, was laid to rest in Aernen churchyard, where a headstone was erected to his memory by his old employers and friends, Messrs. V. Hawkins, F. F. Tuckett, and Professor Tyndall. A liberal collection was made in England for his dependents.

Not least bright among mountain memories and pictures comes the thought of the guide who is our friend, with whom we delight to work; and as among the race of dwellers in the Alps we hope for a maintenance of his sterling powers and qualities, so we find pleasure in recalling some, now beyond earth's highest summits, who were leaders in the lands of our Alpine enjoyment, and were upright, and kindly, and brave. H. C.

Jakob Anderegg.

This well-known Oberland guide was a cousin of Melchior Anderegg, and for some years rendered excellent service to many first-rate mountaineers. He took to his profession rather late in life—in the year 1864—when he was thirty-seven years old. He was a man of great physical strength, and of invincible cheerfulness and good-humour. One at least of his employers, who bears ample testimony to his physical powers and great courage, admits that the "virtue of prudence was in Jakob's case conspicuous chiefly by its absence."

It is recorded of him that on one occasion in descending an unusually difficult icefall he interpreted a joking remark made by one of his employers into a challenge to pass a spot of great danger. He instantly accepted the supposed challenge, and although he succeeded, he exposed himself and his Herrschaft to grave risk. Mr. A. W. Moore, who was one of the party, said sharply to him, "Das war eine Dummheit, Jakob." With a face half bashful, yet full of fun, he replied, "Don't tell Melchior;" for whom he had an almost superstitious reverence.

He guided the late Monsieur Cordier when that gentleman was killed on the

Meije; but for this melancholy accident Jakob was in no way responsible. It was because he disregarded his guides' earnest warning that M. Cordier perished, and Jakob's efforts to save the unfortunate traveller were heroic though unavailing.

In 1865, Messrs. A. W. Moore and Horace Walker took him as their sole guide, an experiment at that time almost without precedent, and Mr. Moore wrote that "the complete success which attended the experiment was evidence enough of Jakob's merit."

For a man who was only in the field of mountaineering for the comparatively short period of fourteen years, he did an unusually large share of general work, and the first ascents recorded under his auspices were of the highest order. In company with his cousin, Melchior Anderegg, he led Mr. Leslie Stephen and Mr. F. C. Grove up the Rothhorn from Zinal in 1864, and shared in the honour of the first passage over Mont Blanc from Courmayeur to Chamonix by the Brenva Glacier in the following year. In 1865, also, he made the first ascent of the Piz Rosegg with Messrs. Moore and Walker, and the Gabelhorn from Zermatt with the same gentlemen, but unaccompanied by any other guide. In company with Mr. G. E. Foster and Hans Baumann, he first climbed the Gspaltenhorn, and the first passages of the Dom Joch and the Agassiz Joch, and the ascent of the Grand Paradis from Cogne must also be credited to his account.

From 1864 to 1874 he was continually employed by well-known members of the Alpine Club, and gave great satisfaction.

His chief characteristic was his daring. It never seemed to occur to him that prudence is sometimes the better part of valour. The idea of difficulty never seemed to suggest itself to his mind, and the word "impossible" was not in his vocabulary. He was entitled to an honourable place in the front rank, he was devoted to his employers, had a keen mountaineering instinct, and a sweet, unselfish nature.

He died at Meiringen, in 1878, in the fifty-second year of his age.

C. E. M.

Michel Croz.

MICHEL AUGUSTE, the younger brother of JEAN BAPTISTE CROZ, lived at the village of Tour, in the valley of Chamonix, where he was born on the 22nd April, 1830. My first acquaintance with him was in an ascent of Mont Blanc in 1859, but it was not until 1860 that he took part in mountaineering beyond the limits of the Mont Blanc district. From that year till his death in 1865, in the lamentable accident on the Matterhorn, he was in the very front rank of the guides then available for difficult mountain expeditions.

In the beginning of August, 1860, Michel met me at Moutiers Tarentaise. He acted as guide in an ascent of the Aiguille Sassière near Tignes, and in the first ascent of the Grande Casse, the highest mountain of Southern Savoy. We then joined the Rev. T. G. Bonney and Mr. Hawkshaw in Dauphiné, made an attempt on the Pelvoux which was defeated by bad weather, and passed by way of the Viso to Turin. Michel then went to Zermatt with my two friends, and accompanied them in several excursions in that neighbourhood, including the ascents of the Breithorn, Monte Rosa, and the Lysjoch, the passage of the Col Durand, Triftjoch, and Adler Pass, and the ascent of the Strahlhorn. In some of these excursions, and notably in the ascent of Monte Rosa, he was sole guide.

In August, 1861, I was travelling with Mr. F. W. Jacomb, with the two brothers Croz as guides. While I was laid up by a temporary illness at Aosta, Mr. Jacomb made, in their company, the first passage of the Col du Sonadon and the first ascent of Mont Gelé. They subsequently accompanied us in an exploration of the Ruitor, in the first ascent of the Col de la Sache, or southern peak of the Pourri, in the first passage of the Felik Joch, the first ascent of Castor, and the first ascent of Monte Viso. Mr. Jacomb then took Jean Croz with him to Mont Blanc, while Michel went with me to Modane, whence we ascended the Aiguille de Polset, the peak immediately to the west of the Col de Chavière.

In July, 1862, Michel, in conjunction with Peter Perrn, of Zermatt, and Bartolomeo Peyrotte, of Bobbio, was attached to my friend Mr. Tuckett in the remarkable series of explorations in the Alps of Dauphiné which first opened up that district to mountaineers. In the course of this journey the party followed Messrs. Whymper and Macdonald in the ascent of the Pelvoux, and crossed three new cols—the Col des Écrins, the Col de Sélé, and the Col du Glacier Blanc.

In August of the same year I travelled with my friend, the Rev. T. G. Bonney, with Jean and Michel Croz as guides. The first expedition was to the summit of Mont Pourri, of which Michel had made the first ascent, alone, on the 4th of October, 1861. This was followed by an ascent of the highest peak of the Ruitor from La Thuile, on the Italian side of the Little St. Bernard, and of the Pic de Grivola, from Cogne. We subsequently went through the Viso district into Dauphiné, made an unsuccessful attempt on the Écrins, and crossed the Col du Glacier Blanc to La Grave. In 1863, the same party, with the addition of Mr. G. S. Mathews, made the first ascent of the Grandes Rousses in Dauphiné, explored the Glacier de Lans, reached the top of the Col de la Casse Déserte, and crossed the Col des Cavales and the Col de Sélé. They subsequently made the first passage of the Col de Monci, south of Cogne, between the Rossa Viva and the Tour du Grand St. Pierre.

In 1864, Michel was engaged by Mr. Whymper, who was accompanied by Mr. Horace Walker and the late Mr. A. W. Moore, with Christian Almer, of Grindelwald. In the month of June, the combined party made the expeditions in Dauphiné, the history of which is related in the 8th, 9th, and 10th chapters of Mr. Whymper's 'Scrambles amongst the Alps,' and in Mr. Moore's Journal, 'The Alps in 1864.' The journey included the first passage of the Brèche de la Meije, the memorable first ascent of the Pic des Écrins, and the first passage of the Col de la Pilatte.

In July, Michel accompanied Mr. Whymper and the late Mr. Reilly in a series of new expeditions in the Mont Blanc district, including the Col de Triolet, the Mont Dolent, the Aiguille de Trélatête, and the Aiguille d'Argentière. Mr. Whymper and Michel subsequently joined Mr. Moore and Christian Almer in the first passage of the Moming Pass from the Arpitetta Alp to Zermatt. Later in the year, in the month of August, we find him again with Mr. Reilly, engaged in the first passage of the Col du Dôme du Goûter from the châlets of Miage to the Grand Mulets.

In the year 1865, Michel Croz was again with Mr. Whymper, who had also engaged Christian Almer and Franz Biener. The party ascended the Grand Cornier from Zinal and descended to Abricolla, whence they made the ascent of the Dent Blanche. They subsequently crossed the Col d'Érin to Zermatt, and after some attempts upon the Matterhorn went on to Courmayeur. They next ascended the western summit of the Grandes Jorasses and crossed the Col Dolent to Chamonix. Here Croz was obliged to part from Mr. Whymper, having made an engagement with another employer, who failed to keep his appointment at the time agreed upon, and was obliged to return to England on account of ill-health. Croz, considering that he was bound to wait for his new employer, remained in enforced idleness at Chamonix, and so missed the honour of acting as leading guide in the first ascent of the Aiguille Verte, accomplished by Mr. Whymper, with Almer and Biener, on the 29th of June. The success of this expedition, in which Oberland guides only were engaged, created great jealousy at Chamonix, and gave rise to an angry demonstration against the Oberlanders, in which it is needless to say that Croz took no part. Soon after this incident he was engaged by the Rev. Charles Hudson, with whom he made, on the 5th of July, the second ascent of the last-named peak. The Rev. G. Hodgkinson and Mr. T. S. Kennedy, with the guides Michel Ambroise Ducroz and Peter Perrn, were also members of the party. Then came the accidental meeting with Mr. Whymper at Zermatt, the ascent of the Matterhorn of the 14th of July, and its fatal termination.

Of Michel Croz's qualities as a guide it is almost impossible to speak too highly. He was admirable both on rock and ice, but like every Chamoniard he preferred the latter. As an ice-man he had few equals and no superiors. He was an excellent and unwearying step-cutter, and his great physical power enabled him to contend successfully with sudden difficulties where muscular strength was required, such as cutting through an ice cornice or crossing a difficult bergschrund. His geographical instinct was extraordinary. On his first visit to the valley of the Casse Déserte in Dauphiné, he indicated with unerring accuracy the point where, as we mounted higher, the summit of the Écrins would appear above the boundary ranges.

Mr. Whymper has given an excellent portrait of Croz on p. 180 of his 'Scrambles amongst the Alps,' followed by words which give a faithful picture of his character. He was happiest, Mr. Whymper writes, "where he was employing his powers to the utmost. Places where you and I would 'toil and sweat and yet be freezing cold,' were bagatelles to him, and it was only when he got above the range of ordinary mortals, and was required to employ his magnificent strength, and to draw upon his unsurpassed knowledge of ice and snow, that he could be said to be really and truly happy. Of all the guides with whom I travelled, Michel Croz was the man who was most after my own heart. He did not work like a blunt razor and take to his toil unkindly. He did not need inquiry or to be told a second time to do anything. You need but to say what was to be done and how it was to be done, and the work was done, if possible. Such men are not common, and when they are known they are valued. Michel was not widely known, but those who did know him came again and again. The inscription that is placed upon his tomb, truthfully records that he was 'beloved by his comrades, and esteemed by travellers.'"

It is interesting to note, in turning over the pages of Mr. Whymper's book,

in how many of the woodcuts of that fascinating volume Michel Croz occupies a prominent place. In the engraving opposite p. 217 he is the principal figure on the jagged ridge of the Écrins; on p. 220 he is represented in a midnight bivouac under a rock on the Pré de Madame Carle; in the engraving opposite p. 229 he appears as the foremost actor in the passage of the bergschrund on the Col de la Pilatte; in that opposite p. 259, perhaps the most beautiful engraving of ice scenery ever produced, he is seen hacking his way through the cornice of the Moming. Of this feat Mr. Whymper writes: "He acted rather than said where snow lies fast, there man can go; where ice exists, a way may be cut, it is a question of power; I have the power, all you have to do is to follow me." Again, in the woodcuts on pp. 390 and 392 he occupies the highest point on the crowning ridge of the Matterhorn. These two cuts have a mournful interest: they represent one of the last incidents in his life. For the next record of him we must turn to the tomb in the churchyard at Zermatt, where the inscription on the memorial stone "bears honourable testimony to his rectitude, his courage, and his devotion."

W. M.

Peter Rubi.

PETER RUBI, a native of Grindelwald, was born in 1833. He became a guide considerably later in life than the generality of those who afterwards rise to any pre-eminence in the profession. Although we find mention of him as early as 1862, yet it was not till some ten years later that his name began to be classed among those of the then great guides of the Alps. This is to be accounted for by the fact that he seldom left his native valley, and never sought for engagements which would take him far from the Oberland. He had an intense love for the peaks and glaciers among which he had been brought up, and never could be persuaded that any other place offered such a tempting field for the mountaineer as Grindelwald. Though it is probable that Rubi would have made a name for himself as a first-rate guide, much earlier in life, had he travelled farther afield, yet it is certain that during this time he was working among the mountains and glaciers around his home, gaining knowledge of the difficulties, and especially of the precautions necessary, on snow and rock, a knowledge  which led him eventually to be considered one of the safest and most cautious of guides.

In appearance below rather than above middle height, but gifted with greater strength than many, Rubi trudged contentedly through a long day under a heavy load, while from amid the wrinkles of an ugly, but good-humoured face, a pair of grey eyes smiled upon his friends. His hand, ever ready in difficulties, was so obtrusively large as to provoke on the part of his more frivolous employers, the inevitable contrast with that "small white hand" of his feminine namesake, rendered some years ago a household word by the most popular songwriter of that day. His weatherbeaten face and nautical roll gained for him the not unfitting *sobriquet* of 'the Bosun.' He dabbled, too, in the healing art, although his remedies were often more homely than pleasant, as any one treated by him for a sprained sinew or snow-blindness would allow. He always carried in his pocket a small phial of ether, and, unless you were careful, a piece of sugar soaked in this was thrust into your mouth at each breathing halt on an ascent. At Zermatt he was frequently to be seen, hastening to the bedside of a sick companion, bearing some nauseous brew in a dilapidated teapot. The chief trait in his character was his extreme simplicity. Possessing the true courage of the mountaineer, boldness tempered with caution, disliking, and even suspicious of any guide but an Oberländer, he placed a child-like trust in his old employers. I never met him at the beginning of a season without his feelings finding vent in almost boyish antics, nor left him at its termination without the tears raining unchecked down his rugged cheeks.

On the 21st July, 1862, Rubi acted as porter to Mr. Leslie Stephen and his companions, when making the first passage of the Jungfrau Joch. On this occasion, he carried a ladder, some twenty-four feet long, from Grindelwald to the Wengern Alp, and thence over the Jungfrau Joch to the Grindelwaldes Eismeer. The party met with exceptional difficulties in forcing its way through the séracs of the Guggi Glacier, owing to the instability of the towering ice-pinnacles around them. "Rubi," writes Mr. Leslie Stephen, "appeared to think it rather pleasant than otherwise in such places to have his head in a kind of pillory between two rungs of a ladder, with twelve feet of it sticking out behind, and twelve feet before him."

I first met Rubi in 1873 at the village of Saas, and this, I believe, was one of the earliest occasions on which he was, for any length of time, away from the Oberland. He was then acting as leading guide to Mr. Hulton, with whom we joined forces on several expeditions. I was so much impressed by Rubi's great caution amid difficulties, as well as by his unfailing good-nature, that I asked him to join me as soon as his then engagement was completed. It is characteristic of him that he at once prevailed upon me to abandon the Zermatt district, and return with him to his beloved valley. From this time either my brother or I engaged him every season till the year before his death.

The following are the new expeditions in which Rubi took part as far as I am able to name them. With Mr. Hulton, he made the first ascent of Monte Rosa from the Grenz Gletscher in 1874; and in the same year he found what was apparently a new route up the Gabelhorn from Zinal. Later in that season, he led my brother and myself up the Blümlis Alp from the Tschingel Gletscher for the first time; and across the Mitteleggi arête of the Eiger, from the Wengern Alp to the Lower Grindelwald Glacier, a route only famous for its uselessness, and for the formidable steepness of its ice-slope, which prevented a change of leaders, and compelled one guide to cut steps for five and a half hours, continuously, without a halt. In 1875, he guided me over a pass between the two Schreckhorns, while we were beaten back when close to the summit of the Wetterhorn by way of the Hühnergütz Glacier. In 1877, accompanied by Mr. H. S. Hoare and Mr. W. E. Davidson, we found a new route up the Weisshorn by the Schallenberg arête; and, with Mr. Davidson, we climbed the Gabelhorn direct from the Gabelhorn Glacier; while we were beaten by weather on the Zäsenberg ridge of the Ochsenhorn, when close to the top. In 1879, with Dr. Moseley, he made the first passage of the Viescherjoch from the Aletsch Glacier to Grindelwald, a pass only once previously crossed, and in the opposite direction; and later in the same year had the misfortune, along with Christian Inäbnit, to be of the party when Dr. Moseley lost his life, while descending the rocks of the Matterhorn. Dr. Moseley having, against reiterated advice, unfastened the rope, and having declined the assistance offered to him by Rubi, endeavoured to vault over a projecting piece of rock, when he slipped and was killed. In the account of the accident, Mr. C. E. Mathews describes the guides as "two of the ablest of the Oberland guides," and says that "no blame whatever attaches to Rubi or Inäbnit." It seems doubly hard that such an accident should have happened under the leadership of a guide so well known for his prudence and caution. It is written of him in the *Alpine Journal*, " No guide could surpass him for caution and attention in whatever concerned the security of the traveller. Towards the end of a long day, knowing that weariness is apt to bring heedlessness, he was always ready and on the watch." It was indeed a picture to see him the last in descending a nasty piece of snow, soft from the afternoon sun, how he buried the stock of his ice-axe almost up to the head, and planted his feet, as though he expected at each step to be called upon to prevent the consequences arising from a slip of one of the party.

On one occasion, at least, my brother and I owe our lives to Rubi's watchfulness and endurance. Having been obliged in crossing the Jungfrau from the Wengern Alp, to make a détour over the summit of the little Silberhorn, we were stopped by darkness and by a large crevasse just below the Roththal Sattel, where no crevasse should be. Here we passed a miserable night in the snow. The weather was bad, and we had consumed all our wine and brandy, and although we had food, our mouths were too parched to eat. In addition, my brother was so severely attacked by exhaustion and mountain sickness, that we momentarily expected he would succumb, but, thanks to Rubi's unremitting care, he gradually revived. Then came the fight against the fatal sleep, and this I shall never forget, when Rubi's energy was again severely taxed, and many were the friendly kicks bestowed by him to keep our senses alive, during this apparently endless night.

On July 17th, 1880, Rubi, in company with his brother-in-law, F. Roth, and a Swiss traveller, Dr. A. Haller, left the Gleckstein to cross the Lauteraarjoch. None of the party were ever seen again; they probably perished among the higher séracs of the Upper Grindelwald Glacier. More it is unlikely we shall ever know, and here Rubi may well be content to rest, his grave in no foreign land, but at the foot of the noblest peak of the valley he loved so well.

J. W. H.

Johann Fischer.

JOHANN FISCHER was born in 1834, at Zaun, a scattered hamlet on a shelf of the mountain above lower Hasli Thal. Melchior Anderegg and his brother live there; Jaun lives below them at Unterbach, where, too, Jakob Anderegg used to be, and Andreas Maurer lived further south on the same shelf at Lugen; so the place has produced many good guides. Of Fischer's early doings I know nothing beyond what is written in his guide's-book, which his widow has been kind enough to send to me. In 1867, my friend Dr. T. C. Allbutt and I went to the Eggischhorn from the Grimsel over the Oberaarjoch, in charge of the two Almers. The next day was wet and thick, and we stayed at the hôtel and amused ourselves by doing small gymnastic feats. After we had done as many as we were capable of, a powerful man came forward out of a corner, and without saying a word straddled his legs apart, clasped his calves with his hands, and stooping down bit the very short grass off the ground with his teeth. This quite eclipsed other performances, and was my first introduction to Fischer. He turned out to be Herr Wellig's chief guide at the Eggischhorn inn, the best man, as Herr Cathrein told me years after, who has served there in that capacity. The work he did there was sometimes tremendous. He stayed for nights together at the

Faulberg hut, fresh travellers being sent up to him nightly for the Jungfrau or Finsteraarhorn. I remember him telling me that he went in one week twice up the Jungfrau, and thrice up the Finsteraarhorn. In less favourable weather he would take travellers over the Mönchjoch to Grindelwald, or help to carry a fat woman down to or up from Viesch. In 1869 he carried Mr. Squires, an American gentleman who was exhausted and insensible, on his back for an hour or two up the last part of the Mönchjoch. In 1872 I engaged him at Melchior's advice, and found him, to my mind, a perfect guide, sober, willing, courteous, possessed of a good head, and, perhaps, the strongest of all the guides. We made glacier excursions from Contamines and Cogne, up the Grivola, without local help, amongst others. Then Jean-Antoine Carrel came from Breuil to help us, and we went up Mont Blanc from the Miage glacier by the direct way to the top. We were enveloped in mists soon after reaching the top: Carrel had never been there before; Fischer and I once each, years before, by the passage between the two Rochers Rouges, somewhat impracticable for tired men, late in the day in mists. However, a couple of hours' search brought us to the Mur de la Côte, and we were then not long in getting down to Chamonix. We also ascended the Aiguille de Léchaud, a new ascent from Courmayeur, and made other expeditions in the Mont Blanc chain. After finishing with me, he returned to his old work at the Eggischhorn.

In 1873 we ascended the front Aiguille de Blaitière, a new ascent in which we were joined by my friend, J. A. G. Marshall and Ulrich Almer; crossed the Cols d'Argentière, Maison Blanche, Bertol, the Col d'Érin, and up the Aiguille de la Za and Mont Blanc de Cheillon. All these walks were new to him, and were done single-handed with me. We also made for the first time the Col des Hirondelles, as Marshall called it—a name suggested to him by a few dead swallows which were lying on the glacier at the foot of the apparently inaccessible rocks—between the big and little Jorasses. M. Loppé joined us on this expedition; Marshall was tied to Ulrich Almer, and Leslie Stephen hooked on to Fischer, and so we had a cheery day. After this he again went to the Eggischhorn, where he was always welcome, and I thkin Mr. Hulton had him in some high excursions from Zermatt up the Matterhorn, Lyskamm, and other places.

In 1874 he guided me over the Buet to Chamonix, where we failed to climb the Aiguille de Charmoz by the couloir, now found to be the proper way; this failure arose from my want of perseverance. We also failed to climb Mont Blanc from the head of the Fresnay glacier, by the ridge up to Mont Blanc de Courmayeur. This failure, after sleeping out at about 12,000 feet, was caused by misty weather and a thunderstorm in which we were caught in the morning. We made other excursions up the Brenva glacier, and up a point of the great Aiguille de Peuteret ridge from Courmayeur; up the Pigne d'Arolla and the Aiguilles Rouges of Arolla by a new way, where the local guides with another party would not follow even after they had gained the main ridge. He also crossed from Stachelberg to the Maderauer Thal, ascended the Grosse Windgälle on a windy day, and crossed the pass from Geschenen to the Rhone glacier inn, all, as usual, without a second man and without mistakes.

He left me to join my old friends, Frank and J. A. G. Marshall, with whom he made, I believe, the first ascent of the Aiguille de Triolet from the southern side. With Mr. J. A. G. Marshall, he was killed at midnight on August 31st, in descending the steep and crevassed Glacier de Brouillard. Ulrich Almer fortunately was not injured by falling into the crevasse, and was able to extricate himself. He left a widow, who still lives at Zaun, and several children, of whom the eldest is now a schoolmaster near Solothurn. He was forty years old. No better guide has been seen in the Alps; he was absolutely honest and upright in everything he did.

T. S. K.

Laurent Lanier.

LAURENT LANIER was born at the village of La Saxe, in the Commune of Courmayeur, about the year 1840.

To describe his personal appearance is in many ways to describe his character, for each was so strikingly exemplified the one by the other. Shrewdness, independence, self-reliance, and determination one could read in every feature. The keen black eye which seemed to be always searching for something not actually present, the merry laugh which betrayed his appreciation of a joke, even when at his own expense, the genial *bonhomie* and eagerness of his whole expression when entertaining his friends with some detailed account of his mountaineering or hunting experiences, and the very reverse when relating the sins and iniquities of his enemies, were all evidence of his Italian nationality. This was also betrayed by the vein of superstition which ran through his whole character, and which we would hardly have expected to find in a man of such strength of mind and determination. For all creeping things he had an unreasoning and honest terror, which continually led to practical jokes being made at his expense. I shall never forget his horror and terrified flight when first teased with a toy wooden serpent at Chamonix. An unfortunate cook happening to be in his way, she and the dishes with which she was laden were flung to the ground, while Laurent himself was eventually found safely hidden under the landlord's bed. On another occasion, while returning from chamois-hunting, having killed a snake, I pretended to be about to throw the body in his face, when, hastily cocking his rifle, he swore he would shoot me if I did not desist.

As an instance of his self-reliance and presence of mind in the emergency of a sudden danger, may be mentioned his conduct on the steep snow slope leading to the final arête of the Mischabel Dôm. He was ascending that mountain with two gentlemen and another guide, when the party became involved in, and carried away by, a large snow avalanche. The other guide completely lost his head, and, with the two gentlemen, was swept unresistingly down the slope. By some supreme effort, Laurent wrenched himself out of the mass of snow, and when the party were pulled up at the brink of a large crevasse into which the avalanche had disappeared, the deeply-cut track of his axe upon the ice slope above showed to what a powerful and desperate resistance they owed their escape.

Laurent took to guiding early in life, soon attaining a high position in his profession, and, being taller than his fellows, with a clear olive complexion and black hair, he was a conspicuous figure in any assembly of mountaineers. Brave, but not rash, no one appreciated better than he the dangers of the mountains. Before all, a 'safe' guide, in none of the ascents in which he was engaged did an accident happen to any of his companions. On rocks, sure rather than brilliant, he was excelled in icemanship by none.

The first important climb in which he took part, was an attempt to cross the Petites Jorasses from Courmayeur to Chamonix with Mr. Marshall Hall, in August, 1866. Mr. Hall says, "We met with snow up to the waist, and avalanches were falling on all sides every few minutes. After attaining a point on the glacier close under the last rocks, we were obliged to abandon the attempt, from the imminent danger we should have incurred in the fresh state of snow upon those rocks. Laurent Lanier behaved in the most courageous and unexceptionable manner on untried ground."

In August, 1869, he accompanied Mr. T. Middlemore over the summit of Mont Blanc by way of the Glaciers du Taoul and Mont Maudit, an ascent which he repeated with Mr. E. Millidge in August, 1871, and again in September of the same year with Mr. H. W. Parkes. In August, 1872, he made, with Mr. F. Pratt Barlow and Mr. S. F. Still, the first ascent of the Grand Paradis from Cogne, while in July, 1877, he led Lord Wentworth straight up the north-east face of the same mountain from the Plan de la Tribulation, and also found a new route up the Grivola from the Val Savaranche. In 1879, with Mr. G. FitzGerald, he made the first ascent of the Aiguille de Talèfre. With Mr. W. E. Davidson, he made, amongst many others, the following noteworthy expeditions. In August, 1874, the passage of the Old Weissthor from Macugnaga; in July, 1875, the first passage of the Arbenjoch, when the difficulties encountered on the Durand Glacier were extreme, the ascent from the Roc Noir to the Col occupying ten hours. Mr. Davidson writes, "The ascent from Zinal we should certainly not have been able to make, but for the great determination and skilful icemanship of Lanier, who led throughout." In September, 1876, the first ascent of Castor from the Zwillingejoch, and the first descent of the Jägerjoch from the Riffel to Macugnaga. In 1878, the first descent from the summit of Mont Blanc to Courmayeur by the Aiguilles Grises route; the first passage of the Col Dolent from Chamonix to Courmayeur, this being the second passage of that Col, and an attempt on the Aiguille de Charmoz, which proved unsuccessful, the rocks just below the summit being covered with a glaze of ice. (In these two last climbs I had the good fortune to take part.) In 1880, with Mr. Davidson and Mr. F. C. Hartley, he was beaten in a second attempt on the Aiguille de Charmoz, a slightly higher point being reached than in 1878; while, with the same gentlemen and Mr. James Eccles, he was obliged by bad weather to retreat when close to the summit of the Aiguille Verte, by a new route from the Charpoua Glacier.

During the latter years of his life he suffered greatly from a frost-bitten foot, which was aggravated by the severe weather met with in the last-named expedition, and which caused him to decline, as far as possible, all arduous climbs, especially those in which many hours would have to be spent in the snow. The last important summit he reached was that of the Dent du Géant, up which, with his old friend, Hans Jaun, he guided me in 1883.

Famous as he was as a guide, it was in chamois-hunting that he chiefly excelled—and in this he had no equal. I doubt if any hunter in the Pennine Alps could claim, to his own rifle, so good a bag of chamois as Lanier, which, at the time of his death, fell just short of 250 head. He was, indeed, absorbed in the sport, and possessed every qualification necessary for a successful stalker: an eye which nothing could escape, patience in working out the habits and favourite passages of the game, an endurance which neither ill-success, bad weather, nor want of food could conquer, and, above all, a seeming knowledge of what was passing in the mind of the animal, and what course, under any given circumstances, it would take. I may mention an instance in which these qualities were pre-eminently displayed. For two days we had been unsuccessfully searching for chamois from early morning till evening—spending the nights at his chàlet, and our food supply was rapidly running out. On the third morning we started again at 4.30, intending to make a short day and be down at Courmayeur in time for dinner. We found chamois at 9 o'clock, but they were unapproachable, and it was not until late in the evening that I got a shot, breaking a buck's shoulder, which got away in the dusk. We did not reach the châlet till 10 p.m., faint from want of food, but 5 o'clock next morning saw us again on the march. We found the wounded buck, as Laurent had foretold, on a patch of grass some two hours' scramble beyond where it had been hit, but it was after midday before we could approach and kill it. As for myself, I was utterly used up from want of food, and could hardly drag my legs along; Laurent was still as keen as ever, even giving me what little he had to eat, though he himself must have been starving, and would not hear of retreat till we had got the buck.

The privations which he had to endure while chamois-hunting doubtless undermined his constitution, and I was much struck, during the summer before his death, by his loss of energy on ordinary occasions, though when shooting he was as keen as before. In January, 1884, having killed a chamois late one evening on the slopes of the Grapillon, he was obliged to take refuge in a hut at Satjoan, which was half filled with snow. Here, without fire or food, exhausted by his exertions, and with soaking clothes, he passed the night alone. This brought on an attack of pleurisy, and although at one time he seemed to be shaking it off, a fresh chill caused a renewal of the attack, to which he succumbed on the 1st of May. Of his love for chamois-hunting it may well be said,—

"Oh, it was a sport
Dearer than life, and but with life relinquished!"

A more delightful companion no mountaineer could desire, his quaint wit and unfailing good temper shortened many a wearisome day. A constant source of amusement was to pass the afternoon of a wet day in his workshop, listening to his tales of sport and mountain adventure, and here any one who knew him spent much of his spare time. Kind and affectionate to his parents, he has left an aged mother to mourn his death; true and staunch to his employers, his loss will be felt by a large circle of acquaintances, while to his friends it is indeed irreparable.

J. W. H.

Andreas Maurer.

A STURDY, determined-looking fellow of 5 ft. 9 in., deep of chest and thick of limb, a head to match, but remarkably well poised, light, almost yellow, hair and moustache, nondescript features, a pair of laughing, honest blue eyes, and a skin, once fair, now ruddy from exposure to sun and weather. Dress him in thick gray homespun with snow-gaiters and mittens, sling a rifle across his shoulder, give him an ice-axe in his hand, and you have a sketch of Andreas Maurer, as I saw him last in the winter of 1881-2, six months before the accident that robbed us of a faithful guide, true friend, and keen chamois-hunter.

ANDREAS MAURER was born in the Hasli Thal in 1842, and obtained his guide's certificate at the age of twenty-six. Prior to this he had, as *Träger*, ascended many of the Oberland Peaks, and crossed most of its snow passes. His knowledge of the Engelhörner was probably unrivalled, certainly unsurpassed. In his frequent winter expeditions after chamois he had traversed or climbed almost every couloir, rock face, or peak of them before he got his *Führerbuch*. Besides the practical knowledge thus gained, he had the advantage of being brought up on terms of close friendship and intimacy with some of the best Oberland guides. Melchior and Jakob Anderegg and Hans von Bergen were his neighbours, while Johann Jaun, whose name is now a household word amongst those who know and love the mountains, was his intimate friend and companion.

With such associates, no wonder that Maurer became imbued with the best traditions of the Oberland guides. He had that rarest gift, true courtesy, while his happy temperament made him always cheery and light-hearted even in the greatest difficulties. Nature had endowed him, too, with a physique that made light of all fatigue, and he possessed a reserve of strength which in an emergency was little short of marvellous.

Yet withal Maurer will never be ranked amongst the half-dozen leading guides of his generation. He was not born to be a leader; he lacked that great essential which, for want of a better word, we call "head." He was not the man to organize an expedition or to discover a new route, but give him the idea, and he would work it out with a determination and ability that are invaluable in a lieutenant.

Amongst the many virtues that have made the Oberland guides conspicuous, apart from their ability as mountaineers, there were two that Andreas Maurer possessed to an eminent degree—he was absolutely ungrasping, even to the verge of improvidence, and thoroughly staunch. One felt instinctively that, whatever happened, one could rely upon him to the death.

In the late summer of 1880, a friend of mine, accompanied by Andreas Maurer and Emile Rey, made an attempt to reach the summit of the Aiguille du Plan by the precipitous ice face above the Chamonix Valley. After step-cutting the whole day, they reached a point where to proceed was impossible, and retreat looked hopeless. To add to their difficulties, bad weather came on, with snow and intense cold. There was nothing to be done but to remain where they were for the night, and if they survived it, to attempt the descent of the almost precipitous ice slopes they had with such difficulty ascended. They stood through the long hours of that bitter night, roped together without daring to move, on a narrow ridge, hacked level with their ice-axes. I know from each member of the party that they looked upon their case as hopeless, but Maurer not only never repined, but affected rather to like the whole thing, and though his own back was frozen hard to the ice-wall against which he leaned, and in spite of driving snow and numbing cold, he opened coat, waistcoat, and shirt, and through the long hours of the night he held, pressed against his bare chest, the half-frozen body of the traveller who had urged him to undertake the expedition.

The morning broke still and clear, and at six o'clock, having thawed their stiffened limbs in the warm sun, they commenced the descent. Probably no finer feat in ice work has ever been performed than that accomplished by Maurer and Rey on the 10th of August, 1880. It took them ten hours of continuous work to reach the rocks and safety, and their work was done without a scrap of food, after eighteen hours of incessant toil on the previous day, followed by a night of horrors such as few of us can realize. The proverbial caprice of mountain weather was the thread on which depended the lives of the party. Had not the day been still and warm, there would have been an "In Memoriam" chapter in the *Alpine Journal*, and this act of unselfish devotion would have been left unrecorded!

During the last ten years of his life Andreas Maurer travelled almost exclusively with members of the Alpine Club, and during this time acquired an extended knowledge of the Alps. He knew the Bernese Oberland by heart—amongst the Zermatt mountains he was quite at home—while he had a large experience both of the Chamonix group and the Dauphiné Alps. In 1880 he accompanied M. de Déchy in his expedition to the Himálayas, where, to quote M. de Déchy's words, "He showed the highest qualities as an able traveller-assistant in scientific observations and photographic work, and a most obliging and cheerful man . . . developed all the qualities of a first-rate guide, strong, active, and willing to any work."

Most of the great peaks of the Alps had been already ascended before Maurer won his spurs, but a reference to the pages of the *Alpine Journal* will show that he took more than his share of what was left. Among these were:—

The first ascent of Aiguille Verte from Argentière Glacier.
First ascent of Les Courtes from Argentière.
First ascent of Aiguille des Droites.
First ascent of Aiguille d'Alvau.
First ascent of Râteau from the north.
First passage of Col de Roche d'Alvau.
First ascent of Bietschhorn from the south, descending to Ried.
First ascent of Lauteraarhorn by the western face.

Maurer's great strength was proverbial in the Hasli Thal; amongst many of the feats he performed, one instance will suffice as an illustration. He was chamois-hunting in the depth of winter, and had, with U. Zurflüh, followed a herd of chamois on to the Stollehorn, the highest of the Engelhörner, and, as sometimes happens, they had gradually forced the herd upwards to a point about 300 feet below the summit, where the rocks are so precipitous that their further upward progress was barred, while there was no escape to the right or left of the couloir up which the chamois had retreated, the result being that the hunters killed five; this happened an hour after daybreak, about 8.30 a.m. Maurer carried three of these, besides a heavy rifle, to his home near Lungen, where he arrived about five the next morning. Taking a low average weight of each beast at fifty pounds, he with his rifle must have carried nearly a hundredweight and a half, down some of the steepest and most difficult rocks in Switzerland, and then through the deep winter snow for over twenty hours!

But, alas! with all his strength and endurance, Andreas had to succumb to a power greater than his, and on the 3rd of August, 1882, he, to whose readiness in emergency many a man now living owes his life, was lying dead at the foot of the couloir on the Wetterhorn—a mountain which he knew as well as the pathway to his own châlet. He was accompanied by Mr. Penhall on this their last expedition, and Andreas started for it with a strange presentiment of impending evil, as a few minutes before leaving the Bear at Grindelwald he gave his pipe to Emil Boss, saying that he should probably never want it again. How the accident occurred will never be known. In all probability they were swept away by a small avalanche while traversing the couloir high up on the western face of the mountain. Their bodies were found at the base of the couloir, still roped together, resting on the *débris* of the avalanches that sweep down it. That Maurer had made desperate efforts to arrest their fall is proved by the fact that his finger-tips were torn off by the rocks as he clutched them in their descent. Knowing as I do the character of the rocks, which are by no means precipitous, and Maurer's enormous strength, I cannot help thinking that Mr. Penhall must have been struck insensible in the first fall, and so rendered incapable of assisting himself; had it been otherwise I feel convinced Maurer could have halted him. But, alas! it was not to be, and two victims were added to the long death-roll of the Alps.

And so farewell, a long farewell, Andreas—no more scrambles up rock face and couloir—no more step-cutting up ice slope, nor weary plodding across snow fields—our cheery mountain bivouacs are but memories, and our last camp-fire is burnt out.

But still, though years roll on, staunch friend and gallant *Bergsteiger*, you are well remembered by your *Herr*, and by your fellow-guide and trusted companion. We stood together this autumn on the Dossen Horn, watching the sunlight dying out on the peak of the Wetterhorn, and our thoughts were of you. And as the gloom of night settled down on this your grand memorial stone, Johann Jaun turned with tears in his eyes to me, and said, "Ich habe Andreas sehr geliebt," and the answer came—"Ich auch!"

J. O. M.

Ferdinand Imseng.

FERDINAND IMSENG was born at Saas in 1845. He was related to the well-known curé of that place. When about twenty years of age he removed to Macugnaga. He was a hunter by profession, and the Macugnaga district possesses advantages for chamois-hunting over the districts within the Swiss frontier. The close time for chamois being much shorter in Italy than Switzerland, Italian huntsmen just across the border profit by the more stringent and wise regulations of their neighbours. They are able to hunt what are practically Swiss chamois when the Swiss themselves may not. When Imseng was not hunting he worked in the mines of the Val d'Anzasca. In his case, as in that of so many others, chamois-hunting was the apprenticeship for guiding.

Imseng took part in several remarkable expeditions in his time, but his name will be remembered chiefly in connection with one of them, the ascent of the Höchste Spitze of Monte Rosa from Macugnaga. How well I remember sitting by him one day with all the wondrous height of that snow wall cloudless and dazzling before us, whilst he pointed out his route to me, step by step, and urged with an enthusiasm almost rising into anger, that the climb was altogether safe if taken at the right time, in the right way, and by good men. Exactly three years later an avalanche overwhelmed him on the very spot to which his finger had pointed.

Imseng was the most venturesome guide I ever knew. He was ambitious of distinction and greedy of adventure. He had neither wife nor children and wanted none, being in this respect also an exception among his fellows. He liked to earn money and to make himself well-to-do, but money was not the object for which he was willing to peril his neck. As far as I could make out, he delighted in the excitement of danger. He would not go out of his way to get into danger, but he liked an expedition with some risk in it that he might show his ability in avoiding the risks. The ascent of Monte Rosa from Macugnaga had been the dream of his youth. In the pursuit of chamois he had traversed the lower slopes of the mountain and found the route on the safety of which he was willing to pledge his reputation. It was a happy day for him when in July, 1872, he at last over-persuaded a party to undertake the expedition, and that notwithstanding the protests of their own trusted guide. This is not the place to recount the incidents of an ascent destined to be memorable in the history of mountaineering. The toil of it was what remained in Imseng's memory. The party was large, the slope steep, and the snow soft; they had to wade through it for the best part of eight hours. At last they came near to the foot of the rocks of the final peak. Then Imseng went ahead with all the rope behind him, and, waist deep in snow, forced with his body a deep furrow up the steep and slushy slope. He remembered that piece of work as the hardest he ever had to do.

By this ascent, the whole credit of which belonged and was yielded to Imseng, his reputation as a bold and competent guide was fixed. Thenceforward he probably seldom lacked employment. A sort of alliance sprang up about this time between him and Franz Andermatten. The two used to work together in perfect harmony, and their unfailing fund of high spirits made mountaineering with them specially delightful. They played incessant pranks and small practical jokes upon each other, and the most burning snow-field scarcely relaxed the torrent of their good-humoured chaff. Each was eager to do more than his share of the work; neither was in the least jealous of the other. I cannot remember any new ascents of first-rate importance made by them together, but they accomplished all the principal climbs in their district and others in the Oberland and about Mont Blanc.

I well remember making Imseng's acquaintance one bright afternoon in the summer of 1877, when he came rollicking in to the Riffel from some ascent of Monte Rosa or the Cima. Thenceforward I never willingly climbed without him. Together in 1878 we accomplished the first ascents of the Rothhorn up the face from Zinal, of the Dom from the Domjoch, and of Monte Rosa by one of the Grenz glacier buttresses. Our great aim at this time was the ascent of the Matterhorn from the Stockje. Fresh snow always came the day before we intended to start, and Imseng's impatience knew no bounds. He could not bear that another party should accomplish before him anything that his *Herren* desired to do. When the Dom was our goal he found out that another party in the hôtel was likewise waiting for the same expedition. Without telling us why, he insisted upon our starting one evil day, and forced us to climb the desired ridge in a storm of wind and snow.

The following year I was unable to accompany Penhall to Switzerland. He and Imseng settled themselves down at Zermatt with the Z'mutt arête of the Matterhorn as their aim. Already that year Imseng had conquered the Weisshorn from the Zinal side, thus accomplishing what is perhaps the longest scramble up difficult slabs of rock anywhere in the Alps. The Matterhorn was likewise destined to yield to them, after three days and two nights spent upon the mountain. They started one morning from Zermatt, spent the night out on the shoulder, and then, despairing of the weather, returned to Zermatt, but only to find that another party had gone for the self-same expedition. They dined and then started again, and walked and climbed the long night through and all the following day, eventually reaching the top some hours after the rival party, who, guided by Alexander Burgener, had ascended by a somewhat different route.

Imseng could not bear to be beaten. He would have climbed till every vein in his body burst rather than have yielded to another. The dogged perseverance of the man was one of his leading qualities. No one could be more light-hearted and joyous than he, however wretched the surroundings; but if he was opposed, no one could envelop himself in a more thundrous cloud of anger. In an attempt upon the Nord End, which he and I made alone together, his character declared itself in a very attractive fashion. He insisted upon starting from Zermatt though not a star pierced the thick cloud-blanket above our heads. He led off at express speed and never once halted till in something less than four hours we reached Auf dem Felsen, and the sun of a brilliantly clear day rose upon us. He kept up nearly the same pace over the hard snow and up the rock face of the final peak, joking and jodelling whenever he had the breath to spare. At last we were brought up by a rock eight feet high, the top edge of which was part of the final arête, about five minutes below the summit. I was ladder; he climbed on to my shoulders and got his hands over the edge of the rock. Then he gave a mighty tug, and all the four fingers of one hand were gashed on it as by a knife. He howled and jumped down by my side. For half an hour we tore up handkerchiefs and bound his fingers one by one. Then he wanted to try again. I insisted that he should not. His hand was in no state for scrambling. He protested, and would only agree to return on condition that I expressly recognized that he wanted to go on. He hated to be turned back from anything. He prided himself that he knew what could be done, and what could not. Once, after three days of fresh snow, he took us from the Riffel to Macugnaga over the Old Weissthor, leading straight down the couloir. All the Zermatt guides advised us not to go. Imseng contemptuously dismissed their advice. He knew Macugnaga better than they, he said, and that time he was right. The couloir was in perfect condition.

The day came when he was confident overmuch, and he paid the penalty for it with his life. On August 8, 1881, he started away from Macugnaga with Signor Marinelli and another guide and porter. The day was very hot. They mounted to the Jäger Rücki, where the former party had slept in 1872, but instead of staying there they crossed the great couloir and got off on to the opposite rocks, over which great avalanches sometimes fall. One was due that very afternoon, and about five o'clock it fell, carrying death to all members of the party except the loitering porter. Thus ended the short life of one of the most fearless and joyous of the Alpine guides. Like the conquerors of the Matterhorn, he died at the foot of the mountain it had been his pride to overcome. He lies in the churchyard of Macugnaga, and a cross of Monte Rosa granite marks the place of his rest.

W. M. C.

APPENDIX.

As the remarks made regarding the climbing qualification necessary for membership of the Alpine Club have evoked much criticism, the following examples are given in proof of the statements made on page 20. Number I. is prob,bly the best mountaineering record ever laid before the Committee by a candidate, and is that submitted by a well-known *German* mountaineer. Numbers II to VII. are taken from the Candidates' Book, now in use in the Alpine Club rooms.

I.

Mont Blanc, from Gl. du Brouillard.
Grandes Jorasses.
Aiguille Verte.
Aiguille de Trélatête.
Matterhorn.
Weisshorn.
Gabelhorn.
Rothhorn.
Dent Blanche.
Lyskamm.
Dom.
Täschhorn.
Monte Rosa.
Dent d'Hérens.
Bruneckhorn.
Breithorn.
Grand Combin.
Aletschhorn.
Blümlis Alp.
Eiger.
Mönch.
Jungfrau.
Finsteraarhorn.
Schreckhorn.

Wetterhorn.
Gross Nesthorn.
Piz Rosegg.
Piz Bernina.
Ortelor Spitze.
Silvrettahorn.
Wildstrubel.
Diablerets.
Rheinwaldhorn.
Balmhorn.
Eiger Joch.
Jungfrau Joch.
Agassiz Joch.
Finsteraarjoch.
Lauteraarjoch.
Oberaarjoch.
Schmadri Joch.
Wetterlücke.
Mönch Joch.
Tschingel Pass.
Lötschen Lücke.
Cevedale Pass.
Strahleck.
Beich Grat.
Bietschjoch.

Petersgrat.
Weissthor.
Schwarzenberg Gletscher Pass.
Ried Pass.
Matterjoch.
Adler Pass.
Alphubel Joch.
Col de Sonadon.
,, de Mont Tondu.
,, de Talèfre.
,, du Tour.
,, du Miage.
,, de Trélatête.
,, d' Argentière.
,, de Cheillon.
,, de Chermontane.
,, du Grand Cornier.
,, du Géant.
,, d'Hérens.
,, delle Loccie.
,, de la Maison Blanche.
,, Durand.
Moming Pass.
Tiefenmatten Joch.
&c., &c., &c.

II.

Monte Rosa.
Strahlhorn.
Breithorn.
Matterhorn.
Rothhorn.
Weisshorn.
Täschhorn.
Rympfischhorn.
Pollux.

Aig. du Midi.
Grivola.
Jungfrau.
Eiger.
Wetterhorn.
Finsteraarhorn.
Piz Morteratsch.
High Level route, from Zermatt to Chamonix.

Col Durand.
Adler Pass.
Alphubel Joch.
Oberaarjoch.
Trift Pass.
Col du Géant.
Col des Hirondelles.

APPENDIX.

III.

In 1880 and 1882.

Eiger.	Dom.	Petersgrat.
Weisshorn.	Breithorn.	Col d'Herens.
Monte Rosa.	Mönchjoch.	

Expedition to recover bodies after accident on Dent Blanche, in August, 1882. A work of difficulty and danger.

IV.

Author of "The King Country; or, Exploration in New Zealand." First ascent of Mount Ruapehu, (N. Island, N.Z.), 9000 feet. Mount Tongariro, active volcano, 7000 feet. Mount Tanhara. Mount Te Aroha. Southern Alps of Australia. Volcano in Tanna (New Hebrides). Mount Fusiyama, Japan (to snow line). Sierra Nevadas, California, Rocky Mountains, 10,000 feet.

V.

Tofana.	Pelmo.	Marmolata.
Monte Cristallo.	Antelas.	Cristall Pass.

Attempts on Besso di Mezzodi and Croda di Lago, without guides.

VI.

Mont Blanc.	Sidelhorn.	Eiger.
Titlis.	Finsteraarhorn.	Strahleck.

VII.

Wetterhorn.	Mittelhorn.	Monte Rosa, first ascent of season.
Petersgrat.	Mont Blanc, first ascent of season.	
Tschingel Gl.		Matterhorn.

INDEX.

Adai Khokh, the, 104.
Adamello, the, 111.
Adler Pass, from Sans to Zermatt, 17; the, 137, 154; discovery of, 146.
Agassiz Joch, the, 82, 85.
Aiguille d'Alvau, first ascent of, 165.
Aiguille d'Argentière, the, 113, 155; first ascent of, 116.
Aiguille des Arias, the, 86.
Aiguilles d'Arves, the, 86.
Aiguille de Blaitière, ascent of, 27, 70, 92, 160; first ascent of, 82.
Aiguille de Chambeyron, the, 86.
Aiguille du Chardonnet, by the Glacier du Tour, 98.
Aiguille de Charmoz, both peaks ascended, 27; the, 103, 160.
Aiguille du Dru, ascent of, 27; the earliest serious attempt on the, 88; first ascent of, 103; ascent of the higher and lower peaks, 132.
Aiguille du Géant, first ascent of, 125.
Aiguille du Goûter, the, 84, 151.
Aiguilles Grises, the, 130.
Aiguille de Lechaud, the, 160.
Aiguille du Midi, 77, 88, 113; a new way up the, 111; winter ascent of, 122; first ascent of the lower peak, 132; from Mont Fréty, 144.
Aiguille de Péclet, the, 86.
Aiguille (Blanche) de Peuteret, 29, 102, 132.
Aiguille (Noire) de Peuteret, 132.
Aiguille de Peuteret ridge from Courmayeur, 160.
Aiguille de Polset, the, 155.
Aiguille du Plan, first ascent, 116; from the Plan des Aiguilles, 132; an attempt to reach the summit—a night of horrors, 164.
Aiguille de Rochefort, first ascent of, 116.
Aiguilles Rouges of Arolla, the, by a new way, 160.
Aiguille de la Sassière, the, 86, 154.
Aiguille de Talèfre, first ascent of, 132, 162.
Aiguille de Trélatête, first ascent of, 116, 155.
Aiguille de Triolet, first ascent from the southern side, 160.
Aiguille Verte, the, 12, 84; from Argentière, 75; by the Charpoua Glacier, 104, 118; from the Argentière Glacier, 165.
Aiguille de la Za, the, 160.
Ailefroide, the, 86, 92.
Aletsch Glacier, the, 158.
Aletschhorn to the Faulberg, 152; first ascent of, 150; first ascent by a lady, 152.
Algeria, a visit to, 112.

Allalin Glacier, the, 138.
Allalinhorn, first ascent of, 147; from the Fee Pass, 147.
Allalin Pass, first passage of, 147.
Almer, Christian—born in 1826—is cheesemaker, then shepherd—takes part in the advance on Luzern in 1847, 83; takes part in the famous ascent of the Hasli Jungfrau—the conquest of the Mönch—ascent of the Klein Schreckhorn, the Eiger, the Jungfrau Joch, the Gross Viescherhorn, the Sesia Joch, the Mischabel Joch, and the Finsteraar Joch—makes the perilous passage of the Col du Tour Noir—in 1864 passes from the Col de Voza to the Valley of Chamouix, over Mont Blanc, by way of the Aiguille du Goûter—the marvellous campaign of ten days in Dauphiné—crosses the Morning Pass and the Schallen Joch—surmounts the Grand Cornier, the Grandes Jorasses, the Col Dolent, the Aiguille Verte, the Col de Talèfre, and Ruinette—third ascent of Dent Blanche—attempts the Matterhorn, 84; ascends the Lauterbrunnen Breithorn—remarkable climb of the Silberhorn—up the Jungfrau from the Wengern Alp—first ascent of the Nesthorn—visits the Eastern Alps—surmounts the Cevedale, the Fornaccia, and the Saline—a night adventure in the Suldenthal—the Ehnefluh Joch, the Schmadri Joch, and the Agassiz Joch—crossing of the Jägerhorn from Macugnaga to the Riffel—the Lyskamm from Gressoney—the Weisshorn from the Bies Glacier—the Täschhorn from the Mischabel Joch—the dog Tschingel, 85; a list of Almer's important ascents and passages, 86; he tries the Jungfrau in winter, gets frostbitten, and becomes a cripple for life, 87.
Almer, Ulrich—born at Grindelwald in 1849—the first ascent of the Gross Nesthorn—the second ascent of the western summit of the Grandes Jorasses—visits the Tyrol, and Dauphiné—visits England first ascent of the Pic Central—a new route up the Pointe des Ecrins—the first ascent of the Ailefroide—first ascent of the Weisshorn from the Bies Glacier—first ascent of the Aiguille de Blaitière—first passage of the Col des Hirondelles, 92; his extensive experience—ascent of the Schreckhorn by the western arête—the Dent Blanche from Montet—the Breithorn from the Schwarzthor—ascends the Wetterhorn and Jungfrau in January, also the Schreckhorn—the Mönch

in February, and the Finsteraarhorn in March—ascends Mont Blanc by the Brouillard route, 93; is precipitated into a crevasse—saves a party of four through extraordinary presence of mind—a successful ascent of the Jungfrau—ascent of the Ober Gabelhorn—a huge mass of cornice falls—arrests the fall of his entire party, 94; the descent of the Dent d'Hérens—is struck by an enormous stone—down to the Stockje with broken ribs, 95.

Alphubel, the, 65.

Alpine Club was founded, 18.

Alpine Journal established, 24.

Alps of Dauphiné, explorations in, 155.

Alps of Glarus, the, 93.

Ampezzo Dolomites, the, 93.

Anderegg, Jacob—the ascent of the Rothhorn from Zinal—took part in the first passage over Mont Blanc from Courmayeur to Chamonix by the Brenva Glacier—made the first ascent of the Piz Rosegg, of the Gabelhorn from Zermatt, and first climbed the Gspaltenhorn, 154.

Anderegg, Melchior—born at Zaun—his first glacier expedition, 64; ascent of Mont Blanc by Les Bosses du Dromadaire—from Courmayeur to Chamonix by the Brenva Glacier—the first ascent of the Rympfischhorn, the Alphubel, the Oberaarhorn, the Blümlis Alp—the Monte della Disgrazia—the Rothhorn from Zinal—a new way to the top of the Jungfrau—the first on the summit of the Mont Mallet—first on the Dent d'Hérens—first on the Balmhorn—first on the highest peak of the Grandes Jorasses, 65; death of Mr. Birkbeck—a visit to London, 66; down a coal-mine—he is a genuine artist, 67; his marriage, 68.

Andermatten, Franz Josef—born at Almagel, 145; the discovery of the Adler Pass—the first passage of the Allalin Pass, the Ried Pass, and ascent of the Ulrichshorn—from the Thälihorn to the Zwischebergen, 146; to the top of the virgin Laquinhorn—first ascent of the Allalinhorn—ascent of the Nadelhorn—ascent of the Biesjoch and the Balfrinhorn, 147.

Andes of Ecuador, the great, 129.

Apennines in the Abruzzi, 112.

Ararat, 111.

Arben Gletscher, the, 98.

Arben Joch, the, 71; first passage of the, 162.

Argentera, the ascent of, 85.

Armenian Highlands, the, 111.

Auf dem Felsen, 168.

Auldjo, Mr. John, 8.

Balfour, death of Prof. F. M., 30.

Balfrinhorn, the, 147.

Balmat, Auguste—a native of Chamonix, 136; born in 1808—the way over the Col du Géant—" un véritable diable pour la glace," 137; the Allalin Glacier—the ascent of the Wetterhorn, 138; an act of devotion—an amusing adventure—ascends Monte Rosa—spends a night on Mont Blanc—his death caused by grief, 139.

Balmat, Jacques, 4, 5.

Balmat Monument, the, 5.

Balmhorn, the, 65.

Bans, Les, 86.

Barry, Dr., 10.

Baumann, Johann—born at Grindelwald, 1830—first expedition in 1862, the first passage of the Jungfrau Joch, 87; the earliest attempt on the Aiguille du Dru—ascents of Mont Collon and the Gspaltenhorn, the Dom from Saas—the passage of the Dom Joch—ascent of the Mönch from the Eiger Joch—the Eiger from the Eiger Joch—the first passage of the Ochsen Joch—the Tiefenmatten Joch crossed—ascents of the Grande Aiguille, the Roche Faurio, the Sommet des Rouies, and the Brèche de la Charrière—a new route up the Wetterhorn—the passage of Mont Blanc—the ascent of the Grandes Jorasses—ascends the Matterhorn from Zermatt—the incident on the Schreckhorn, 88; a most serious misadventure on the Aiguille du Midi—" Ich lebe noch," 89.

Baumann, Peter—born at Grindelwald in 1833—his best known first expeditions, the Jungfrau Joch and Viescher Joch—a new route up the Schreckhorn from the Lauteraarsattel, 90; the Schreckhorn accident and relief expedition, 91.

Becca de l'Inverguan, the, 126.

Beichgrat, first passage of the, 142.

Bennen, Johann Joseph, of Laax—born in 1824, 148; ascent of the Finsteraarhorn, 149; early attempts on the Matterhorn—first ascent of the Aletschhorn, Weisshorn, and Weissthor—first recorded passage of the Zwillinge Joch, the Col de la Reuse d'Arolla, and the Col du Mont Tendu—attempts on the Matterhorn—passage of the Old Weissthor, 150; first passage of the Col de la Reuse—attempt on the Lyskamm—Mont Blanc direct from the Aiguille to the Dôme du Goûté, to the Bosses du Dromadaire, 151; the accident to Mr. Birkbeck on the Col de Miage—the rescue of the entombed porter on the Aletsch Glacier—the Oberaar Joch passed—an attempt upon the Zinal Rothhorn from Zermatt—Monte Rosa surmounted—first ascents of the Aletschhorn and Jungfrau

made by a lady—the ascent of the Haut de Cry, 152; a snow-field split in two—the avalanche—" Wir sind alle verloren," 153.
Ben Nevis, ascent of, 133.
Bergen, Johann von—born at Meiringen, 68; pre-eminently a rock climber, 69; saves the life of an Englishman—consummate skill displayed on the Aiguille de Blaitière—the ascent of the Finsteraarhorn by the southeastern arête—the first ascent of the Engelhörner—first ascent of Mont Maudit, 70; ascent of the Gabelhorn—from the Blümlis Alphorn to the Weisse Frau, 71.
Bergli Joch, the, 111.
Bernina, the, 111.
Bies Joch, the, 147.
Bietschhorn, the, 76; a new way, 110; first ascent of, from the south, 165.
Birkbeck, accident to Mr., 152.
Blanc, Mont, 1, 3, 4, 8, 10, 71, 84, 115, 120, 139; ascent of, from St. Gervais, 37; ascended by an Englishwoman, 40 ; by Les Bosses du Dromadaire, 65; from the Miage Glacier, 75, 160; from the Glacier de la Brenva—in winter, 86; from Courmayeur, 88; by the Brouillard route, 93; survey of, 112; from Chamonix by Les Bosses, 113; by Broglia and Fresnay Glaciers, 116, 118; first ascent of, from the Italian side, 130; ascent of, by way of the Glaciers du Tacul and Mont Maudit, 162; the first ascent of, 150; passage of, from the Aiguille to the Dôme du Goûté, and thence to the Bosses du Dromadaire and summit, 151; from Courmayeur to Chamonix by the Brenva Glacier, the first passage over, 154.
Blanc Mont de Cheillon, 160.
Blanc Mont de Courmayeur, the, 160.
Blümlis Alp, the, 65; from the Tschingel Gletscher, 158.
Blümlis Alphorn, the, 71.
Bohren, Peter, 143; ascent of the Klein Schreckhorn—crosses the Col de Minge—ascent of the Aiguille du Midi from Mont Fréty—first passage over the Mischabel Joch—ascends the Lyskamm, 144; first ascents of the Ebnefluh and the Dreieckhorn—the first winter campaign from Grindelwald, 145.
Boss, Herr Emil, 93, 96.
Bosses du Dromadaire, the, 10, 151.
Bourrit, Marc Theodore, 3, 4.
Bourrit and De Saussure, 2.
Brèche de la Charrière, the, 88.
Brèche de la Meije, the, 84; first passage of, 155.
Breithorn, the, 76, 154; from the Schwarzthor, 93, 100; from the north, 101.
Brenva Glacier, the, 154, 160.

Breuil Joch, from Breuil to Zermatt, 130.
Brinnen and Laug Thals, the, 142.
Buet, ascent of, 2, 113; over the, to Chamonix, 160.
Burgener, Alex., 27; born at Eisten in 1846—a successful sportsman—an attempt on the Lyskamm in bad weather—the first ascent of the Aiguille du Dru—both peaks of the Aiguille de Charmoz, 103; ascends the Rothhorn from Zermatt—passage of the Col du Lion—the sensational descent of the Mitteleggi arête in the Eiger—up the Matterhorn from the Zmutt Glacier—first ascent of the Aiguille Verte by the Charpoua Glacier—Burgener appears as an author—the first ascent of Adai Khokh in the Caucasus—visits South America, falls ill, expedition abandoned—the first ascent of Tetnuld Tau, Central Caucasus, 104.

Cachat, Zacharie, 12.
Calotte de Rochefort, first ascent of, 132.
Canary Islands, the, 121.
Canons, Austin, 4.
Carrara, the marble heights of, 112.
Carrel, Jean Antoine, 29; born in the year 1829—takes part in several of the first attempts to gain the summit of the Cervin—his first scramble on the Matterhorn, 127; Mr. Whymper's ascent of the Matterhorn on the 14th of July—Carrel's party discovered and driven off, 128 ; Carrel gains the summit two days later by the Italian side—he visits the great Andes of Ecuador—the ascents of Chimborazo and Cotopaxi—extracts from Mr. Whymper's diary, 129; thirty-six nights passed at elevations over 14,000 feet—Carrel's first ascent of the Tête du Lion—the first passage of the Pic du Grand Tournalin from Val Tournanche, and of the Breuil Joch from Breuil to Zermatt—first ascent of Mont Blanc from the Italian side—the first passage of the Col Budden—ascent of the Punta Sella, 130; crossing the Col d'Hérens—a slip—Carrel known as the "Bersagliere"—was "out" in two campaigns, and fought at Solferino, 131.
Castor, the first ascent of, 155; from the Zwillinge Joch, 162.
Caucasus explored, 29; visit to, 101; the, 104, 111.
Cervin, see Matterhorn.
Cevedale, the, 85.
Chamonix Aiguilles, the, 113.
Chimborazo, ascent of, 129, 130.
Cima di Brenta, the, 82.
Cima di Jazzi, the, 98.
Cimon della Pala, the first ascent of, 82.
Cinta, the Monte, 112.

INDEX.

Clarke, Dr., 9.
Cogne, 160, 162.
Col des Aiguilles d'Arves, the, 84.
Col de l'Aiguille du Plan, the, 118.
Col d'Argentière, winter ascent of, 122 ; the, 160.
Col des Avalanches, the, 86.
Col Bertol, the, 160.
Col Budden, first passage of, 130.
Col de la Casse Déserte, the, 155.
Col des Cavales, the, 155.
Col de Chardonnet, winter ascent of, 122.
Col Dolent, the, 84.
Col du Dôme du Goûter, 155.
Col Durand, 154.
Col d'Erin (see Col d'Hérens).
Col des Ecrins, the, 155.
Col du Géant, the, 3, 14, 137.
Col du Glacier Blanc, the, 155 ; to La Grave, 155.
Col du Grand Cornier, the, 82.
Col de la Grande Rousse de Valgrisanche, 126.
Col des Grandes Jorasses, the, 75, 76 ; from Chamonix, 121.
Col des Grands Montets, winter ascent of, 122.
Col de Gros Jean, the, 86.
Col d'Hérens, crossing the, 131, 140, 155, 160.
Col des Hirondelles, 18, 111, 160 ; the first ascent of, 92.
Col dit Infranchissable, the, 118.
Col du Lion, the, 104.
Col Maison Blanche, the, 160.
Col de Miage, the, 113, 116, 144.
Col de Monci, passage of, 155.
Col du Mont Tendu, first recorded passage of, 150.
Col de la Pilatte, 84 ; first passage of, 155.
Col de la Reuse d'Arolla, first recorded passage of, 150 ; first passage of, 151.
Col de Roch d'Alvau, first passage of, 165.
Col de la Sache, first ascent of, 155.
Col de Sélé, the, 155.
Col du Sonadon, first passage of, 155.
Col du Tacul, the, 121 ; first actual passage of, 122.
Col de Talèfre, the, 84.
Col de Trélatête, the, 111 ; passage of, 116.
Col de Triolet, first passage of, 116 ; the, 155.
Col du Tour Noir, the, 84.
Col du Tour, passage of, 117.
Col de Vacornère to Breuil, 100.
Col de Voza, the, 84.
Collon, the Mont, 88 ; by the S.S.E. buttress, 100.
Confinale, the Monte, 142.
Contamines, 160.
Cook, Mount, New Zealand, first ascent by Ulrich Kaufmann, 29 ; ascent of, 97.
Corridor, the, 71.
Corsica, a visit to, 112.
Cortina Dolomites, the, 86.

Cotopaxi, ascent of, 129.
Cottians, the, 85.
Courmayeur to Chamonix by the Brenva Glaciers, 65.
Courtes, the, 76 ; from Argentière, first ascent of, 165.
Couttet, François, 11 ; born at Chamonix in 1828—surveying the chain of Mont Blanc, 112 ; an ascent of the Buet—the first to cross the Col de Miage—ascends the Aiguille du Midi—Mont Blanc from Chamonix by Les Bosses—attempt on the Aiguille d'Argentière, and driven back by a gale—becomes maître d'hôtel, 113 ; the visit of Napoleon III. to Chamonix, 115.
Crête de la Bérarde, the, 86.
Crête de l'Encula, the, 86.
Cristallo, Monte, the first ascent of, 142.
Croda Rossa, the first ascent of, 82.
Croz, Michel—born at Tour in 1830—ascends Mont Blanc in 1859—ascends the Aiguille Sassière near Tignes—the first ascent of the Grande Casse—attempt on the Pelvoux—ascent of the Breithorn, Monte Rosa, and the Lysjoch—the passage of the Col Durand, Trift Joch, and the Adler Pass, and the ascent of the Strahlhorn, 154 ; the first passage of the Col du Sonadon, and first ascent of Mont Gelé—exploration of the Ruitor—first ascent of the Col de la Sache—first passage of the Felik Joch—the Castor, and ascent of Monte Viso, also the Aiguille de Polset—crosses the Col des Écrins, the Col de Sélé, and the Col du Glacier Blanc—ascent of Mont Pourri, the highest peak of the Ruitor from La Thuile, and the Pic de Grivola from Cogne—an attempt on the Écrins—crosses the Col du Glacier Blanc to La Grave—first ascent of the Grandes Rousses—explores the Glacier de Lans—reaches the top of the Col de la Casse Déserte—crosses the Col des Cavales and the Col de Sélé—the first passage of the Col de Monci and of the Brèche de la Meije—the memorable first ascent of the Pic des Écrins, and passage of the Col de la Pilatte—the Col de Triolet, Mont Dolent, Aiguille de Trélatête, and the Aiguille d'Argentière—passage of the Col du Morning Pass, and first passage of the Col du Dôme du Goûter—ascent of the Grand Cornier and Dent Blanche—across the Col d'Erin to Zermatt—ascent of the Grandes Jorasses, 155 ; his geographical instinct, 156.
Cupelin, Edouard—born in 1840—his first ascent of Mont Blanc, 120 ; surmounts the Col des Grandes Jorasses—visits the Canary Islands, ascends Teneriffe—first ascent of the Schwartzhorn—scales Mont Mallet by a new route—makes the first passage of the Col du Tacul,

INDEX.

121; the first winter ascent of the Aiguille du Midi, the Col des Grands Montets, the Col de Charlonnet, the Fenêtre de Saleinaz, the Col d'Argentière, and the first actual passage of the Col du Tacul—meets with an accident while making the ascent of the Aiguille Verte, 123.
Curé of Champéry, the, 4.
Curé of Saas, 17; murder of, 18.

Dante's Pietra Pana, 112.
Dark Eagle Peak, the, 149.
Dauphiné, the, 86, 92, 93; ten days in, 84.
Della Disgrazia, the Monte, 65.
De Luc, the brothers, 2.
Dent Blanche, by an entirely new route, 82; the, 84, 100; from Montet, the, 93; relief expedition to, 99; by the great southern arête, 101.
Dent d'Hérens, 65; descent of, 95; from the Italian side, 130.
Dent du Géant, ascent of, 27.
Dent du Midi, the, 1, 4.
De Saussure, Horace Benedict, 3, 4.
Dévouassoud, François Joseph, 28; born in Les Barats in 1831, 105; is ten years treasurer to the Guides' Company, 107; saves three lives—the first ascent of the Sass Maor of Primiero—scales the eastern face of the Rosengarten Spitze, 109; ascends Mont Blanc—a cross-country ramble from Thonon to Trent in South Tyrol—the first ascent of the Presanella—a long journey through the Dolomites, the Tyrolese and Graubünden Alps—among the Oetzthaler Ferner—a new way up the Bietschhorn, 110; a tour of the Levant—the Hill of Bashan—the by-ways of the Armenian Highlands—the Central Caucasus—the ascent of Kazbek and of Elbruz—through the séracs of the Karagam Glacier, 111; climbs Dante's Pietra Pana, the marble heights of Carrara, and the Gran Sasso d'Italia—visits Corsica, Algeria, and Spain—ascends the Finsteraarhorn and Jungfrau on two successive days, 112.
Dolent, first ascent of Mont, 116, 155.
Dolomites, the, 110.
Dom, the, 100; from the Dom Joch, 167; a new ascent of, 98; the ascent of, from Saas, 88.
Dôme de Rochefort, the first ascent of, 116.
Dôme du Goûter, the, 4, 116.
Dom Joch, the passage of, 76, 88.
D'Oro, the Monte, 112.
Dreieckhorn, first ascent of, 145.
Droites, Les, 76.
Dufour Spitze, the, 125.
Durand Glacier, the, 162.

Eagle's Nest, the, 3, 139.
Ebnefluh Joch, the, 82, 85; first ascent of, 145.
Ecrins, the, 84.
Eggischhorn to Zermatt, a new mountain route, 142; the, 159.
Eiger Joch, the passage of, 80.
Eiger, the, 83, 84, 98, 143; from the Eiger Joch, 88; from the Bergli, 100; from the Mittelleggi arête, 132.
Elbruz, the, 101, 112.
El Kleib, discovering the foundation of a temple on the top of, 111.
Engelhörner, the first ascent of, 70.
Eschia Pass, the, 142.
Ewig Schneehorn, the, 141.
Expedition, the first winter, 39.
Expeditions, list of, 14; by notable amateurs, 38.

Fatal accidents, list of, 32.
Faulberg Cave, the, 152.
Fee Pass, the, 147.
Felik Joch, first ascent of, 155.
Fellaria Alp, the, 142.
Fellaria Glacier, the, 142.
Fenêtre de Saleinaz, winter ascent of, 122.
Fifre, the, 86.
Finsteraar-Firn, the, 145.
Finsteraarhorn, the, 14, 70, 112, 149; the first ascent of, 23; from the Rothloch, 75; from the Agassiz Joch, 93; the first ascent by English travellers, 140.
Finsteraar Joch, the, 84; the village of, 145.
Fischer, Johann—born in 1834, at Zaun, 159; in one week twice up the Jungfrau, and twice up the Finsteraarhorn—carries Mr. Squires up the last part of the Mönch Joch —glacier excursions from Contamines and Cogne up the Grivola—ascent of Mont Blanc, also the Aiguille de Lechaud—ascent of the front Aiguille de Blaitière—crosses the Cols d'Argentière, Maison Blanche, Bertol, the Col d'Erin, up the Aiguille de la Za and Mont Blanc de Cheillon—the Col des Hirondelles —over the Buet to Chamonix—excursions up the Brenva Glacier, up a point of the great Aiguille de Peuteret ridge from Courmayeur — up the Pigne d'Arolla and the Aiguilles Rouges of Arolla—from Stachelberg to Maderaner Thal, ascends the Grosse Windgalle and crosses the pass from Geschenen to the Rhone Glacier line—is killed in descending the Glacier de Brouillard, 160.
Fletschhorn, the, 75.
Fletsch Joch, the, 142.
Forbes, Dr., 13.
Fonds, Les, 3.

INDEX.

Fornaccia, the, 85.
Founders' Day, 1.
Fresnay Glacier, the, 160.
Fuorcla Crast' Agüzza, the maiden passage of, 142.
Fuorcla Sella, the, to the Fellaria Alps, 142.
Fuorcla Zupo, first ascent of, 142.

Gabelhorn Glacier, the, 158.
Gabelhorn from the Arben Joch, 71; the, 76, 158; from the Arben Gletscher, 98; from Zinal, a new route, 158; from Zermatt, first ascent of, 154.
Gauli Joch, the, 141.
Gelé, first ascent of Mont, 155.
Gesner, ascent by, 2.
Glacier de Brouillard, 132, 160.
Glacier de Charpoua, the, 118.
Glacier de Lans, the, 155.
Glacier de Trient, 117.
Glacier du Tour, the, 98.
Gletscherhorn, the highest point reached, 82.
Gorner Glacier, the, 101.
'Grand Col,' the, 3, 14.
Grand Combin, the, 140.
Grand Cornier, the, 84; from Zinal, 155.
Grand Hôtel Couttet, the, 114.
Grand Paradis, the, 125; the first ascent from Cogne, 162.
Grand Plateau, the, 4.
Grande Aiguille, the, 88.
Grande Casse, first ascent of, 154.
Grande Ruine, the, 86.
Grandes Jorasses, the, 65, 74, 76, 84, 88, 92; across the Col Dolent to Chamonix, 155.
Grandes Rousses, first ascent of, 155.
Grands Mulets, the, 70.
Grassen Joch, the, 142.
Graubünden Alps, the, 110
Gran Sasso d'Italia, 112.
Great Tasman Glacier, the, 96.
Grimsel Hospice, the, 141.
Grimsel over the Oberaar Joch, the, 159.
Grindelwald Eismeer, the, to the Viescher Glacier, 141.
Grisons, the, 142.
Grivola from the Val Savaranche, 162; the, 160.
Gross Lauteraarhorn, the, 1.
Gross Nesthorn, first ascent of, 92.
Gross Schreckhorn, ascent of, in winter, 86; the first ascent of, 141.
Gross Viescherhorn, the, 84.
Grosse Windgalle, the, 160.
Gspaltenhorn, the, 27, 88; when first climbed, 155.
Guggi Glacier, the, 158.
Guicho La Pass, the, 98.
Guidecraft, 48.

Hailer, loss of Dr. A., and party, 159.
Hasli Jungfrau, the, 83.
Hasli Thal, 164.
Haut de Cry, the, 152.
Hill of Bashan, the, 111.
Himálayas, the, 28, 97, 98, 165.
Höchste Spitze of Monte Rosa, 166.
Höhe Gaisl, the first ascent of, 82.
Hühnergütz Gletscher, the, 88, 158.

Ice-axes, description of, 42.
Imboden, Josef—born at St. Niklaus in 1840—his characteristic commencement as a guide, 97; up the Cima di Jazzi and Monte Rosa—is a good rock climber—a new ascent of the Dom—ascends the Lyskamm—a new route from the Glacier du Tour up the Aiguille du Chardonnet—attempts the Eiger by the Mittelleggi arête—ascends the Gabelhorn—visits the Himálayas—ascends a peak over 20,000 feet—crosses the Guicho La—is attacked by fever, 98; the two imitation snakes—the search expeditions on the Lyskamm and the Dent Blanche, 99.
Imseng, Ferdinand, 26; born at Saas in 1845—the ascent of the Höchste Spitze of Monte Rosa from Macugnaga, 166; first ascent of the Rothhorn up the face from Zinal, of the Dom from the Dom Joch, and of Monte Rosa by one of the Grenz Glacier buttresses—ascent of the Matterhorn, 167; an attempt upon the north end—from Riffel to Macugnaga over the old Weissthor—meets his death in an avalanche on 8th of August, 1881, 168.
Imseng, Johann, 17.

Jägerhorn, from Macugnaga, to the Riffel, 85.
Jäger Joch, first descent of, from the Riffel to Macugnaga, 162.
Jaun, Johann—was born near Meiringen—served his 'apprenticeship' under Melchior Anderegg—generally called "Hänserli," 72; his excellent powers of observation—crossing the Mönch Joch in bad weather, 73; ascent of Mont Blanc—a sworn alliance—Jaun called out on frontier service—an incident on the Lyskamm—Jaun's coolness—ascent of the Grandes Jorasses, 74; ascent of the Matterhorn—a new ascent of the Fletschhorn—first ascent of the Schallenhorn and Mont Blanc from the Miage Glacier—the expedition of the Col des Grandes Jorasses—the feasibility of the Finsteraarhorn from the Rothloch is demonstrated—an attempt upon the Aiguille Verte—the attack repeated, 75; the first ascent of the Courtes and Droites—fail to ascend the Piz Bernina—successful attack

on the Rosegg—a fortnight's chamois-stalking
—up the Breithorn and down to the Riffelhaus in eight hours, 76; a search party—
on the Aiguille du Midi, 77; Jaun's
merits as a wood-carver — he visits the
Himálayas, 78.
Joch Pass, the, 141.
Jumeaux de Valtournanche, Les, 132.
Jungfrau, the first ascent of, 22; by the Roththalsattel, 65; from the Wengern Alp, 85, 159;
the, 86, 87, 94, 112; ascent in winter, 93;
first ascent by a lady, 152.
Jungfrau Joch, the, 84, 87, 90; first passage,
158, 141.

Kaltenwasser Joch, the, 142.
Karagam Glacier, the, 111.
Kaufmann, Ulrich, 29; born in Grindelwald in
1846—laurels gained in his campaigns in the
Himálayas and New Zealand—his great
strength—wearisome work on the great Tasman
Glacier, 96; the ascent of Mount Cook—
serious hardships in the Sikkim Himálaya, 97.
Kazbek, crossing the, 111.
Kien Gletscher, the, 98.
Klein Schreckhorn, the, 84, 144, 145.
Knubel, Peter—born at St. Niklaus in 1833—the
first to ascend the Matterhorn from the Swiss
side after the accident in 1865, and the second
ascent from Zermatt—visits the Caucasus
—ascends the Elbruz — makes the first
ascent of the Breithorn from the north- the
first passage of the Rothhorn —ascents of the
Sommet des Rouies, the Roche Faurie and
the central peak of the Meije—the Dent
Blanche by the great southern arête—a gallant
performance on the Lyskamm ridge, 101; loses
three brothers, and his brother-in-law, 102.
Königs Joch, the, 142.
Konigsspitze, the, 110, 142.
Kuhe Gletscher, the, 88.

Langtauferer Spitze, the, 110.
Lanier, Laurent—born at La Saxe - the adventure
on the Mischabel Dom—gets carried away in a
snow avalanche, 161; an attempt to cross the
Petites Jorasses—over Mont Blanc—ascent of
the Grand Paradis from Cogne—a new
route up the Grivola—ascent of the Aiguille
de Talèfre—the passage of the Old Weissthor—
the Arben Joch and Castor—first descent
from Mont Blanc to Courmayeur by the
Aiguilles Grises route—the Col Dolent from
Chamonix to Courmayeur—an attempt on the
Aiguille de Charmoz—the retreat from the
Aiguille Verte—the summit of the Dent du

Géant reached, 162; a chamois hunt—cause
of death, 163.
Laquinhorn, the, 142, 147.
Lauener, Christian — born at Lauterbrunnen —
Johann Lauener killed, 81; ascents of the
Marmolata and Cima di Brenta—first ascents
of the Cimon della Pala and Höhe Gaisl or
Croda Rossa - first passage of the Lauinen Thor
— the Weisse Frau—the Col du Grand Cornier
and the Silberhorn— the Ebnefluh Joch,
Schmadri Joch, and Agassiz Joch—the highest
point of the Gletscherhorn—ascent of the
Schallhorn from the Moning Pass—Dent
Blanche by a new route—the first ascent of
the Aiguille de Blaitière, 82; a plucky
incident, as described by Prof. Tyndall,
83.
Lauener, Ulrich—born at Lauterbrunnen the
ascent of the Wetterhorn, 79; the passage of
the Eiger Joch—ascent of Monte Rosa,
80.
Lauinen Thor, the first passage of, 82.
Lauteraarhorn, the first ascent of, 22; first ascent
of, by the western face, 165.
Lauterar Joch, the, 159.
Lauterbrunnen, 79, 81.
Lauterbrunnen Breithorn, the, 85.
Leone, Monte, 4.
Lesser Atlas, the, 112.
Levanna, the, 86.
Levant, the, 111.
Lombard Alps, the, 110.
Lysjoch, 77, 154; to Zermatt, 126.
Lyskamm, the, 74, 98, 144; from Gressoney,
85; relief expedition to, 99; ridge, the,
101; attempted in bad weather, 103; the
summit reached by the S.W. arête, 126; first
attempt, 151.

Macugnaga, 166.
Madatsch Joch, the first passage of, 142.
Maderaner Thal, 160.
Mallet Mont Glacier, the, 75.
Maquignaz, Jean Joseph—born at Val Tournanche
in 1829—crosses the Matterhorn, 124; first
ascent of the Aiguille du Géant—ascends the
Dufour Spitze—the Grand Paradis from Val-
savaranche, 125; the Lyskamm — crosses the
Lysjoch—ascends the Signal Kuppe—the Becca
de l'Invergnan and the Col de la Grande
Rousse de Valgrisanche - the Tour du Grand
St. Pierre, 126.
Maritime Alps, the, 85.
Marmolata, the, 82.
Matterhorn, successfully ascended, 24; from Zermatt
to Breuil, 75; attempt on the, 84, 150; from
Zermatt, 88; the, 100, 101, 167; from the

N

Zmutt Glacier, 104; from Breuil to Zermatt, 124, 125; from the Italian side, 129; early attempts, 127, 150.
Maudit, Mont, 5; first ascent of, 70; scaled by a new route, 121.
Maurer, Andreas, 26; born at Hasli Thal in 1842—his knowledge of the Engelhörner unsurpassed—an attempt to reach the summit of the Aiguille du Plan—a night of horrors—an act of unselfish devotion, 164; accompanies M. de Déchy to the Himálayas—list of ascents: the first ascent of Aiguille Verte from the Argentière Glacier, of Les Courtes from Argentière, of Aiguille des Droites, of Aiguille d'Alvau, of Raten from the north, of Bietschhorn from the south, of Lauteraarhorn by the western face, and the first passage of Col de Roche d'Alvau—a chamois hunt—a feat of great strength—killed on the Wetterhorn on 3rd of August, 1882, 165.
Meije, the central peak of the, 86; the highest point of the, 86; the, 101.
Mer de Glace, the, 70, 77, 144.
Mingo Glacier, the, 75.
Michel, Christian—his first ascent of the Gross Schreckhorn—over the Strahleck, the Gauli Joch, the Ewig Schneehorn, the Urner Alp, and the Weitsattel—the first passage of the Jungfrau Joch—a maiden passage of the Viescher Joch—the ascent of the Silberhorn—first passage of the Bergli Joch, 141; a new route from the Eggischhorn to Zermatt—visits the Eastern Alps in 1864—the first passage of the Beichgrat—ascent of the highest summit of the Piz Viesch—crossed the Fuorcla Sella to the Fellaria Alp—the maiden passage of the Fuorcla Crast' Agüzza—the first ascent of the Piz Zupo—first passage of the Fuorcla Zupo—first ascents of Monte Confinale, Madatsch Joch, and Monte Cristallo—the second ascent of the Königsspitze—first passage of the Königs Joch, and a new route up the Ortler—first ascent of the Wellhorn—the Mönch from the little Scheideck, 142; ascent of the Eiger, 143.
Misauna Gletscher, the, 76.
Mischabel Dôm, the, 161.
Mischabel Joch, the, 84; first passage of, 144.
Mittelleggi arête, the, 104, 158.
Moming Pass, the, 75, 84; from the Arpitetta Alp, 155.
Mönch Joch, the, 73.
Mönch, the, 84; from the Eiger Joch, 88; a winter ascent of the, 93; from the Little Scheideck, 143.
Mons Fractus, 1.
Mont Mallet, 65.
Moro Pass, the Monte, 148.

Morteratsch, the, 76.
Moseley, death of Dr., 158.
Mummery, Mr., 27.
Mur de la Côte, the, 71, 160.

Nadelhorn, first ascent of, 17; the, 147.
Napoleon III. at Chamonix, 115.
Nesthorn, first ascent of the, 85.
Nord End, the, 168.
Notable expeditions by amateurs without guides, 38.

Oberaarhorn, the, 65.
Oberaar Joch, the, 152.
Ober Gabelhorn, the, 94.
Oberland sacks, 47.
Ochsenhorn, the, 158.
Ochsenjoch Pass, first passage of the, 88.
Oetzthaler Ferner, the, 110.
Old Weissthor, passage from Macugnaga, 162; the, 150.
Ortler, the, 111.
Ortler, a new route up the, 112.

Palü Glacier, the, 142.
Pavé, the, 86.
Payot, Alphonse—born at Les Moussons in 1852—his first expedition, the Col dit Infranchissable—the passage of the Col de l'Aiguille du Plan—a campaign in the Bernese Oberland—ascent of Mont Blanc by the Broglia and Fresnay Glacier—a noteworthy display of skill on the Aiguille Verte, 118.
Payot, Michel Clement, 29; born at Les Moussous in 1840—joins Tyndall's ascent of Mont Blanc—rescues a fellow-porter—gains a "médaille d'honneur" and a diploma of merit, 115; the first ascents of the Mont Dolent, the Aiguille de Trélatête and the Aiguille d'Argentière—the first passage of the Col de Triolet—crosses the Dôme du Goûté—first ascents of the Aiguille du Plan, the Aiguille de Rochefort, Mont Blanc by Broglia, the Dôme de Rochefort and the Aiguille de Rochefort, the Col between the Southern Miage and the Trélatête Glaciers, and two new Cols between the Tour Ronde and the Aiguille du Géant—through the Central Rocky Mountains, 116.
Pélérins, village of Les, 4.
Pelvoux, the, 86, 154, 155.
Pennines, the, 93.
Petites Jorasses, an attempt to cross from Courmayeur to Chamonix, 162.
Petrus, Johann, killed, 102.
Pfarrer Strasser of Grindelwald, 30.
Pic des Agneaux, the, 86.
Pic Central of Meije, the, 92.
Pic Charlet, the, 28.

Pic Dent, the, 28.
Pic des Ecrins, the memorable first ascent of, 155.
Pic du Grand Tournalin from Val Tournanche, 130.
Pic de Grivola, the, 155.
Pic sans Nom, 28.
Pic d'Olan, the, 86.
Pigne d'Arolla, the, 160.
Pilatus, legend of, 1.
Pinzolo, the, 86.
Piz Bernina, the, 76.
Piz Palü, the, 110.
Piz Rosegg, the, 154.
Piz Kesch, the, 142.
Pizzo de Verona, the, 142.
Piz Zupo, first passage of, 142.
Plan de la Tribulation, 162.
Pointe des Ecrins, the, a new route, 92.
Pointe des Henvières, the, 86.
Pointe du Sélé, the, 86.
Pointe Haute de Mary, the, 85.
Pollinger, Aloys—born at St. Niklaus in 1844—his first expedition—ascent of the Weisshorn—the Dent Blanche by two new routes—the Breithorn from the Schwarzthor—his special gift of finding new peaks and passes, 100.
Pourri, Mont, 86 ; first ascent of, 155.
Prarayen, 100.
Pré de Madame Carle, a midnight bivouac under a rock on the, 156.
Presanella, the first ascent of, 110.
Primiero, the, 86.
Punta Sella, the, 130.

Râteau, the, 86, 165.
Rey, Emile—born at Courmayeur in 1846—attempts the Aiguille du Plan from the Plan des Aiguilles, and the Eiger from the Mitteleggi arête—Rey, alone and unroped, succeeds in turning a very difficult rock—he ascends the Aiguille (Noire) de Peuteret and Les Jumeaux de Valtournanche—takes part in the first ascent of the Aiguille de Talèfre—ascent of the Calotte de Rochefort—the Aiguille de Talèfre from the Italian side—the first ascent of the lower peak of the Aiguille du Midi—first ascent of the Aiguille Blanche de Peuteret—reaches the Col connecting the Aiguille Blanche with the massif of Mont Blanc from the Glacier de Brouillard—the second ascent of the higher and lower peaks of the Aiguille du Dru, 132 ; ascent of Ben Nevis—leader of two search parties in 1882 and 1886, 133.
Rheinwaldhorn, the, 110.
Ried Pass, the, 146.
Riffel, from the, to Macugnaga over the Old Weissthor, 150.

Ritter Joch, to Cormi, over the, 142.
Roche de la Muzelle, the, 86.
Roche Faurio, the, 88 ; first ascent, 101.
Rocher Rouge, the, 5, 10, 71.
Rocky Mountains, visit to, 116.
Roc Noir, ascent of, 162.
Ropes, 46, 47.
Rosa massif, the Monte, 1 ; first ascent of, 22.
Rosa, Monte, 80, 82, 98, 110, 139, 152, 154, 166 ; from the Italian side, 130 ; by one of the Grenz Glacier buttresses, 167 ; first ascent from the Grenz Gletscher, 158.
Rosegg, the, 76.
Rosengarten Spitze, the, 109.
Rossbodenhorn, the, 142.
Rothhorn, from Zinal, 65, 154, 167 ; the, 76 ; first passage of the, 101 ; from Zermatt, 104.
Rousseau, J. J., 2.
Ruan, Mont, 5.
Rubi, Peter—born in 1833, 157 ; makes the first passage of the Jungfrau Joch—carries a ladder some 24 feet long from Grindenwald to the Wengern Alp, over the Jungfrau Joch to the Grindelwald Eismeer—first ascent of the Monte Rosa from the Grenz Gletscher—a new route up the Gabelhorn from Zinal—up the Blümlis Alp for the first time—Mitteleggi arête of the Eiger—Weisshorn by the Schallenberg arête, 158 ; lost with party in crossing the Lauteraar Joch, 159.
Ruinette, the, 84.
Ruitor, exploration of the, 155 ; the highest peak of, 155.
Russein Alp, the, 4.
Rympfischhorn, first ascent of, 65.

Saas im Grund, 142.
Saas Maor of Primiero, first ascent of, 109.
Saline, the, 85.
Scersen, Monte de, 76.
Schallenberg arête, the, 158.
Schallenhorn, the, 75.
Seballen Joch, the, 84.
Schallhorn, ascent from the Moming Pass, 82.
Scheuchzer, 6.
Schmadri Joch, the, 82, 85.
Schreckhorn, the, 88, 145 ; from the Lauteraarsattel, a new route, 90 ; accident, the, 91 ; ascent by the western arête—ascent in winter, 93 ; by the north-west arête, 100.
Schwartzhorn, first ascent of, 121.
Schwarzthor, the, 100.
Séracs de Géant, the, 114.
Sesia Joch, the, 84.
Sherwill, Capt., 9.
Signal Kuppe, the, 126.
Sikkim Himálaya, campaign in the, 97.

Silberhorn, ascent from the north, 82; that remarkable climb up the northern face of the, 85; first ascent of the, 141.
Simond, Auguste—born 1816, died 1870—ascent of the Matterhorn from Grindelwald—the early ascents of Monte Rosa—the first ascent of the Finsteraarhorn by English travellers—first ascent of the Grand Combin, 140.
Sixt, 3.
Smith, Albert, 13.
Société des Guides, founding of, 11.
Sommet des Rouies, first ascent of the, 88, 101.
Sonderbund War, the, 83.
Southern Alps, N.Z., the, 96.
Spain, through, 112.
Spescha, Placidus à, 4.
Stachelberg to Maderauer Thal, from, 160.
Strahlegg to Grindelwald, passage of, 14, 64, 141.
Strahlhorn, the, 154.
Studer's "Über Eis und Schnee," 1.
Suldenthal, a night adventure in the, 85.

Table au Chantre, la, 3.
Tarentaise, the, 86.
Täschhorn from the Mischabel Joch, the, 85.
Teneriffe ascended by Edouard Cupelin, 29; ascent of, 121.
Tête du Lion, first ascent of, 130.
Tetnuld Tau, the, 104.
Thälihorn, the, 146.
Thebes, the crags above, 111.
Théodule Pass, the, 3, 14; to Courmayeur, 74.
Thonon to Trent, 110.
Tiefenmatten Joch, the, 88.
Tinzenhorn, first ascent of the, 110.
Titlis, the, 1, 2, 4.
Tödi, the, 1, 4, 108.
Tour du Grand St. Pierre, 126.
Tour Ronde, the, 111.
Tour, the Col du, crossed under difficulties, 117.
Training of Mountaineers, 52.
Trélatête Glacier, the, 117.
Trift Joch, 154.
Tsantaleina, the, 86.
Tschierva Gletscher, 76.
Tschingel, the dog, 85.
Tschingel, the, 14.
Tyrolese, the, 110.

Ulrichshorn, the, 146.
Upper Grindelwald Glacier, 158.
Urner Alp, the, 141.

Val d'Arpette, 117.
Val de Bagnes, the, 140.
Val de Levigno, the, 76.
Vallée Blanche, 77.
Valley of Chamonix, 84.
Val Masino, the, 111.
Val Orsino, 3.
Valpelline Pass to Prarayen, 100.
Vélan, Mont, 1, 4.
Viescher Glacier, the, 93, 141.
Viescher Joch, the, 90, 141; first passage of, 158.
Visolotto, the, 86.
Viso, Monte, 86, 110; first ascent of, 155.
Voirons, Les, 3.

Walker, Miss, the first lady to climb regularly, 65.
Watt, Joachim von, 2.
Weisse Frau, the, 71, 82.
Weisshorn, the, from the Bies Glacier, 85, 92; ascent of, by the S.E. face and the S. arête, 100; from Zinal, 167; first ascent of, 150, 151; by the Schallenberg arête, a new route, 158.
Weiss Kugel, the, 110.
Weissthor, first recorded passage of, 150.
Weitsattel, the, 141.
Wellhorn, first ascent of the, 142.
Wengern Alp, the, 158.
Wetterhorn, first ascent of, 1, 10; the, 79, 83, 86, 138, 144, 145; from Grindelwald, 140; a new route, 88; ascent in winter, 93; the accident of the 3rd of August, 1882, on the, 165.
Wildspitze, the, 110.
Wills's ascent of Wetterhorn, Mr. Justice, 1.
Windham, Mr., 6.

Zäsenberg ridge of the Ochsenhorn, the, 158.
Zillerthal, the, 93.
Zinal, ascent of the, 162.
Zinal ridge, the, 100.
Zinal Rothhorn, the, from Zermatt, 152.
Zmutt Glacier, the, 104.
Zwillinge Joch, first recorded passage of, 150; the, 152.
Zwischbergen Pass, the, 146.

www.ingramcontent.com/pod-product-compliance
Lightning Source LLC
Chambersburg PA
CBHW021815230426
43669CB00008B/754